VITAL AND VALUABLE

THE RELEVANCE OF HBCUs TO AMERICAN LIFE AND EDUCATION

JAMES V. KOCH,

OLD DOMINION UNIVERSITY

OMARI H. SWINTON,

HOWARD UNIVERSITY

Columbia University Press   *New York*

Columbia University Press
Publishers Since 1893
New York   Chichester, West Sussex
cup.columbia.edu

Copyright © 2022 Columbia University Press
All rights reserved

Library of Congress Cataloging-in-Publication Data
Names: Koch, James V., 1942- author. | Swinton,
Omari H., 1980- author.
Title: Vital and valuable : the relevance of HBCUs to American life
and education / James V. Koch, Omari H. Swinton.
Description: New York : Columbia University Press, 2023. |
Series: Black lives in the diaspora : past, present, future |
Includes bibliographical references and index.
Identifiers: LCCN 2022018606 | ISBN 9780231208987 (hardback) |
ISBN 9780231208994 (trade paperback) |
ISBN 9780231557726 (ebook)
Subjects: LCSH: African American universities and
colleges—Evaluation. | African Americans—Education (Higher) |
Education, Higher—Aims and objectives. | Higher education
and state—United States.
Classification: LCC LC2781 .K66 2023 |
DDC 378.1/982996073—dc23/eng/20220706
LC record available at https://lccn.loc.gov/2022018606

Columbia University Press books are printed on permanent and
durable acid-free paper.
Printed and bound by CPI Group (UK) Ltd, Croydon, CR0 4YY

Cover design: Elliott S. Cairns
Cover image: hxdbzxy/Shutterstock.com

CONTENTS

VITAL AND VALUABLE

BLACK LIVES IN THE DIASPORA:

PAST / PRESENT / FUTURE

PREFACE

This book came to pass because two individuals who had never met face to face concluded there was much to be said empirically about Historically Black Colleges and Universities (HBCUs) that had been overlooked or neglected. True, the literature on HBCUs often is rich and extensive, but frequently the suppositions in that literature have not been based on rigorous empirical analysis.

We intend this book to fill some of this evidentiary gap by providing well-grounded empirical bases for statements about HBCUs. We focus on several issues that have not received substantial attention. For example, what determines HBCU campus enrollments? How are their competitive positions with respect to PWIs (predominantly white institutions) affected by factors such as the net prices they charge, the household incomes of their students, the percentage of Black individuals in their home states, and the racial composition of their student bodies?

Because the funding of public HBCUs always has been an issue, we devote considerable time to assessing the extent to which this has changed over time.

Despite efforts to the contrary, the presence of Black men on HBCU campuses continues to decline and fell to only 36.2 percent of headcount undergraduate enrollments in fall 2020. At the same time, it also is true that Black men are more likely than Black women to choose to attend a PWI. This caught our attention, and we trace this phenomenon and offer a preliminary analysis.

Our own observations told us we should give attention to the role of intercollegiate athletics on most HBCU campuses. We provide the first substantive estimates of the impact of football teams and intercollegiate athletics spending on HBCU admissions applications and on enrollment, retention, and graduation statistics. And, as is our habit, we provide context for this information by performing the same analysis for PWIs.

Early on, we perceived that one cannot address the needs of Black students or HBCUs without speaking to the effect that the diminishing size of inflation-adjusted Pell Grants has had on HBCUs and their students, both of whom typically exhibit significant financial need. This circumstance has been exacerbated by the dysfunctional federal student loan program, and we suggest reforms.

Some of the stresses faced by HBCUs today reflect their governing boards—including the manner in which the members are selected, general absence of relevant training for their positions, failure of too many board members to view themselves as fiduciaries, and incentives they place in front of their presidents. We suggest improvements.

By no means do we contend that this book deals with every important topic that pertains to HBCUs. We do, however, believe we have made substantive progress in terms of providing additional evidence, some of which is at odds with mainstream beliefs.

We emerged from our work with the conclusion that HBCUs represent an invaluable national resource, one too often ignored in non-Black communities. HBCUs have been "out of sight, out of mind" for significant numbers of Americans. We hope to change this situation by supplying a grounded rationale for their support and thereby stimulating other researchers to pay more attention to HBCUs.

We perceive the time is ripe for change. Our hope is that this book will inform the transformational process by providing a solid evidentiary basis to support well-scripted improvements.

ACKNOWLEDGMENTS

Scholarly contributions of substance do not emerge magically out of the ether. This book would not have appeared but for the patient mentoring and support of a host of individuals and institutions.

James V. Koch wishes first to thank his always supportive, very perceptive wife, Donna L. Koch, who rivals Job in her patience. He also owes much to mentors such as James Fisher, David Sweet, Eleanor McMahon, Robert Bell, John Worthen, Richard Barry, George Dragas, Arthur Diamonstein, and Helen Dragas. Old Dominion University continues to provide critical support for his efforts, as does the Strome College of Business at Old Dominion and its dean, Jeff Tanner.

Omari H. Swinton wishes first to thank his wife, Phyllis Swinton, for her support during the writing process. He would additionally like to thank his mother and father, Patricia and David Swinton, for their guidance and support. He owes a debt of gratitude to his mentor, Rhonda Vonshay Sharpe, and his colleagues Nicholas Hill, Haydar Kurban, and William Spriggs for their support. Howard University hired him and had faith in him, and for that he is forever grateful.

Both authors would like to thank the college presidents and governing board members who took time out of their busy schedules to answer a wide range of questions. We also owe a debt to several anonymous referees who offered helpful guidance, to Eric Schwartz of the Columbia University Press and Ben Kolstad of KGL for their useful guidance and suggestions, and in particular to Lois Smith for her superb copyediting.

Among the individuals who provided valuable advice, assistance, and critiques of our work are Vinod Agarwal, Alonzo Brandon, William A. Darity Jr., Robert Fenili, Kevin James, Dominique Johnson, Faisal Mahmud, Julianne Malveaux, Robert McNab, Kurt Schmoke, David Selover, Macki Sissoko, Michael J. Sorrell, Cecelia Tucker, Ziniya Zahedi, and Donald Zimmerman.

VITAL AND VALUABLE

1

REMOVING THE VEIL

For many years, there has been a veil
that has obscured what we do.

—Comment by an HBCU president to the authors

"If you come here, you will find something that you will not find anywhere else," noted a college administrator when talking about her campus. "I wanted to learn from someone who looked like me," said one undergraduate student, while another forthrightly stated that her campus years "made me want to do better." "My campus experience was 'unapologetically Black,'" observed an alumnus, and this enabled him to understand his roots.

Each of these comments refers to experiences of individuals on the campus of a Historically Black College and University (HBCU). The U.S. Department of Education reported that 102 HBCUs existed in 2021, and collectively they enrolled approximately three hundred thousand students.[1] Their annual operating revenues approached $5.8 billion, with an estimated annual economic impact of a hefty $15 billion.[2] These are attention-getting numbers.

HBCUs have produced an impressive flow of graduates. The list includes difference makers such as Vice President Kamala Harris, the Reverend Dr. Martin Luther King, Jr., Oprah Winfrey, the Reverend Jesse Jackson, Thurgood Marshall, Spike Lee, Toni Morrison, Alice Walker, Samuel L. Jackson, Marian Wright Edelman, Langston Hughes, Ralph Ellison, W. E. B. Du Bois, and Booker T. Washington. The athletic exploits of HBCU graduates such as Walter Payton, Wilma Rudolph, and Robert Lee Hayes are legendary. Three-quarters of Black military officers, three-quarters of Black doctoral degree holders, and four-fifths of all Black federal judges earned their bachelor's degrees at an HBCU.

Another fact not to be ignored is that HBCUs have achieved a remarkable record in enabling upward economic and social mobility for their student bodies. Consider the evidence provided by Harvard University's Opportunity Insights Project, which tracked 2014 earnings of students who graduated around the year 2000. At Georgia's Albany State University, a modestly sized HBCU, 42.1 percent of its undergraduates came from a family whose income ranked in the lowest quintile nationally. However, roughly fifteen years later, 90.2 percent of those students had risen at least into the next-higher income quintile, and fully 40.9 percent had progressed into one of the top two income quintiles.[3] This is upward economic mobility writ large, and HBCUs typically outperform PWIs (predominantly white institutions) in this regard.

Nonetheless, despite these impressive feats, knowledge of the achievements of HBCUs is hazy in the minds of many individuals who are not a member of or connected to any Black communities, and perhaps such accomplishments are even unappreciated and unacknowledged by some Black individuals. The degree of familiarity with HBCUs on the part of many

Americans—especially those who are white, Asian, and Hispanic, or those who reside outside the South—may be limited to occasional glimpses of HBCU intercollegiate athletic teams or their famed marching bands. The reality is that the location of the nearest HBCU is one thousand or more miles away for tens of millions of people. Hence, it cannot be surprising that large numbers of Americans (perhaps a majority) do not know anyone who attends an HBCU or has graduated from one. If challenged to identify what the abbreviation "HBCU" stands for, most Americans likely would fail to respond correctly.[4]

With respect to public awareness, a veteran HBCU president pithily commented to us, "We've been hiding in plain sight." In a nutshell, his observation captures the rationale for this book. To many individuals, HBCUs are an unknown quantity. There is a need to inform and enlighten many readers about them—why they exist, what they do well, where they appear to be falling short, and how enlightened public policies might improve the current situation. HBCUs constitute too important a part of the American social fabric to be burdened by misinformation or ignorance.

We seek to repair a portion of the knowledge deficit that afflicts many Americans concerning HBCUs. No study can capably evaluate all aspects of the performance of HBCUs, and therefore we focus on retention and graduation rates, the extent to which the students are able to improve their economic status, campus resource allocations and administrative expenses, and fundraising. We leave issues such as accreditation, faculty quality, and curriculum to other analysts.

Our approach to these questions is primarily empirical. We let the evidence speak for itself rather than offer passionate normative statements concerning what we or someone else fervently believes ought to be true. Each of us is entitled to our own views on the issues of the day, but in an ideal world, those views will have a visible connection to reality.

The evidence we generate, in turn, will lead us to policy recommendations.

WHY ARE HBCUs A MYSTERY TO MANY?

The work we report here would not have been undertaken if Americans had a better understanding of HBCUs than we perceive is the case and/or more scholars had applied rigorous statistical methods to the analysis of HBCU behavior and performance. These two conditions are related. A significant reason that HBCUs have not received more research attention is that they pose a cultural mystery to many.

To some Americans, especially those who are white or did not grow up in the South, HBCUs represent a semi-exotic permutation of American higher education—one that some admire, others question the relevance of, and many know relatively little about. The reasons are complex. At the forefront, however, is the specter of racism. With some exceptions, HBCUs historically operated on the periphery of the majority, non-Black society. As a veteran white legislator once opined to one of the authors, "We don't mess with them as long as they don't cause us any problems." This political and social positioning meant that only in recent years have the promise, possibilities, and plight of HBCUs emerged as topics demanding serious attention from non-Black elected officials and the larger society. Clearly, one reason for this was the emergence of Black voters as a large and attractive voting bloc that commanded attention.

Nevertheless, "out of sight, out of mind" also is an important reason that the circumstances, triumphs, and challenges associated with HBCUs are not widely known. Only about seventy-five thousand non-Black individuals (0.4 percent of all American college students) attended an HBCU in fall 2019.[5] Further, HBCU campuses exist in only nineteen states. Hence, it is fair to conclude that large numbers of Americans have had few to no contacts with HBCUs and therefore are uninformed or ill-informed about them.

HBCUs AND SOCIAL CHANGE

While our analysis focuses primarily on measurable outcomes, often economic in character, we would be remiss if we failed to note that HBCUs have been actively involved in hastening vitally important social changes, such as racial integration, equal housing opportunities, and improved law enforcement policies and behavior. Let's trace a bit of this history, because unless one understands how that bears on the numbers in our empirical analyses, one can miss much of the meaning of those numbers and our conclusions.

Most HBCUs were founded in the 1800s, a time when Black individuals were either prohibited by state law or strongly discouraged from attending existing colleges and universities, public or private. As Adam Harris has ably pointed out in *The State Must Provide*, some states went to extraordinary lengths to keep Black and white people from sitting next to each other in college courses or even on the same campus. The example of the Commonwealth of Kentucky is instructive. The foundation of its approach to educational segregation, the "Day Law," written into Kentucky's constitution in 1904, prohibited Black and white people from attending any school together.[6] The state's only racially integrated college at the time, Berea College, was forced to segregate. Berea challenged this law before the U.S. Supreme Court in *Berea College v. Kentucky* (1908)[7] but lost.

Kentucky went through numerous gyrations to avoid integration. It was one of several states that attempted to satisfy the "separate but equal" doctrine, handed down by the Supreme Court in *Plessy v. Ferguson* (1896),[8] by paying Black Kentuckians to leave the state and attend colleges in the North. It also went through the charade of admitting Black students into select previously segregated professional programs but then forcing them to locate in separate rooms or buildings while taking the same courses as white students.

The separate but equal notion of providing public higher education persisted legally until *Brown v. Board of Education* (1954),[9] and remnants may still be with us. Segregated states might have been able to satisfy the terms of *Plessy*, for example, by establishing free-standing academic programs at HBCUs that were comparable to those at white institutions. However, with few exceptions, this approach was deemed by states to be too expensive and either never implemented or not fully funded. Usually there has been more talk about separate but equal than political and financial will to implement it.

"Separate but equal" strains of thought have not disappeared in higher education. Maryland continues to debate whether seemingly identical graduate and professional programs should be located at both Towson University (26 percent Black) and the HBCU Morgan State University (83 percent Black).[10] The two institutions are situated less than six miles apart.

On issues ranging from civil rights to economic justice, HBCUs often have been at the forefront of movements advocating change in American society. HBCU campuses have served as headquarters, think tanks, training camps, and war rooms for social, political, and economic action. Civil rights icons such as Medgar Evers (Alcorn State), Rosa Parks (Alabama State), Stokely Carmichael (Howard) and, of course, the Rev. Dr. Martin Luther King, Jr. (Morehouse) were educated at HBCUs, and their campuses became hives of civil rights activity.

Shaw University hosted the first meeting of SNCC, the Student Non-Violent Coordinating Committee, and played a key role among Southern HBCUs.[11] South Carolina State University students' attempt to desegregate a bowling alley resulted in the infamous Orangeburg massacre. The Rev. Dr. Martin Luther King, Jr. first encountered Thoreau's essay on civil disobedience at Morehouse College.

The Friendship Nine, a group of Black men who were students at Friendship Junior College, publicized a "Jail, No Bail" strategy after being arrested at a segregated lunch counter in Rock Hill, South Carolina, in 1961. They chose thirty days of hard labor on a prison farm rather than pay a fine.

A large group of peaceful, singing marchers substantially composed of Black collegians from the HBCUs Benedict College[12] and Allen University were arrested and convicted of a breach of peace in Columbia, South Carolina, in 1961 after refusing police orders to disperse. In *Edwards v. South Carolina*,[13] the Supreme Court ruled that their arrest was an unconstitutional attempt by the state of South Carolina to make criminal the peaceful expression of unpopular views.

The captivating story of how HBCUs have contributed to desegregating the United States and challenged the nation to live up to its constitutional obligations has been told with verve and understanding by Jelani M. Favors in *Shelter in a Time of Storm*.[14] Favors, a historian, focuses special attention on student and faculty activism at six HBCUs, beginning with post–Civil War events at Tougaloo College and ending with an analysis of circumstances on HBCU campuses today. He illuminates both the unifying characteristics of their activities and the differences that stemmed from their distinctive histories and locations. At Jackson State, for example, activist students faced opposition from not only the white power structure but also their own college president and campus administration. This was no crystal staircase.

Favors's summary assessment is piercing: "Black colleges, in particular, primed a critical mass of young minds to reject the corrosive effects of white supremacy, to see themselves as agents for social and political change, and to link that agency to a broader vision of freedom for all marginalized people."[15]

In the early years, not all HBCU campuses were scenes of ferment. Some, especially those in the public sector such as Jackson State, were slower to engage in activism because their state appropriations were threatened by white establishment politicos. This is apparently the reason that in 1962, Southern University expelled sixteen student civil rights activists—among them D'Army Bailey, who would later obtain a law degree from Yale University and serve as a district circuit court judge in Tennessee. However, such actions seemed only to energize civil rights activities, and as Martin Luther King described, "In 1960 an electrifying movement of Negro students shattered the placid surface of campuses and communities across the South. The young students . . . gave America a glowing example of disciplined, dignified non-violent action against the system of segregation."[16]

While the issues and locations may have changed in the intervening half century since the action at Southern University, the struggle of HBCU students against societal injustice has not. Instead of a sit-in at a whites-only lunch counter, today's activities more often focus on police misconduct, unjustified killings of Black individuals, employment discrimination, and economic inequality. The torch continues to be carried by HBCU students.

A degree of the social impact of HBCUs has flowed from their redemptive qualities. Historically, they have generously provided individuals with first, second, and sometimes even third chances to improve themselves and become productive citizens. When mainstream American society has refused to care or even listen, HBCUs have stepped into the breach and provided hope and a road map toward opportunities for advancement. "There is gold in every individual," an HBCU administrator told us. "We simply have to find it and mine it."

The HBCU experience of prominent alumnus Samuel L. Jackson is instructive. The highly acclaimed actor was expelled from Morehouse College in 1969 because he and some other students held members of the Morehouse Board of Trustees hostage for two days to protest a variety of curriculum and governance matters. Morehouse subsequently relented, however, readmitting Jackson. He graduated in 1972, thereby putting an exclamation point on an activist and redemptive story that epitomizes two of the most important roles that HBCUs have played in American society.

The coming of the Biden administration and the presence of Vice President Kamala Harris perhaps may make a difference in how HBCUs are perceived and treated. Further, a spate of large, generous (and substantially unanticipated) financial gifts to HBCUs has brought attention to them, and these gifts have brightened their prospects. In addition, the deaths of George Floyd and others appear to have pricked the conscience of segments of the non-Black American population and caused some individuals to be more open to discussions of economic and social issues that are important to Black individuals.

Taken together, these factors may generate greater public interest in the circumstances of HBCUs. Nevertheless, one must place these developments in the context of the traumatic changes imposed on society by the COVID-19 pandemic, which has altered when and where individuals can attend college or hold a job, who must stay home to care for children, who pays taxes, who can afford to make gifts, and more. These circumstances make it difficult to predict if incipient interest in HBCUs will last.

HBCU ENROLLMENT PROSPECTS

Students who have opted to attend an HBCU often speak appreciatively of the personal growth they experienced on campus and the concern shown for their needs. They applaud the enhanced understanding of the Black experience that they acquired and the absence of their need to fit into artificial racial stereotypes. The 2017 PBS documentary "Tell Them We Are Rising: The Story of Historically Black Colleges and Universities" records these sentiments from students attending a variety of HBCUs.[17]

Hanging over these benefits, however, are deteriorating overall college enrollment trends. A "demographic cliff" looms in the future that will challenge all campuses, but perhaps HBCUs more than others.[18] The cliff reflects the reality that the number of high school graduates will decline during the next two decades in many of the markets traditionally served by HBCUs.[19] In Mississippi, for example, the number of high school graduates is predicted to decline by 19 percent between 2019 and 2037.[20]

While the ultimate impact of COVID-19 has yet to be determined, the pandemic's effects on HBCUs have disadvantaged them. It became unwise or impossible to offer the personalized, high-touch education that traditionally has been their calling card. COVID-19 pushed nearly all institutions, including

HBCUs, to rely on more impersonal, distance education offerings in lieu of face-to-face courses. Thus, much of the individual care, treatment, and understanding that many feel have differentiated HBCUs from PWIs has been lost.

COVID accentuated what has become a ten-year decline in headcount college enrollments in the United States.[21] In the estimation of an HBCU admissions director, "Life in my office is going to get very tough. Not as many people are attending college and not as many kids are graduating from the high schools we serve. It's dog eat dog."[22]

It is safe to say that HBCUs as a group are not going to be sailing into a placid sunset.

TWO BRIEF EXAMPLES

Two brief examples involving HBCUs demonstrate how empirical evidence can make a difference in decision making. First, consider the hypothesis that HBCUs as a group might combat their declining market shares by broadening their student recruitment focus beyond the traditional audience: domestic Black students.[23] Should HBCUs recruit more whites, Hispanic-Latinos, Asians, and international students? A 2019 *Washington Post* story that focused on Morgan State University strongly suggested this approach,[24] but a subsequent report in *University Business* attributed most of Morgan's enrollment prosperity to its status as an HBCU.[25] The evidence on expanding recruitment efforts to non-Blacks is mixed. Headcount enrollments at 102 degree-granting HBCUs declined 14.27 percent between fall 2010 and fall 2020 (21.50 percent among men). Morgan, whose enrollment declined only 2.2 percent during this period, appears to be an exception.[26]

Would the culture and identity of a representative HBCU be altered substantially by the presence of a significantly larger number of non-Black students and thus repel some prospective Black students? No one has been in a position to answer this question or assist HBCUs in deciding if the broadened recruitment of non-Black students would be cost-effective and generate enrollment dividends for them as a group. We provide large-sample evidence on this issue in subsequent chapters and find that it is questionable whether broadened recruitment of non-Black students constitutes a winning strategy for HBCUs.

For our second example, we again focus on the presence of white students on HBCU campuses. Carter and Fountaine,[27] Dennis,[28] and Dent[29] are among several who have examined the experiences of white students at public HBCUs. Their studies are interesting and well worth reading but might leave one with the impression that an important reason we need to know more about the circumstances of white students on HBCU campuses is that their numbers have been increasing. A subsequent Pew Trust study appears to suggest the same.[30]

However, the total number of white students at HBCUs has been declining, not increasing. Between FY 2010 and FY 2018, the number of students who self-identified as white declined by more than 6.1 percent.[31] The proportion of non-Black students who have enrolled at HBCUs has been increasing—by slightly more than 6.0 percent between FY 2010 and FY 2018. This means that the number of self-identified Hispanic/Latino, Asian, and international students, rather than self-identified white students, has been increasing on HBCU campuses.[32]

Thus, when HBCU enrollment data are given closer inspection, we find two apparent trends of importance: an increase in non-Black but nonwhite students at HBCUs and a decline in both the number and the proportion of Black students enrolled at HBCUs. A possible implication of the second point is that PWIs are pulling Black students away from HBCUs. We explore this hypothesis in greater detail in succeeding chapters.

As we seek to draw lessons from our analysis, it is wise to acknowledge that a single policy prescription seldom fits all HBCUs because of the tremendous variety that they exhibit in size, finances, student bodies, physical circumstances, histories, and locations. On occasion, it may be a stretch to mention North Carolina A&T University, which enrolled 12,753 students in fall 2020, in the same breath as the 450-student Paul Quinn College in Dallas, Texas. The realities facing Howard University, located in bustling Washington, D.C., and supported by an endowment valued at $688.56 million in 2019 differ from those confronting Alabama's small-town Talladega College, whose 2019 endowment was less than 0.4 percent of that amount—$2.56 million.[33] Thus, we should be careful to avoid committing either a fallacy of division (assuming that what is true for HBCUs as a group necessarily holds for a single HBCU) or a fallacy of composition (assuming that what holds true for a single HBCU necessarily is true for all HBCUs as a group).

THE PLAN OF THE BOOK

The remainder of this book is organized as follows.

In chapter 2, we present and comment on the six most common arguments supporting the existence and operation of HBCUs. We label this a précis of the affirmative case for HBCUs, because our goal is briefly to identify, clarify, and review empirical evidence concerning the major strands of argument in support of HBCUs rather than present an exhaustive treatment. We want readers to understand the arguments, appreciate the implications of their major claims, and grasp the most important empirical evidence that relates to them. Our aim, however, is to distill rather than treat these topics exhaustively.

Chapter 2 should be viewed as a building block that will enable readers to understand and evaluate the empirical evidence presented in subsequent chapters. For many readers with a sketchy knowledge of HBCUs, this a vital step in comprehending reliable information.

We devote chapter 3 to addressing questions relating to the enrollments at HBCUs. This is a topic that surged to the forefront because HBCU headcount enrollments declined more than 10 percent between FY 2010 and FY 2019. COVID-19–restricted 2020 influences seem likely to have continued this downward trend. In this topsy-turvy world, which institutions have suffered losses and which have expanded? Can we explain why? Have for-profit institutions and the increased presence of distance learning harmed HBCUs? Is the increased interest expressed by many PWIs in enrolling more Black students just talk, or does it have substance? What do demographic projections tell us about the future prospects of HBCUs?

While we provide answers to these questions, we also find that significant variations often exist among individual HBCUs, and this makes it more difficult to generalize about enrollments. As a factual matter, HBCU enrollments over the years have been more variable than those of PWIs.[34] This is another reminder that HBCUs are not a monolithic entity.

Our attention in chapter 4 is devoted to explaining the sample of institutions that are the backbone of our empirical work and describing the variables we utilize. Quality empirical work, if it is to be taken seriously, must be accessible and replicable. While we do not shy away from citing anecdotal evidence on the issues we address, the *sine qua non* of serious research is the ability of other parties to access and utilize the data and models on which a study is based. Storytelling and reliance on individual testimony clearly have valuable uses and often are very influential, but the danger is that they perpetuate stereotypes and misapprehensions rather than speak to reality. Our focus is on large-sample empirical evidence, which we illustrate and spice with specific examples. This chapter makes that possible.

In chapter 5, we begin the presentation of our empirical findings. We examine the factors that determine oft-cited measures of HBCU performance, including enrollments, graduation rates, retention rates, student/faculty ratios, administrative expenditures, and student debt. We also critique the relevance of some of these variables to the world of HBCUs.

We banish to appendices the formal regressions that generated our empirical results and instead translate our empirical results into more easy-to-understand changes that are related to policy actions. For example, in chapter 5, based on our empirical work, we find that even after accounting for the impact of more than a dozen other factors, institutions with larger enrollments exhibit higher graduation rates than those with lower enrollments. Holding other factors constant, we estimate that a one-thousand-student increase in a representative institution's fiscal year enrollment is associated with a 0.25 percent to 0.53 percent increase in its six-year graduation rate for first-time full-time freshmen. We supply a host of similar estimates for the performance measures noted earlier.

We present additional intriguing results in chapter 6. Our focus here is on admissions yield rates, male versus female graduation rates, institutional endowments, and a performance metric central to the purpose of HBCUs—the extent to which specific campuses enable their student bodies to move upward in economic terms.

Chapter 7 addresses "What does it all mean and where do we go from here?" We summarize our findings and consider their policy implications for a variety of interested parties. Some of our evidence is directly relevant to the choices made by administrators (especially presidents and provosts), faculty, and staff on individual campuses. Other implications focus on the decisions made by governing boards, groups that are often ignored in higher education discussions but nevertheless legally in charge.

Our empirical results are replete with implications for public policies. In chapter 7, we divide this discussion into several parts, including one on matters primarily state focused and another on matters that have stronger federal considerations.

Readers will find that we do not sugarcoat the evidence. HBCUs have not excelled at all tasks; for example, we detail the tendency of many HBCUs to become top-heavy in the area of administration. However, we temper this judgment by pointing out appropriately that significant economies of scale exist in the performance of many administrative tasks. This means that the relatively smaller sizes of most HBCUs[35] prevent them from realizing some potentially available administrative economies. Thus, we seek to place evidence in context.

As always, however, the proof of any pudding is in the eating. Translated to this book, this means it is time for us to make our case. Let's begin that process in chapter 2.

2

A PRÉCIS OF THE CASE
FOR HBCUs

A Haven for Hungry Souls.

—Originally invoked by W. E. B. DuBois, this phrase
is often heard in Black churches and HBCUs.

S
hortly we will begin to wade through substantial
amounts of empirical evidence relating to the performance of HBCUs. Such evidence, however, does
not appear out of a void and in the case of HBCUs the data
describing them unavoidably reflect their origins and struggles.
It is essential that readers less familiar with HBCUs understand
something of the complex histories and environments that have
produced the HBCUs we see today and have generated the
numbers we will analyze. Context matters.

This chapter is billed as a précis of the case for HBCUs
because it is designed to give readers a short course in the rationale for their existence. While we believe the overall brief in
favor of HBCUs is strong, as we will see, not all aspects of the
supporting arguments are equally persuasive.

But first, let us review a bit of history, which will provide context for the analysis that follows.

THE ADVENT OF HBCUs

Most HBCUs were founded in the years after the Civil War, when all but a few institutions of higher education enrolled only white students—a legal requirement in the South and a sometime practice elsewhere. HBCUs therefore constituted a response to the exclusion of Black students from American college campuses.

The appearance of HBCUs simultaneously satisfied the demands of segregationists for racially exclusive campuses, assuaged some of the guilt that whites may have felt concerning the treatment of Black individuals under slavery, and responded to Black individuals' demand for opportunities to pursue higher education. Consequently, the establishment of HBCUs in racially segregated states such as Alabama and Mississippi often enjoyed support from both whites and Blacks even if their funding was parsimonious.

Nevertheless, the nation's first HBCU was established in the North. Cheyney University was founded by Pennsylvania Quakers in 1837. It was followed in 1849 by the now defunct Avery College in Pittsburgh and in 1856 by Ohio's Wilberforce University—named after the British abolitionist William Wilberforce. Religious beliefs were a prominent motivation for the founding of these early HBCUs and continue to loom large today. Slightly more than half of HBCUs were established by a religious group—most often, the African Methodist Episcopal Church, the United Methodist Church, or various groups of Baptists. But a variety of other religious groups have created HBCUs, including Lutherans, Presbyterians, and Roman Catholics.

The first HBCU in the South (Shaw University) was established in 1865 in North Carolina. Other institutions created after the Civil War included the well-known Dillard, Fisk, Hampton, Howard,

Rust, and Simmons Universities. Developments in the public sector were more modest and included North Carolina's State Colored Normal School (now Fayetteville State University) and Alabama's Lincoln Normal School (now Alabama State University).

Howard University represents a special hybrid case. Though private, it is a federally chartered (1867) research university, receiving an annual appropriation from the U.S. government. If any HBCU can be considered to be the flagship institution, it is Howard; its propitious location in Washington, D.C., places it at the center of public policy debates and helps to ensure that graduates will occupy significant positions. After experiencing several years of declining enrollment, Howard's numbers have surged and recently enrolled the largest freshman class in its history. Its student body now exceeds eleven thousand. Howard's professional programs in areas such as medicine, law, and business are highly regarded. It was a Howard University Law School graduate, Thurgood Marshall, who successfully argued the groundbreaking *Brown v. Board of Education* case before the Supreme Court in 1954.[1]

The first publicly supported HBCU, the University of the District of Columbia, was founded in 1851 as Miner Normal School. Taxpayer-supported HBCUs received impetus from the passage of the Morrill Act of 1890, which required states to establish racially separate land grant colleges for Black individuals if they were excluded from existing colleges. In the South, this led to the founding of HBCUs such as Delaware State, Fort Valley State, North Carolina A&T, South Carolina State, and West Virginia State. Existing normal schools in states such as Florida were anointed with land grant status in the process, producing institutions such as Alabama A&M, Alcorn State, Florida A&M, Kentucky State, Prairie View, Southern University and A&M, and Virginia State.

Although the first HBCUs were founded in the North, this rarely signaled that Black individuals could attend other colleges there. Yale University provides an illustration. Slave labor was used to construct some buildings at Yale, and the institution honored Confederate veterans. Yale personnel actively proposed an initiative to build a college for Black students in New Haven in 1831 rather than have Black students attend Yale itself.

Not until 1965, however, were HBCUs recognized formally as a distinct group of institutions by the federal government. The Higher Education Act of 1965 asserted that HBCUs included "any historically Black college or university that was established prior to 1964, whose principal mission was, and is, the education of Black Americans, and that is accredited by a nationally recognized accrediting agency or association."[2]

For most of their histories, state-supported HBCUs have not been provided the same financial support as that of comparable PWIs.[3] As figure 2.1 reveals, however, things have changed in some states, at least if we focus on the median HBCU. The funding data in figure 2.1 have been adjusted for changes in the Consumer Price Index.[4] One can see that the median (50th percentile) real state appropriation per calendar year full-time equivalent (FTE) student of HBCUs was $9,692 in FY 2004, almost $1,800 below the median state support provided to the typical flagship state university (though larger than the comparable appropriations given to the metro leader and regional institutions). By FY 2019, however, the median real state appropriation per calendar year FTE student of the thirty public HBCUs exceeded that of the flagships by more than $500.

The data in figure 2.1 merit interpretation. First, there was a dawning recognition—even a sense of guilt—among many legislators and governors that for many decades, HBCUs had not been treated well financially and the time had come to make

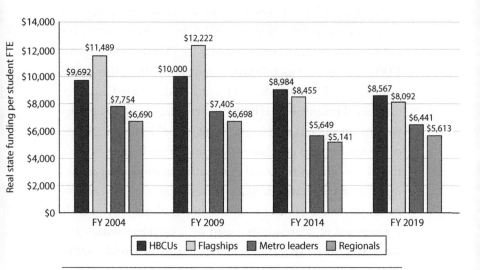

FIGURE 2.1 Median real institutional state appropriation per calendar year FTE student, public institution types, FY 2004–FY 2019

Note: Sample sizes: 30 HBCUs, 73 flagships, 55 metro leaders, 68 regionals.

Source: U.S. Department of Education, Integrated Postsecondary Data System (hereafter cited as IPEDS), https://nces.ed.gov/ipeds. The sample is drawn from James V. Koch and Richard J. Cebula, *Runaway College Costs: How College Governing Boards Fail to Protect Their Students* (Baltimore: Johns Hopkins University Press, 2020).

recompense. In the aftermath of that action, some HBCUs acquired the financial equivalent of most-favored nation status. In Maryland, for example, after extended negotiations, Governor Larry Hogan signed off on a $577 million decade-long injection of funds into Maryland's four HBCUs (Bowie State University, Coppin State University, Morgan State University, and the University of Maryland Eastern Shore). The president of Morgan State, David Wilson, commented, "This infusion of money will enable us to put in place new high-demand academic degree programs that are in alignment with the work of the future."[5]

Second, the Great Recession of 2008–10 saw state universities endure substantial funding cuts, which in some cases still have not been reversed. However, funding for HBCUs and regional PWIs was not cut proportionately during (and after) this period compared with the flagship and metro leader institutions. This differential treatment of HBCUs reflected legislative and gubernatorial perceptions that larger, "name brand" institutions could cope with financial cuts better than smaller institutions because those larger universities could increase tuition without experiencing adverse enrollment declines. For example, the University of Michigan, where 47 percent of the undergraduate student body is composed of nonresidents, raised its nonresident tuition and fee by $5,455 between FY 2009 and 2013, whereas Florida A&M, where 22 percent of undergraduates are not residents, raised its non-residents' fees by $2,212 during the same period. Michigan's ability to deal with state financial cuts by means of tuition increases was dramatically greater than that of the typical HBCU.

Third, between FY 2010 and FY 2019, the median loss in calendar year FTE student enrollment at the HBCUs in our sample was 13.1 percent.[6] Practically speaking, this reduced the size of the denominator in the real state appropriations per FTE student variable.

Fourth, what holds true for HBCUs as a group does not necessarily apply for specific campuses. In Mississippi, between FY 2009 and 2019, Jackson State University lost 18.70 percent of the value of its real state appropriation per FTE student. Neighboring HBCUs Alcorn State and Mississippi Valley State lost 14.03 percent and 4.67 percent, respectively.[7] HBCU funding is a "coat of many colors," and often this makes it difficult to generalize from one to another institution.

Fifth, one cannot overcome a century of underfunding and neglect with a single decade of generosity. The impacts of increased

It seems unlikely that any new HBCUs ever will be founded. The politics and economics are simply too complicated. Therefore, the demise and disappearance of any of today's HBCUs might be compared with the extinction of a species. Once gone, it will never reappear, and we will have lost the distinctive characteristics that it brought to American higher education.

(or decreased) funding disperse over time, and it may take many years to build academic assets such as quality faculties, academic programs, equipment, and research specialties. Thus, one cannot look at the improved financial fortune of public HBCUs and conclude their battle is over.

A similar analysis for private HBCUs cannot be undertaken because with few exceptions, they do not receive state appropriations. One can, however, track the median real net tuition and fee revenues of private HBCUs, which are heavily dependent on tuition. As figure 2.2 reveals, median real net tuition and fee revenues vary substantially by institution type. Flagship state universities have prospered in this regard; their collections more than doubled between FY 2004 and FY 2019. Both metro leader and regional institutions saw their real tuition and fee collections increase during the first decade of this century, but since then, this revenue source has become stagnant.

By contrast, public HBCUs' revenue tuition and fee collection increased modestly (6.37 percent) over the same fifteen-year period, but the analogous revenue stream declined 9.68 percent at the independent HBCUs. The primary causes of this reversal for independent HBCUs have been declining enrollments and the rising tuition discounts they have granted their students in

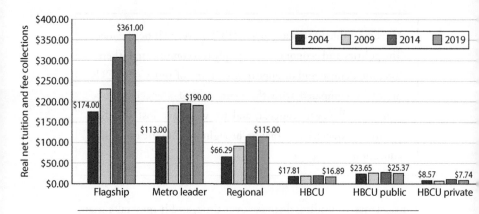

FIGURE 2.2 Median institutional real net tuition and fee revenues, by institution type, FY 2004–FY 2019

Note: The sample consists of 73 flagships, 55 metro leaders, 68 primarily regional institutions, 30 public HBCUs, and 20 independent HBCUs.

Source: IPEDS. Financial magnitudes reflect July 2018 prices. The sample is drawn from Koch and Cebula, *Runaway College Costs*.

the form of institutionally funded scholarships and grants. Thus, if we set aside leadership HBCUs such as Hampton, Howard, Morehouse, and Spelman, the financial threat posed by falling real tuition and fee revenues for a typical private HBCU could spell the end for some. Simply put, these institutions will find it difficult to survive, much less prosper, if their revenues continue to decline, having little margin for error due to their small size. We preface our future discussions by stating that both federal and state policy makers must take this new financial reality into account. Otherwise, an entire sector of American higher education is likely to disappear.

Having established the background for the coming discussion, we now focus on six of the most prominent assertions that explain the need for HBCUs and why they must continue to exist.

- HBCUs provide opportunities not otherwise available.
- HBCUs are more affordable than PWIs.
- Black students underperform at PWIs because they are uncomfortable on those campuses.
- HBCUs excel at providing students with upward economic mobility.
- HBCUs are key to the maintenance of a Black talent pipeline that cannot be replicated at PWIs.
- HBCUS have a substantial positive social and economic impact on their communities.

Let's begin by examining the opportunities hypothesis.

HBCUs Provide Opportunities Not Otherwise Available

While there is abundant, unarguable historical evidence that for more than a century, Blacks in America were denied entrance to many colleges and universities, to what extent does this continue to hold true? Contemporary evidence of continued barriers to higher education is nuanced. Consider that every state with a substantial Black population has a community college system that pursues open admissions policies and offers low prices. Approximately 40 percent of all undergraduate students in the United States attend a community college.[8] In states such as Florida, most community colleges now offer some baccalaureate degrees. The doors to these institutions are open to all, and Black individuals take advantage of this opportunity; they account for more than 30 percent of all students who complete a program and obtain a credential at community colleges.[9]

In all but one state containing an HBCU, several essentially open admission four-year public PWIs compete for students. In Mississippi, for example, the University of Southern Mississippi admitted 97 percent of its applicants in 2019–20, while Delta State University admitted 94 percent. In that same period in Alabama, the University of Alabama in Huntsville admitted 83 percent, and Auburn University at Montgomery admitted 90 percent.[10] Delaware is the only state where an open admission PWI does not exist alongside an HBCU.

Nevertheless, there is an unavoidable "lobster for me, but hardtack for you" sense attached to the argument asserting that because Black individuals are now able to attend PWIs, HBCUs are no longer necessary. This proposition would have relevance if all American colleges and universities had open admission and provided all admitted students with necessary financial assistance. Of course, this is not the case.

The Pew Research Center reported that in 2016, self-identified Black individuals accounted for only 9 percent of the undergraduate student bodies of institutions that Pew deemed "very selective" in admissions but 18 percent of the student bodies of minimally selective and open-admissions institutions.[11] To be more specific, in Fall 2019, only 4 percent of undergraduates at the University of Michigan, Ann Arbor, self-identified as Black, and at the University of California, Los Angeles (UCLA), it was even lower, 3 percent.[12] Highly ranked public institutions that *U.S. News and World Report* classifies as regional exhibit the same general pattern with respect to self-identified Black individuals in their student bodies: California Polytechnic Institute (San Luis Obispo), 1 percent; James Madison University (Virginia), 5 percent; Truman State University (Missouri), 4 percent; and the College of New Jersey, 6 percent.[13]

Further, Black students tend to attend institutions that have fewer financial resources, and therefore these institutions end up spending less money educating their students. In 2015, the median white student attended an institution that spent about $11,000 annually per FTE student, whereas the median Black student attended an institution that spent $1,000 less.[14]

Suffice it to say that the doors to PWI campuses do not magically open because an applicant is Black. Much depends on the admissions selectivity of the PWI and the financial aid packages it offers to those it chooses to admit. UCLA, for example, received 111,231 undergraduate applications in fall 2019 and admitted only 12 percent. The University of Illinois at Urbana-Champaign received 43,509 applications and admitted 59 percent, and the University of Massachusetts Amherst campus received 42,157 applications and admitted 64 percent.[15]

Institutions seldom categorize their admissions acceptance rates on the basis of race because they fear this might increase their vulnerability in legal actions brought by white and Asian applicants whom they choose not to admit. In the most recent Supreme Court decision in this arena (*Fisher v. University of Texas*, 2016), the court narrowly upheld the admissions processes then used by the University of Texas. Undergraduate applicant Abigail Fisher argued unsuccessfully that the university had discriminated against her because she was white.[16]

Table 2.1 demonstrates the gaps that exist between enrollments of self-identified Black undergraduates at a representative group of PWI flagship institutions and the percentage of Black citizens in these institutions' homes states. Georgia and South Carolina are outliers in this regard; there, the proportionate representation of self-identified Black undergraduate students at flagship institutions is less than one-quarter of the proportionate representation of Black individuals. For whatever reason,

TABLE 2.1 PERCENTAGE OF BLACK POPULATIONS IN SELECTED STATES AND OF BLACK UNDERGRADUATE STUDENTS AT FLAGSHIP INSTITUTIONS, 2019

Institution and state	Percentage of Black undergraduates	Percentage of Black individuals in home state	Ratio of home state Black individuals to campus Black individuals
U. Alabama Tuscaloosa	10	26.8	2.80
Auburn U.	5	26.8	3.60
U. California Berkeley	2	6.5	3.25
U. California Los Angeles	3	6.5	2.17
U. Florida	6	16.9	2.82
Florida State U.	9	16.9	1.88
U. Georgia	7	32.6	4.66
Georgia Tech	7	32.6	4.66
Louisiana State U.	13	32.8	2.52
U. Maryland College Park	11	31.1	2.83
U. Michigan Ann Arbor	4	14.1	3.53
Michigan State U.	7	14.1	2.01
U. South Carolina	6	27.0	4.50
Clemson U.	6	27.0	4.50
U. Tennessee Knoxville	6	17.1	2.83
U. Texas Austin	4	12.9	3.23
Texas A&M U.	3	12.9	4.30
U. Virginia	7	19.9	2.84
Virginia Tech	4	19.9	4.98

Sources: National Center for Education Statistics, College Navigator, www.nces.ed.gov, for Black enrollments; U.S. Census Quick Facts, https://www.census.gov/quickfacts, for state racial data.

Dr. Tony Allen, who chaired President Joseph Biden's Inaugural Committee, became president of Delaware State University in 2020 and proclaimed his wish that it become "the most diverse, contemporary Historically Black College and University [HBCU] in the nation." Said President Allen, "We're looking for students with a fire to succeed, regardless of the color of their skin." Prior to COVID-19, this strategy appeared to be paying dividends for Delaware State, whose fall 2020 headcount enrollment exceeded five thousand for the first time in its history.

Michael T. Nietzel, "A New President Wants to Make Delaware State University the Most Diverse HBCU in America," *Forbes*, March 5, 2020, https://www.forbes.com/sites/michaeltnietzel/2020/03/05/a-new-president -wants-to-make-delaware-state-university-the-most-diverse-hbcu-in -america/?sh=3499ffb47f2d.

---

it is fair to observe that Black students do not wish to attend the flagship institutions in these states, are not admitted, or cannot afford to attend.

While these states offer many higher education alternatives to their flagship institutions, it is a telling commentary on the fundamental values of the flagships that the percentage of those states' Black citizens range from 1.88 to 4.98 times greater than the percentage of Black undergraduate students attending those institutions.

Much larger percentages of self-identified Black individuals enroll at institutions we refer to as "metro leaders." These are large public urban institutions that, though not flagships, have become influential in their regions. We include in this group of almost forty institutions the University of Central Florida, Georgia State University, the University of Texas San Antonio, and Portland State University. Table 2.2 reports the percentage

TABLE 2.2 PERCENTAGE OF BLACK POPULATIONS IN SELECTED STATES AND OF SELF-IDENTIFIED BLACK UNDERGRADUATE STUDENTS AT METRO LEADER INSTITUTIONS, 2019

Institution and state	Percentage of Black undergraduates	Percentage of Black individuals in home state	Ratio of home state Black individuals to campus Black individuals
U. Alabama Birmingham	24%	26.8%	1.12
San Diego State U. (CA)	4%	6.5%	1.63
San Jose State U. (CA)	3%	6.5%	2.17
U. Central Florida	11%	16.9%	1.54
U. South Florida	10%	16.9%	1.69
Georgia State U.	41%	32.6%	0.80
Wichita State U. (KS)	6%	6.1%	1.02
U. Maryland Baltimore County	19%	31.1%	1.64
Wayne State U. (MI)	15%	14.1%	0.94
U. Toledo (OH)	10%	13.1%	1.31
Portland State U. (OR)	4%	2.2%	0.55
Temple U. (PA)	13%	12.0%	0.92
U. Tennessee Chattanooga	10%	17.1%	1.71
U. Texas San Antonio	8%	12.9%	1.61
Old Dominion U.	32%	19.9%	0.60
Virginia Commonwealth U.	20%	19.9%	0.96

Source: National Center for Education Statistics, College Navigator, https://www.nces .ed.gov, for percentage of Black undergraduates; U.S. Census Quick Facts, https:// www.census.gov/quickfacts, for percentage of Black individuals in states.

of self-identified Black students for a sample of these schools compared with the percentage of self-identified Black individuals in their home states. There is a visible difference between metro leaders and flagships. Five institutions enrolled larger proportions of self-identified Black students than the proportions of self-identified Black people in their home states. None of nineteen flagships did so. Only one of the metro leaders (San Jose State University) exhibits a ratio higher than the lowest ratio among the flagships. The average flagship ratio is 3.36; the average metro leader ratio is 1.26. It is apparent that the undergraduate student bodies contain much larger percentages of self-identified Black students than is true at the flagships.

One reason for the greater representation of Blacks at the metro leaders is that they are located in large urban areas, where more Blacks reside. However, one should not make too much of this, because in several Southern states, large numbers of Black citizens live in small towns and rural areas. It appears that metro leader institutions are cost competitive and large numbers of Black students perceive them to be acceptable places to go to college.

Not only do most of the metro leaders have significant Black enrollments, but their Black student bodies are growing. This is relevant to our study for two reasons. First, it suggests that the "comfort" argument cuts different ways. Black students are voting with their feet, and their choices suggest that they find metro leaders tolerably comfortable places to go to school. Second, these data unambiguously suggest that these non-flagship metropolitan institutions represent significant enrollment competition for HBCUs. It is these institutions, rather than elite public and private institutions, which appear to present the most meaningful enrollment challenges to HBCUs. At Georgia State University, for example, the percentage of self-identified Black students rose from 29.65 percent in FY 2004 to 41.39 percent in FY 2019.[17] At

Old Dominion University, Black student enrollment increased from 19.63 percent to 31.40 percent over the same period.[18] We will have more to say about this later in this chapter and test several hypotheses relating to these matters in chapter 5 and 6.

While significant differences exist among states in terms of the proportions of Black individuals who attend college, it remains true that the rate of college-going Black Americans trails that of students who self-identify as white, Hispanic/Latino, or Asian. Figure 2.3 reveals that even though the rate of college-bound recent Black high school graduates has increased significantly since 1990, it declined 8.6 percent between 2010 and 2020 and remains well below the rates of college-bound whites, Hispanics/Latinos, and Asians. The gap between races is particularly large among young Black men, and in fall 2020, that rate fell 5.1 percent—many times more than the 0.7 percent decline in

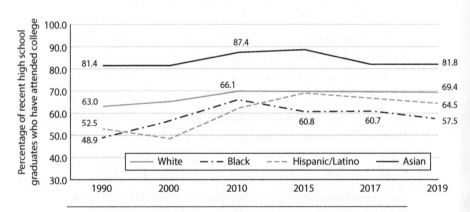

FIGURE 2.3 Percentage of recent high school graduates who have attended college: racial and ethnic differences, 1990–2019

Note: The data represent three-year moving averages and that "recent high school graduates" includes all graduates who were between sixteen and twenty-four years old.

Source: National Center for Education Statistics, *Digest of Education Statistics, 2020,* table 302.20, "Percentage of Recent High School Completers Enrolled in College, by Race/Ethnicity, 1960 Through 2019."

the rate for Black women.[19] In light of these trends, it would be perverse if public policy were to allow the HBCU college-going option for Black individuals to wither. The demise of HBCUs likely would send the rate for college-bound Black individuals tumbling further and translate into economic and social problems with which the society at large would have to deal.

HBCUs Are More Affordable Than PWIs

The evidence in favor of the affordability hypothesis is not as conclusive as some might believe. Reputationally, public HBCUs are inexpensive places to go to school. The Thurgood Marshall College Fund's website, for example, forthrightly states that "Most Expensive HBCUs Keep Tuition Costs Lower Than National Average."[20] This statement is true as it stands but not as useful a distinction as it might first appear. Let's see why.

The key cost variable insofar as students and their families are concerned is not the full "sticker price" that institutions advertise in their catalogs (and the Thurgood Marshall College Fund was referencing). Instead, it is the net price paid by a typical student after grants and scholarships have been deducted (but not loans, because those must be repaid). Figure 2.4 demonstrates this point. In the far-left portion, one can see that the average sticker price advertised by the 30 public HBCUs in our sample was only $21,425 in 2017–18. That was more than $8,000 below the $29,915 average sticker price advertised by the 186 PWIs that we have assembled for purposes of comparison. At first glance, this seems supportive of the "less expensive" hypothesis.

However, let's focus on the net fees paid by students who come to campuses from households with annual incomes between $0 and $30,000—an important constituency for HBCUs, given that Opportunity Insights reports that almost one in four students attending an HBCU comes from a household in the lowest quintile (lowest 20 percent) of the income distribution.[21] As we move from left to right in figure 2.4, we can see that in FY 2018, the PWIs in our sample actually charged less than the 50 HBCUs we are tracking by a considerable amount (average of $10,829 versus $13,210). This means that it was less expensive on average for a student from a very low-income household ($0–$30,000) to attend a public PWI than to attend a public HBCU in their same state.

Figure 2.4 provides several examples. Consider Florida A&M University, which is located in the same city (Tallahassee) as flagship Florida State University. Florida State charges dramatically lower prices than Florida A&M for the lowest-income

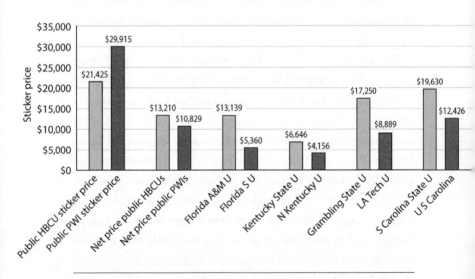

FIGURE 2.4 Sticker and net prices paid by in-state on-campus undergraduate students from $0–$30,000 income households at four-year public colleges, FY 2018

Source: IPEDS.

students: its average net price for a student from a $0–$30,000 income household was only $5,360 in FY 2018, compared with $13,139 at Florida A&M.

Nor, as one can see in figure 2.4, is this pricing differentials limited to Florida. Consider Grambling State University and Louisiana Tech University, located a stone's throw from each other in north central Louisiana. Louisiana Tech undercuts Grambling by more than $8,000 per year for these lowest-income students.

Hence, while it may be true that HBCUs advertise lower sticker prices than PWIs, PWIs may turn out to be the less expensive choice for a large segment of Black students. Why is this the case? There are two primary reasons. First, unlike HBCUs, many PWIs have private foundation scholarship funds to draw on. Second, most PWIs engage in price discrimination by charging much higher prices for students from upper-income households. They use some of those revenues to subsidize lower prices for lower-income students. This is most obviously the case at PWIs that enroll significant numbers of out-of-state students, who pay high nonresident tuition rates.

Let's focus for a moment on the University of South Carolina's flagship Columbia campus, where in fall 2019, 49 percent of the undergraduates came from out of state. Sticker price tuition and fees for these students were $33,928 but only $12,688 for South Carolinians. The University of South Carolina used these price differentials to redistribute income from students paying higher prices to those paying lower prices by means of targeted grants and scholarships to the lower-income students. To a substantial degree, this dynamic exists on virtually every campus in the United States. The extent to which it occurs depends on how successfully a university is able to attract students from upper-income families who are willing to pay higher prices. It does not describe the circumstances of many HBCUs.

There is nothing intrinsically underhanded or evil about the redistribution of financial burdens we have just outlined. Indeed, institutions sometimes highlight this situation and argue that it increases equity in American society and enables many individuals to attend college who otherwise might be denied. The central point, nevertheless, is that only a few HBCUs have the ability to engage in this tactic on a large scale, because they do not attract large numbers of upper-income students and some do not attract large numbers of nonresident students, both of whom might be capable of paying higher prices.[22]

This important distinction involving pricing differentials between HBCUs and PWIs deserves a more concrete example. HBCU Delaware State University advertised a $7,968 sticker price in tuition and fees for its approximate 1,705 undergraduate Delaware residents in FY 2018 but posted a price of $16,904 for its approximately 2,760 out-of-state undergraduates. Meanwhile, the University of Delaware, a PWI located only 50 miles away, quoted $13,160 to its approximately 7,680 in-state undergraduates but $33,150 to its roughly 12,000 nonresident undergraduate students.[23] This means that if all Delaware State's nonresident students were full-time, it could have earned about $24.66 million over in-state tuition and fees .[24] Similarly, the University of Delaware could have earned $239.99 million over its in-state rates.[25] This disparity in semi-discretionary revenues helps to explain why the University of Delaware's average net price for its lowest-income students ($0–$30,000 annual income) was $10,397 in FY 2018, while Delaware State's was $12,265.[26]

The bottom financial line is that in many states, public HBCUs are not the low-cost alternative. Instead, a state's flagship state university may be, if our focus is on students from the lowest-income households. These differentials are even more dramatic when the flagship publics are compared with private HBCUs.

Black Students Underperform at PWIs Because They Are Uncomfortable on Those Campuses

More than a century ago, W. E. B. DuBois, a polymath who excelled as a sociologist, historian, educator, poet, and activist, described the circumstances that many Black people experience that requires them to display "double consciousness."[27] Black individuals must live in two worlds—the Black one that they inhabit in their homes and communities and the white one, representing the world in which they work, study, and undertake other activities such as shopping. DuBois posited even more pointedly that as Black citizens grew up, they soon came to understand that they occupied inferior positions in society and were looked down on by whites. Thus, their achievements might draw resentment rather than congratulations from the majority society. Contrast DuBois's view with that of the legendary Booker T. Washington, who was more inclined to accept the reality of segregation and frequently advocated working within its strictures to enable Black individuals to become educated and productive.

Especially in the South, members of the white establishment visibly preferred Washington's approach over that of DuBois, which some saw as threatening. Opposition to DuBois was fueled at least partly by his dalliances with socialism and certain dictators and his anti-war stance. Life and politics often are complicated.

Contemporary HBCUs reflect both Washington's and Dubois's strains of thought, but the former's approach to higher education issues clearly dominates. Washington's emphasis on preparing Black individuals for tasks such as carpentry, farming, and sewing came to be viewed as far too limited (a form of "neo-slavery"), and DuBois's vision of Black individuals routinely becoming college-educated and prepared to fill professional positions (for example, physicians, attorneys, scientists, and business leaders) easily has carried the day.

Viewed from thirty-thousand feet, one can see that to a considerable extent, HBCUs have had little choice but to work within a system they did not design in order to attain vital academic accreditations, recruit students, help those students grow as individuals and find employment, raise necessary funds, and obtain appropriations, among other things. Though HBCUs seldom have had much say in making the rules that apply to their activities, with few exceptions they must live within those rules.

Thus, some (perhaps many) Blacks find themselves living within DuBois's world of double consciousness in higher education and accordingly seek relief from a bifurcated world—and perhaps from racism at PWIs—by connecting with an HBCU. Inside the arms of the HBCU, they need not pretend or abandon their roots. Hence, they may choose to avoid campuses where perhaps only one of every ten or even only every twenty-five students is Black.

Representative of this sense of comfort are the views of Marissa Stubbs, a student at Florida A&M University: "My HBCU has served as my haven, a place where I can be unapologetically Black. Every time I step on campus, I feel like I belong, and I'm protected."[28] Or consider the experience of Jayla Jones, who started her career at a large public PWI in Texas and then transferred to Prairie View A&M University: "Although UTA was pretty diverse as far as Texas goes, I still considered it a predominantly white institution (PWI). It was hard to find more than a handful of people who looked like me. It was hard to feel like I belonged there."[29]

Let's not forget the role of faculty. The reputation of HBCU faculty is that they provide abundant care and support for their students. As Joe B. Whitehead, provost and vice chancellor of academic affairs at North Carolina A&T University expressed in 2017, "many students who are lower on the socioeconomic scale would be more successful if they didn't have problems outside the classroom. We are looking for ways to make them feel at home, make them feel comfortable discussing issues that may be at play in their lives that are obstacles to their performing at a higher level."[30]

A series of Gallup polls have revealed that graduates of HBCUs usually are more likely to say that their professors cared about them as a person than are graduates of PWIs. HBCU alumni also typically report greater satisfaction with their lives than do PWI graduates.[31] Walter M. Kimbrough, the highly regarded though recently retired president of Dillard University, put it this way: "While Black students have been admitted to some of these 'better' schools, they have not been accepted."[32]

These comments directly imply an obvious and very interesting hypothesis: that Black students attending PWIs are not as comfortable or accepted as they are at an HBCU and therefore do not perform as well as they would at an HBCU. This does not mean that measures of performance such as the six-year graduation rate will be as high at HBCUs as at PWIs; rather, it indicates that similarly situated students will graduate at higher rates at HBCUs than at PWIs. "Similarly situated" is the key phrase.

Versions of the comfort hypothesis have been tested as it relates to the retention and graduation rates of Black undergraduates. Evidence exists that when standardized test scores and household incomes are incorporated as control variables into the empirical analyses of student performance, Black students at HBCUs as a group usually perform as well as or better than Blacks at PWIs. Hardy, Kaganda, and Aruguete[33] provided a mini-review of this evidence in 2020 and supplied some of their own data, which focused on retention and graduation rates and the incomes earned by students after graduation. De Zeeuw, Fazili, and Hotchkiss, researchers at the Federal Reserve Bank of Atlanta, came to a similar conclusion with respect to the earnings of HBCU women graduates. After controlling for institutional characteristics such as Scholastic Aptitude Test (SAT) scores and level of tuition and fees, the authors found that women HBCU graduates out-earned women graduates at PWIs. However, PWIs graduates outperformed HBCU graduates in STEM-related disciplines.[34]

These studies follow up on earlier, similar work by Ehrenberg and Rothstein,[35] Nichols and Evans-Bell (graduation rates),[36] Richards and Awokoya (retention and graduation),[37] and Franke and DeAngelo (graduation rates).[38]

Figure 2.5 provides visual evidence of the comfort effect by means of a naive predictive statistical model that focuses

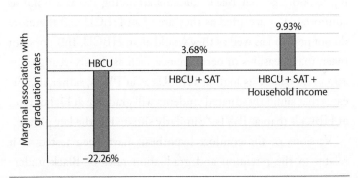

FIGURE 2.5 Impact of HBCUs on graduation rates, FY 2018

Source: IPEDS for graduation rates; U.S. Department of Education, "College Scorecard," https://collegescorecard.ed.gov/data, for SAT scores; Opportunity Insights (2021) for estimated household income.

on graduation rates.[39] We start with a sample of 236 four-year colleges and universities, 50 of which are HBCUs.[40] Suppose our task is to predict the six-year graduation rates of this representative sample of colleges and universities, but the only thing we know about each institution is whether or not it is an HBCU. If this is all we know, then HBCU status is associated with a predicted first-time full-time six-year graduation rate that is 22.26 percent below that of the typical institution in our sample.

This is not a positive outcome, so we refine our predictive model by adding the average SAT score of entering freshmen at each institution. This changes things dramatically. HBCU status now is associated with a predicted graduation rate 3.68 percent higher than the representative institution in our sample. That is, HBCUs are performing better than the typical campus in terms of graduation rates once we consider students' SAT scores.

Next, let's consider the impact of household income on graduation rates by adding to our explanatory model the average percentile rank of the incomes of the students' households. That is, how wealthy, on average, are the students on this campus? This, too, makes a big difference. Figure 2.5 reveals that HBCU status is associated with a predicted graduation rate 9.93 percent higher than the typical institution in our sample.

The salient point of this exercise is straightforward: once one controls for student preparation and considers the impact of family circumstances such as income, HBCUs as a group are seen to be doing an outstanding job in graduating their students. This may not hold true for all HBCUs, but the typical one outperforms the typical PWI insofar as graduation rates are concerned—once we control for household characteristics. We return to this topic with more sophisticated statistical techniques in chapter 4.

PWIs ranked among the elite enroll gifted students with high SAT scores who come from upper-income households. Thus, it is hardly surprising that these students graduate in large numbers. The highly ranked institutions they attend would have to fail conspicuously for that not to occur.

Among other things, this example tells us that raw, unadjusted graduation rates are not very informative. Nor are other unadjusted institutional performance measures, such as retention rates, postgraduation earnings, and loan repayment rates. The relevant consideration is how well institutions perform once we take their circumstances into account.

The simple dynamic illustrated in figure 2.5 constitutes an argument in support of HBCUs because it discloses that a randomly selected Black student is more likely to graduate from an HBCU than from a PWI once we consider that student's SAT score and family income. We will have more to say about this in chapter 5.

Lest you be inclined to regard the previous experiment as a clever statistical quirk, let's repeat the process using a different measure of performance: incomes of college graduates. PayScale annually estimates the salaries earned by individuals at various stages in their careers.[41] We focus this time on predicting median incomes of individuals who are at midcareer, approximately twenty years after graduation.

As figure 2.6 reveals, if all we know about our midcareer individuals is that they graduated from an HBCU, we can predict that their median annual salary will be $22,275 below that of the typical college graduate, according to PayScale. If, however, we add to the statistical mix their average SAT scores, this disadvantage declines significantly, to $771 annually. Next, taking family income into account, let's add to our predictive model the proportion of students on each campus who are Pell Grant

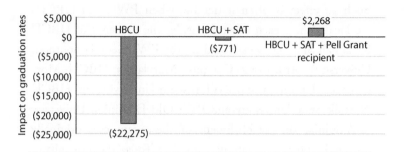

FIGURE 2.6 Impact of HBCUs on midcareer incomes, FY 2021

recipients. This also makes a big difference. Now we predict that the student's annual salary will rise $2,268 above that of a representative student from a representative institution. Here is another instance of how well HBCU students are served by their institutions. Thus, after the typical academic preparation and financial circumstances of their students are taken into account, HBCUs are seen to perform admirably and enable their students to exceed the level of achievement that we would expect from similarly situated students at PWIs.

The point is that HBCUs provide students with valuable support and a sense of ease and comfort, which enables large numbers of them to realize their potential. The graduation rates and incomes of students at HBCUs may not match those of graduates at the nation's elite institutions, but similarly situated students ordinarily progress more at an HBCU than they would at a PWI.

If there is a chink in the armor of the comfort thesis, it is that the proportion of self-identified Black individuals attending many PWIs has increased, sometimes significantly. This suggests that at least on some PWI campuses, the comfort level for Black students no longer deters large numbers of them from enrolling.

Such an effect is often noticeable when PWIs and HBCUs are located near each other. Consider the existence of HBCU Savannah State University and nearby PWI Georgia Southern University's Armstrong Campus, Maryland's HBCU Morgan State University and PWI Towson University, and HBCU Norfolk State University and PWI Old Dominion University in Virginia. The establishment of these campuses originally reflected explicit segregationist impulses. Today, the proximity of such institutions poses competitive challenges for both HBCUs and PWIs, but especially HBCUs, which must maintain or up their game to remain competitive.

These pairs of institutions (and there are many others) compete for Black students and perhaps as well for the academic programs that attract Black students.[42] It is clear that many Black students would rather attend an HBCU than a PWI, but the reverse also appears to be true: some Black students choose a PWI over an HBCU. They may do so because of their perceptions of the relative quality of the institutions, their beliefs about their labor market prospects after graduation, or the reality that some PWIs underprice neighboring HBCUs for low-income students. What cannot be denied is that the increased interest many PWIs have shown in recruiting Black students has had an adverse impact on HBCU enrollments.

HBCUs Excel at Providing Students with Upward Economic Mobility

Another substantive argument in favor of HBCUs is that as a group, they are highly successful in enabling graduates to gain significant upward economic mobility compared with where they started. And, as table 2.3 reveals, "compared with where they started" is an important qualifier.

TABLE 2.3 INCOME MOBILITY CONFERRED BY
VARIOUS TYPES OF UNIVERSITIES ACCORDING
TO OPPORTUNITY INSIGHTS

(1) Institution type	(2) Average household income percentile of students	(3) Average percentage of households in lowest income quintile	(4) Average percentage of lowest-income quantile students who move to highest quintile	(5) Average mobility coefficient
HBCU	43.5	23.4	14.9	2.87
Flagship public	69.3	5.9	35.0	2.07
Metro leader	61.1	9.9	25.8	2.57
Regional public	57.8	11.5	21.3	2.25
Private	65.4	7.3	27.9	1.72
Private selective	77.2	3.9	45.1	1.74

Source: Opportunity Insights, Data Library, "Income Segregation and Intergenerational Mobility Across Colleges in the United States," https://opportunityinsights.org/data.

Column 2 records Opportunity Insights' estimates of the average percentile in the national income distribution of students at various types of universities. One can see that the household of the typical student at an HBCU ranked in the 43.5th percentile, whereas the typical student at a flagship state university came from a household ranked in the 69.3rd percentile.[43] Column 3 records the percentage of students on each type of campus from a household in the lowest income quintile, and column 4 shows the percentage of those students who earned incomes that placed them in the highest income quintile in 2014.

Selective private institutions[44] no doubt point to column 4 to highlight the fact that 45.1 percent of their students from the lowest household income quintile subsequently rose to the highest quintile. At first glance, this seems a superb result. The problem with this interpretation is apparent from column 3, which notes that on average, only 3.9 percent of these institutions' student bodies came from households in the lowest income quintile. Opportunity Insights adjusts for this rather low 3.9 percent value by multiplying the column 3 value by the column 4 value to produce a mobility coefficient that reflects the comparative total size of an institution's contribution to income mobility. We follow Opportunity Insights' practice in column 5, except we multiple the coefficient by 100 so that it is more easily interpreted.

The mobility coefficients in column 5 tell us which institutions are making the largest comparative improvement in income inequality, as measured by the upward movement in the income distribution. One can see that HBCUs shine in this regard and easily lead the pack, followed by the metro leader institutions.

Let's endow the Opportunity Insights data with greater meaning by offering specific examples. Consider Georgia Tech, ranked among *U.S. News and World Report*'s top twenty-five public universities. On average, its graduates earn more than those of any other institution in Georgia, including in the private sector.[45] The Opportunity Insights Project estimated that the average Georgia Tech undergraduate who graduated between 1990 and 2001 was earning an income that ranked them in the 76th percentile nationally in 2014.[46] Interestingly, students also came from households ranked in the 76th income percentile . Thus, this group of graduates maintained the family income percentile that they inherited. Let's assign a value of 76 / 76 = 1.00 to this performance.

The typical HBCU, however, does better, shown by the detail in table 2.4. Consider Alabama A&M, which boasts a ratio of 1.30. This informs us that in 2014, the income of the typical graduate from 1990–2001 had climbed 30 percent above that of their parents. Indeed, the lowest HBCU ratio reported in the table is 1.19, substantially higher than any of the ratios for the comparator PWI campuses.

These data do not mean Alabama A&M graduates earn more in absolute dollars than Georgia Tech graduates; they do not by a large margin. Tech graduates' 76th percentile earnings tower above the 54th percentile earnings of A&M graduates.[47] Proportionately, however, Alabama A&M improves its graduates' circumstances more than does Tech. Table 2.4 provides earnings data for the HBCUs in eight states. In all instances, the HBCUs substantially surpass the PWI institutions in terms of proportionate increases in earnings for their graduates.

TABLE 2.4 RATIO OF GRADUATES' TO PARENTS' INCOMES
(KIDS/PAR) AT SELECTED HBCUS AND PWIS:
2014 INCOMES OF GRADUATES VERSUS
1980-91 INCOMES OF THEIR HOUSEHOLDS

Institution	HBCU ratio	PWI ratio
Alabama A&M U.	1.30	
Miles Coll.	1.33	
Auburn U.		0.84
Jacksonville State U.		1.03
Alcorn State U.	1.46	
Jackson State U.	1.36	
U. Mississippi		0.86
U. Southern Mississippi		1.05

(*continued*)

TABLE 2.4 (CONTINUED)

Institution	HBCU ratio	PWI ratio
Albany State U.	1.32	
U. Georgia		0.85
Georgia State U.		0.97
Florida A&M U.	1.19	
Florida State U.		0.93
U. Central Florida		0.86
Dillard U.	1.25	
Grambling State U.	1.35	
Louisiana Tech U.		1.01
McNeese State U.		1.03
South Carolina State U.	1.33	
Clemson U.		0.92
Coastal Carolina U.		0.91
Prairie View A&M U.	1.31	
Texas Southern U.	1.38	
Texas A&M U.		0.94
U. Texas San Antonio		1.02
Virginia State U.	1.25	
Virginia Union U.	1.23	
Virginia Tech		0.93
George Mason U.		0.96

Notes: Each number is the ratio of the average income percentile rank in the U.S. household income distribution of the graduates of an institution in 2014 to the average percentile rank of students' parents in the U.S household income distribution over the period 1980–91. Therefore, in 2014, if the average income of graduates of a state university ranked those individuals in the 60th percentile but the average income of the household from which they came ranked in the 50th percentile, then 60 / 50 = 1.20. A ratio above 1.00 roughly indicates that the 2014 graduates of this institution were doing relatively better in terms of income than were their parents.

Source: Opportunity Insights, MRC tables 2 and 3.

We note three potential caveats with respect to the results in table 2.4. First, one could argue that it is absolute income changes, not the relative ones we have documented, that should count. However, this is not a disarming critique, because societal mobility often is viewed through the lens of relative, not absolute changes. It is common to speak of incomes growing 10 percent rather than an absolute amount. Similarly, terms such as "middle class" often are used rather than specific income dollar values. The relevant point is that societal mobility can be viewed usefully in terms of relative progress, and this is what we do in table 2.4.

A second caveat is that highly regarded nationally ranked institutions often do very good things for the smaller numbers of lower-income students on their campuses. Opportunity Insights data reveal that 70.2 percent of Georgia Tech students who were born between 1980 and 1991 and were from the bottom quintile of the income distribution subsequently reached the top income quintile in 2014.[48] This is impressive. However, the problem once again is that Georgia Tech admits very few of these students from the lowest income quartile. In 2017–18, only 3.23 percent of its undergraduates were from the bottom income quintile.[49] This profoundly weakens the total impact Georgia Tech has on societal mobility. We have more to say about this in chapter 4.

The third caveat is that the average six-year graduation rate at a representative HBCU typically is below that of non-HBCUs. This is important because if one doesn't graduate, one is much less likely to benefit from the improved income mobility outlined in table 2.4.

The evidence presented in table 2.4 is intriguing because it provides provocative institutional comparisons. It is legitimate to inquire, however, if these patterns hold throughout all of academe. In general, the answer is yes. Take a moment to review the household income percentile data in table 2.3, which shows the average household income percentile of students attending a variety of types of four-year colleges in the United States. The median institutional household income percentile at a selective private institution is more than 35 points higher than at an HBCU. Simply put, these two types of institutions are serving very different student bodies in terms of the economic status of their students' households.

Thus, there is some legitimacy to the charge that American higher education—or at least certain portions of it—now increase economic inequality rather than decreasing it. Thomas Mortensen, a veteran observer of the ability of Americans to afford a college education, has charged, "The rich are getting richer because of higher education."[50] The data presented in this chapter provide some support for this view. HBCUs, however, clearly represent an obvious departure from this model and stand out as beacons of opportunity, given that almost one in four undergraduate students at an HBCU comes from a household in the lowest quintile of the income distribution.

HBCUs Are Key to the Maintenance of a Black Talent Pipeline That Cannot Be Replicated at PWIs

Historically, HBCUs have functioned as the proverbial ladder to success for Black students. They have excelled at producing students who later become valued professionals. The following facts are revealing.

- More than 80 percent of all Black Americans who have received degrees in medicine and dentistry did so at two HBCUs: Howard University and Meharry Medical College.

- Ten of the top eleven campuses producing Black bachelor's degree recipients who subsequently earn a PhD are HBCUs.
- HBCUs were the undergraduate homes of three-fourths of Black individuals holding any doctoral degree.
- Three-quarters of all Black military officers earned their baccalaureate degrees at an HBCU.
- Four-fifths of all Black federal judges are HBCU graduates.
- One-half of all Black faculty holding appointments at PWIs started their careers at an HBCU.[51]

How can we explain this superb performance? Carl Bonner, professor of chemistry at Norfolk State University, says Black students realize that HBCU faculty "care about them, that we will go the extra mile to help them be prepared for what they will encounter."[52] Many HBCUs have earned reputations for being caring institutions.

Can this enviable talent pipeline performance be replicated by PWIs in the future? That remains to be seen, but it is safe to say we will not have to wait decades to find out. Many PWIs now enroll significant proportions of self-identified Black students, and soon it will be possible to conduct large-scale tests to see how these students fare (both on campus and after graduation) relative to those at HBCUs. In the past, Black students at PWIs have not performed as well as comparably situated students at HBCUs.

HBCUs Have a Substantial Positive Social and Economic Impact on Their Communities

Individual HBCU campuses may be experiencing considerable fiscal stress, but collectively, HBCUs are big business. In FY 2018, the 50 HBCUs in our sample had combined operating revenues in excess of $4.41 billion. The average HBCU in our sample boasted operating revenues of $88.2 million.[53]

Those 50 HBCUs are major employers, with more than 32,000 full-time and about 7,000 part-time employees. This is a very big deal in some of the communities where HBCUs are located. Mississippi Valley State University (MVSU) is located in Itta Bena, a community of about 2,000 in the Mississippi Delta region. The city's population peaked at 2,904 in 1980 and has been declining since then. MVSU's enrollment has followed a similar pattern, peaking at a bit more than 3,600 in 2005 and declining almost continuously to slightly less than 2,300 in 2019. Almost 90 percent of the Itta Bena's population is Black, and nearly 36 percent of its population and surrounding LeFlore County were judged to be in poverty in 2019.[54]

It is fair to say that MVSU is by far the most important industry in Itta Bena; in 2018, the university employed 408 full-time and 107 part-time individuals. These employees accounted for about one-quarter of the city's population. The average salary of a full professor at MVSU in 2019 was $64,724, 2.42 times larger than the average household income in LeFlore County.[55] MVSU clearly equates to economic "gold" in Itta Bena and LeFlore County. Were it to disappear, the economic consequences would be severe.

The vital economic character of HBCUs due to the employment they offer is not restricted to rural locations. The District of Columbia's Howard University employed 2,722 individuals (2,390 full-time, 67.6 percent of whom were Black) in FY 2019 and had revenues of $935 million.[56] These are impressive numbers even in D.C. and underline the economic importance of Howard to the region's Black community.

Historically, HBCU campuses were one of the few places Black citizens could expect to be treated fairly in terms of employment. HBCUs have offered employment and salaries that usually were regionally respectable along with some sense of security. Individuals who could not get past the proverbial front door of predominantly white businesses, corporations, and universities nevertheless could compete for attractive jobs at HBCUs. These circumstances remain,[57] and that is one of the reasons HBCUs usually are treasured in their communities. They represent invaluable sources of employment and culture in a sometimes hostile world. Plus, they offer Black individuals a sense of control that may seem absent in the wider economy.

Thus, whether or not Black students gain admission at PWIs, the attachment of Black communities to their HBCUs has remained strong. Consequently, whenever discussions arise about merging HBCUs and PWIs,[58] or even combining HBCUs under one institutional HBCU umbrella,[59] one can count on vociferous opposition from the Black community. More than one white politician has stumbled because they did not understand these dynamics.

There have been occasional downsides to the otherwise favorable impact of HBCUs on Black labor markets and employment. Nepotism is not unknown at HBCUs, and personal connections within the Black community or on campus can be instrumental in one candidate's receiving a job offer over another. These behaviors may not differ dramatically from those in the rest of academe but on occasion have received broad publicity.[60]

Fear of disruption may lead some HBCUs to be wary of outsiders, Black outsiders not excepted. Bill Maxwell, a Black syndicated columnist of the *Tampa Bay Times*, teed up a variety of allegations concerning HBCUs when he averred that "the HBCU practice of hiring from within creates intellectual incest: a culture of arrogance, blind allegiance, cronyism, nepotism, normalization of mediocrity and incompetence, and the inculcation of a bunker mentality."[61] These are serious assertions that in some ways proclaim that conditions can become too comfortable at HBCUs.

Because Maxwell's contentions represent perceptions, it is difficult to formulate them in the form of testable hypotheses. One can, however, examine institutions' internal resource allocations (where they choose to spend their money) and view these allocations as projections of institutional values, mores, and decisions. Reputationally, HBCUs as a group are considered to be administratively top-heavy,[62] which represents a testable hypothesis. Table 2.5 examines the proportion of major expenditures on institutional support. IPEDS describes institutional support expenditures as follows.

> A functional expense category that includes expenses for the day-to-day operational support of the institution. Includes expenses for general administrative services, central executive-level activities concerned with management and long-range planning, legal and fiscal operations, space management, employee personnel and records, logistical services such as purchasing and printing, and public relations and development. Also includes information technology expenses related to institutional support activities. If an institution does not separately budget and expense information technology resources, the IT costs associated with student services and operation and maintenance of plant will also be applied to this function.[63]

Thus, institutional support represents what most individuals associate with "administration."

**TABLE 2.5 MEDIAN PERCENTAGE OF REAL MAJOR
CAMPUS EXPENDITURES ON INSTITUTIONAL SUPPORT,
BY CAMPUS CATEGORY, FY 2004-18**

Category	FY 2005	FY 2008	FY 2013	FY 2018
Flagships	11.95%	13.03%	12.08%	13.64%
Metro leaders	12.37%	13.13%	13.00%	14.48%
Regionals	11.95%	13.03%	12.14%	13.79%
HBCUs	15.51%	15.72%	15.80%	17.37%
Publics	12.42%	13.13%	13.00%	14.03%
Privates	14.71%	14.80%	13.55%	14.41%
FBS football	12.18%	13.36%	13.07%	13.87%
FCS football	13.25%	13.14%	13.55%	14.57%
No football	12.62%	13.69%	13.55%	14.42%
Means of the medians	13.00%	13.67%	13.30%	14.51%

Note: These percentages reflect the proportion of campus expenditures on instruction
as a proportion of total campus expenditures on instruction + academic support +
research + student services + institutional support. Data are price-adjusted.

Source: U.S. Department of Education, Integrated Postsecondary Data System
(hereafter cited as IPEDS), https://nces.ed.gov/ipeds.

Two trends are evident in the table 2.5 data. First, in every class
of institution, the proportion of major expenditures devoted to
institutional support increased between FY 2004 and FY 2018.
Second, HBCUs devote higher proportions of their budgets to
institutional support than other institution types. One empirical
study concluded that this larger expenditure has had a negative
impact on graduation rates at HBCUs,[64] but that counterintuitive finding has not been replicated in any other study.

In partial defense of HBCUs with respect to the claims of
top-heavy administration, one should recognize that economies of scale exist in many administrative functions. The larger

the student body, the greater the potential to realize lower average unit costs. Most HBCUs are too small to be able to spread fixed administrative costs across larger numbers of students. This argument is only partly convincing, because regional public PWIs also tend to be somewhat smaller and devote substantially smaller proportions of their budgets to institutional support than HBCUs.

HBCUs historically have served as a major source of employment for Black individuals. In some instances, an HBCU may have been the only employer willing to hire an appropriately qualified Black applicant. This may have led HBCUs to lean in the direction of spending money on human rather than physical capital. Whether one considers small size and the inability to realize economies of scale as the major reason or prefers an explanation that focuses on rampant employment discrimination, the data in table 2.5 indicate that the representative HBCU consistently has devoted a larger proportion of resources to institutional support than the usual PWI.

Table 2.6 supplies an additional view of HBCU resource allocation by focusing on each institution's expenditures on instruction. HBCUs do not shine in this analysis either, devoting substantially lower percentages of their budgets to instruction than the typical PWI. Further, the position of HBCUs in this regard has deteriorated since FY 2004. This should be a matter of concern on HBCU campuses.

Thus, there is room to question how resources are allocated inside the typical HBCU. The generally impressive performance of HBCUs on the six metrics we have discussed in this chapter might be even stronger if campus decision making and management were modified.

TABLE 2.6 MEDIAN PERCENTAGE OF REAL MAJOR CAMPUS EXPENDITURES ON INSTRUCTION, BY CAMPUS CATEGORY, FY 2004-18

Category	FY 2004	FY 2008	FY 2013	FY 2018
Flagships	43.05%	44.00%	44.10%	42.52%
Metro leaders	53.18%	52.84%	51.88%	51.33%
Regionals	56.44%	55.48%	54.15%	54.81%
HBCUs	43.26%	41.61%	41.45%	39.47%
Publics	50.06%	49.83%	49.38%	48.27%
Privates	40.04%	32.53%	36.88%	34.39%
FBS football	47.56%	47.60%	46.99%	46.43%
FCS football	51.45%	51.13%	49.82%	49.84%
No football	47.95%	47.72%	46.61%	46.77%
Means of the medians	48.11%	46.97%	46.81%	45.98%

Note: These percentages reflect the proportion of campus expenditures on instruction as a proportion of total campus expenditures on instruction + academic support + research + student services + institutional support. Data are price-adjusted.

Source: U.S. Department of Education, Integrated Postsecondary Data System (hereafter cited as IPEDS), https://nces.ed.gov/ipeds.

Source: IPEDS.

SUMMING IT UP

An empirical case can be made for the existence and support of HBCUs. Each of the six hypotheses levied in support of HBCUs is plausible, and there is empirical evidence in favor of each. The three hypotheses that benefit from the strongest empirical evidence in support of their predictions are what we have termed the "comfort" explanation, the tremendous talent pipeline that HBCUs have nurtured and developed, and their ability to provide graduates with impressive upward economic mobility.

Evidence is more mixed with respect to the traditional "we provide opportunities to enroll not available at PWIs" and the assertion that HBCUs are more affordable than PWIs. However, much depends on the location (state and institution within that state) and students' household income.

Our final hypothesis asserted that HBCUs have significant social and economic impact in Black communities. Quantitatively, this is undeniable and an important reason that HBCUs retain fervent support in those communities. In the absence of a post-racial society and the introduction of economic policies that clearly improve the status of Blacks, we should expect to see only modest deterioration of that support even as greater proportions of Black students choose to attend PWIs.

3

DECLINING HBCU ENROLLMENTS— A MYSTERY OR NOT?

"Is there any point to which you would wish to draw my attention?"

—Sherlock Holmes

Some observers of higher education appear ready to write obituaries for HBCUs.[1] They observe that headcount enrollment in the nation's 101 HBCUs fell by more than 46,000 between fall 2010 and fall 2020 (–14.3 percent) and that the COVID-19 pandemic exacerbated serious financial conditions that already existed at a dozen or more small HBCUs. Figure 3.1 demonstrates that while the rate of decline in total enrollments has slackened in recent years, those enrollments have continued to diminish in eight of the past ten years. But headcount enrollments at all degree-granting institutions of higher education declined in all ten.

Figure 3.1 seems to paint a bleak picture, but reality is considerably more nuanced. Among today's HBCUs are some conspicuous successes. Table 3.1 lists institutions where headcount enrollments rose more than 10 percent between FY 2010 and FY 2021. Of these 15 growing campuses, 4 enrolled fewer than a

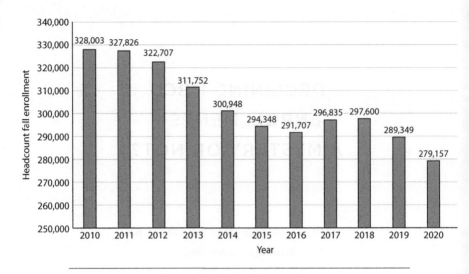

FIGURE 3.1 Headcount student enrollment at U.S. degree-granting HBCUs, fall 2010–fall 2020

Source: IPEDS.

thousand students in fall 2019. Hence, it is not preordained that enrollments at HBCUs in general, or small HBCUs in particular, must decline. Indeed, figure 3.2 illustrates that 26 of 102 four-year degree granting HBCUs expanded enrollments between fall 2010 and fall 2020.

If we limit our focus to four-year not-for-profit institutions (both public and independent), using IPEDS headcount enrollment data for 2,254 institutions for the period fall 2010–fall 2020, we find that enrollments for 1,228 (54.5 percent) grew. Compare this with the 26 / 102 = 25.5 percent of comparable HBCUs that expanded increased enrollments during the same years. Again, though these seem to be unfavorable data, as we will see, HBCUs roughly maintained their enrollment market share during that period.

TABLE 3.1 FOUR-YEAR DEGREE-GRANTING HBCUs WHOSE HEADCOUNT ENROLLMENTS GREW MORE THAN 10 PERCENT BETWEEN FALL 2010 AND FALL 2020

Institution	Enrollment growth rates and headcount enrollment, fall 2010–fall 2020
Albany State University	39.9% (6,509)
Bowie State University	12.0% (6,250)
Central State University	75.7% (4,021)
Delaware State University	26.1% (4,739)
Edward Waters College	195.6% (2,273)
Fayetteville State University	16.3% (6,726)
Fisk University	57.1% (911)
Huston-Tillotson University	17.4% (1,058)
Jarvis Christian College	37.7% (719)
North Carolina A&T University	18.1% (12,753)
Paul Quinn College	107.1% (468)
Philander Smith College	14.8% (799)
St. Philip's College	17.3% (12,696)
Talladega College	63.7% (1,156)
West Virginia State University	14.0% (4,020)

Source: U.S. Department of Education, Integrated Postsecondary Data System (hereafter cited as IPEDS), https://nces.ed.gov/ipeds.

HBCU growth rates have varied substantially in recent years. While a majority of HBCUs were declining in size between fall 2010 and fall 2020, most campuses experiencing those reductions were small, and their contractions were partially counteracted by growth at larger HBCUs.

Inside the HBCU institutional universe, one can find distinctive stories behind the enrollment picture in our tables and figures. A skilled new president can improve the fortunes

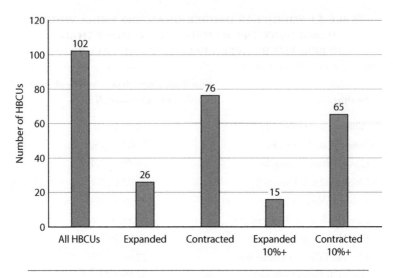

FIGURE 3.2 Expanding and contracting headcount enrollments at
86 four-year degree-granting HBCUs, fall 2010–fall 2019

Source: IPEDS.

of an HBCU dramatically. Consider Talladega College, whose
enrollment at the turn of the century was suffering for a variety of reasons, one of the most important being its probationary
accreditation status with the Southern Association of Colleges
and Schools. Fortuitously for Talladega, William C. "Billy"
Hawkins became president in 2008 and succeeded in restoring
the institution's full accreditation, reducing its debt, relaunch-
ing its intercollegiate athletic programs, improving the institution's physical plant, and obtaining significant financial gifts. The
results speak for themselves: headcount enrollment increased
more than 63.70 percent between fall 2010 and fall 2020. Leadership makes a difference.[2]

Sometimes unusual circumstances have an impact on enrollment; for example, Georgia's 2017 mandated merger of PWI

Darton State College with HBCU Albany State University—
one of the few such consolidations "across the line" ever undertaken.[3] On occasion, enrollment growth has accompanied an
institution's evolution away from its HBCU roots, as has been
the case at West Virginia State University, where in fall 2019,
only 8.0 percent of undergraduate students self-identified as
Black. The university's enrollment grew 14.0 percent between fall
2010 and fall 2020 even while overall higher education enrollments in West Virginia were stagnating.

Consider the State of North Carolina, where the enrollment of the nation's largest HBCU, North Carolina A&T University, expanded by 10.8 percent between 2010 and 2017, even
while enrollment at HBCU Elizabeth City State University
was declining by 57.3 percent. Sometimes a distance of only a
few miles can make a difference. In Baltimore, Morgan State
University is thriving and expanding, while only five miles away,
Coppin State University is confronting major challenges that
include large enrollment declines.

Interestingly, several well-regarded, iconic HBCU institutions—
notably Florida A&M University, Hampton University, and
Morehouse College—experienced declining headcount enrollments between fall 2010 and fall 2020. These contractions ranged
from 16.8 percent at Morehouse to 33.1 percent at Hampton.[4]
In several instances, some or all the reductions were somewhat
deliberate, as the institutions were encountering increasingly
stiff competition from PWIs and declined to lower their admissions standards.

The lesson here is that we need to be cautious about drawing
conclusions about HBCUs overall or in general; their individual
circumstances often vary substantially. Some individuals occasionally tend to characterize all HBCUs in a stereotypical manner that applies no more to those institutions than to all PWIs.

The collection of universities recognized as Historic Black Colleges and Universities were founded to educate newly freed slaves. Each university had a unique mission and goals, which ranged from instructing teachers and farmers to providing a liberal arts education. These missions have evolved over time, but central to all has always been uplifting and educating members of Black communities. Not until the Higher Education Act of 1964, which recognized the issues that segregation historically posed for Black Americans, did the federal government recognize HBCUs as a distinct group of colleges. However, just like many other colleges and universities, the group is heterogeneous. This variety makes them more interesting and often fosters a group of alumni who maintain a strong passion for and love of their universities, more than is the case for many public PWIs. Another example of HBCUs' heterogeneity is that they range in size and complexity, from small rural church-supported institutions such as the 566-student Wilberforce University in small-town Ohio to a federally supported research university in an urban center, such as the 9,399-student Howard University in Washington, D.C. Sometimes pairs of HBCUs are located very close to each other, such as Claflin University and South Carolina State University or Wilberforce University and Central State University.

PROPOSITIONS/HYPOTHESES

With the preceding caveat in mind, let's analyze why HBCU enrollment fell over the past decade. We will learn that, contrary to what some might expect, in the period fall 2010–fall 2020,

HBCUs as a group have performed as well as (or even better than) the typical college or university.

We focus our analysis on nine propositions/hypotheses that relate to higher education enrollments in general and HBCUs in particular. Each purports to speak to the question of why enrollments at HBCUs overall have declined and what that signifies. We will see that the evidence supports some of these assertions, but not others.

- Overall, higher-education enrollments are declining.
- HBCUs are losing market share.
- For-profit private institutions have cut into HBCU enrollments.
- PWIs' increased interest in enrolling more Black students has depressed HBCU enrollment levels.
- The growth of distance learning has stunted HBCU enrollments.
- Falling birth rates and unfavorable demographics have damaged HBCU enrollments.
- Rising labor force participation by Blacks has reduced the number going to college.
- HBCUs are less successful than PWIs at enrolling male students.
- Changes in federal financial aid regulations have disadvantaged HBCUs.

1. Overall, Higher-Education Enrollments Are Declining

We can deal with the primary hypothesis immediately: higher education enrollments in general have been declining, and HBCUs simply are part of this trend. Indeed, in every year between fall 2011 and fall 2020, total headcount enrollments in

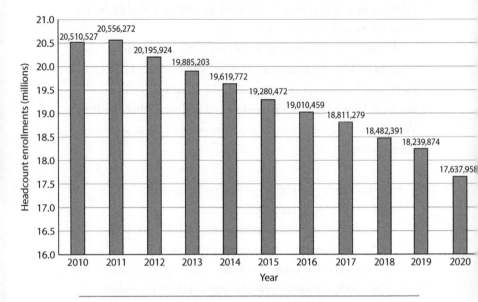

FIGURE 3.3 Headcount student enrollments in American higher
education, fall 2010–fall 2020

Note: 2020 is estimated.

Source: National Student Clearinghouse Research Center, "Current Term Enrollment
Estimates," 2020 and previous years, https://nscresearchcenter.org/current-term
-enrollment-estimates.

American higher education declined. Figure 3.3 illustrates the
loss of 2.92 million students (14.20 percent) in fall enrollments
during this period.

Compare this reduction with the 17.46 percent decline in col-
lective headcount enrollment at HBCUs over the same period.
Conclusion? HBCUs as a group have been damaged by enrollment reductions, and COVID-19 has not been kind to them.
Nevertheless, approximately one-quarter of HBCUs experienced expanding enrollments over the same period.

The decline in enrollment at the 50 HBCUs in our sample was smaller than the national HBCU average—9.9 percent as opposed to 17.46 percent—primarily because our institutional group excludes several dozen relatively small HBCUs for which consistent data were not available. Why don't these institutions comply with the federal government's reporting demands for data? They do not view sending detailed numbers to Washington, D.C., as their highest priority when they are struggling for existence. Such time-consuming reports, grumbled an HBCU administrator, "cost us money but recruit us zero students." This not an isolated phenomenon. Many small institutions find federal reporting requirements onerous.

Sarah Brown, "Colleges Had 3 Months to Overhaul Sexual-Misconduct Policies. Now They're Scrambling," *Chronicle of Higher Education*, August 13, 2020, https:///www.chronicle.com/article/colleges-had-three-months-to -overhaul-sexual-misconduct-policies-now-theyre-scrambling.

If there is an endangered species among HBCUs, it is a small, independent institution with a tiny endowment located in a rural area. The COVID-19 pandemic added to challenges that already existed on such campuses. Painful layoffs and contractions have occurred at some.[5] Major donors have tended to ignore these small HBCUs and focused their gifts on more visible institutions, such as Hampton, Howard, Morehouse, and Spelman.[6]

Even when challenged HBCUs are successful in recruiting students, sometimes they do so by engaging in deep tuition discounting. For several institutions in our sample, records show that in some years, they eventually gave away every dollar of tuition and fees in scholarships and grants—a discount rate of 100 percent.

The HBCUs under stress have another commonality: the market value of their endowments typically is small. Based on oft-cited annual endowment data compiled by the National Association of College and University Business Officers, it seems likely that only 18 among the more than 100 HBCUs were ranked among the top 700 institutions nationally in terms of endowment size.[7] We estimate that the median value of an endowment at a four-year HBCU today is $25 million or less. If an institution spends 4.0 percent each year, the typical HBCU can rely on no more than $1.0 million annually from its foundation. While that income is nothing to sneeze at, it underlines the dependency of most HBCUs on tuition-paying students to remain solvent.

2. HBCUs Are Losing Market Share

This assertion is false. As a group, HBCUs are holding their own, primarily because other sectors (especially two-year institutions and community colleges) have lost market share. The roughly horizontal lines in figure 3.4 tell this story visually. While the percentage of Black individuals attending college has tapered off a bit since 2010, that of Black students who attend an HBCU has increased. Further, the market share of HBCUs in higher education undergraduate enrollment overall has remained roughly constant: 1.59 percent of all students (all races) attended an HBCU in fall 2010 and 1.58 percent in fall 2019.

Thus, it can be seen that HBCUs as a group have not been pushed out of higher education markets. However, the overall

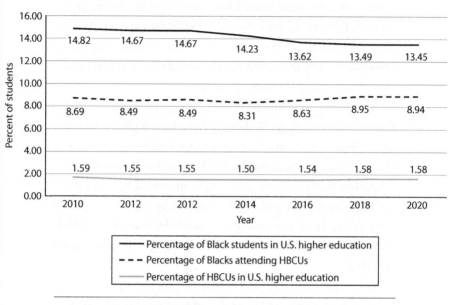

FIGURE 3.4 Black representation in U.S. higher education
and at 102 HBCUs, fall 2010–fall 2020

Source: National Student Clearinghouse Research Center, "Current Term
Enrollment Estimates," for various years.

market for college students has contracted, which presumes that
some HBCUs will suffer enrollment losses as well.

As noted earlier, headcount enrollment at America's colleges
and universities fell over nine consecutive years, resulting in
approximately 2.9 million fewer students in fall 2020 compared
with fall 2010.[8] Inevitably, such circumstances will injure institutions, some of which are HBCUs.

Even so, HBCUs have maintained their share of the higher
education student enrollment market. This is no mean achieve-
ment in a contracting, declining industry that has been turned
upside down. Who would have anticipated at the dawn of this

century that we were headed for a decade of declining enrollments?[9] Few would have forecast that Southern New Hampshire University, an institution that was experiencing falling enrollments early in the first decade, would turn about and enroll more than 113,000 students by 2020.

Amid this turmoil, inspecting the details around these data can be revealing. Although American higher education as a whole was contracting between fall 2010 and fall 2020, the median four-year public PWI grew. The median size of a flagship institution in our sample increased by 1,816 FTE students, by 955 for a metro leader, and by 234 for a regional institution. It is reasonable to conclude that these PWIs enrolled some students who otherwise might have attended an HBCU.

With the total size of the enrollment pie shrinking and PWIs growing, one can ask which other institutional types were experiencing reduced enrollments. The answer is independent for-profit private institutions and community colleges, both of which lost substantial market share (see figure 3.5).

Because community colleges are public institutions closely tied to their communities and regions, realistically they are not going to be shuttered, although it now is incumbent on them to reassess their programmatic mix and approach to prospective students. However, the same "things will muddle on" conclusion does not apply to for-profit independent institutions, about which we will say more shortly. Some clearly are at risk.

Nor should institutions of small size assume their futures are assured. Of the 102 HBCUs that existed in 2020, 32 reported headcount enrollments of less than 1,000, and 49 had enrollments under 2,000. More than 80 percent of the latter campuses experienced declining enrollments between 2010 and 2020. Over that decade, the median size of a public HBCU declined from

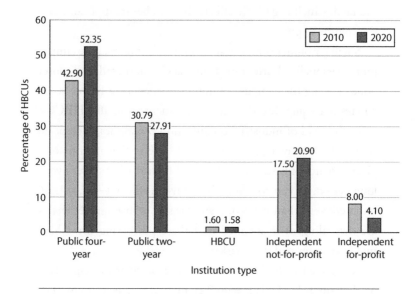

FIGURE 3.5 Headcount enrollment market shares by institution type, fall 2010 and fall 2020

Note: Overlap exists between market shares; for example, between HBCUs and public four-year institutions.

Source: National Student Clearinghouse, "Current Term Enrollment Estimates," for various years; and IPEDS.

4,080 to 3,488, versus the shrinkage at an independent HBCU from 1,048 to 878 students.[10]

Relatively small enrollment size affects HBCUs in a variety of ways—some but not all of which are bad. Institutions with fewer students seldom can realize the potential economies of scale that can be gained in a range of administrative tasks. In addition, such institutions will find it difficult to mount the resources necessary to move forward with complex institutional efforts such as distance learning. Small size also tends to limit the number of admissions and fundraising personnel institutions can put into the field, which negatively affects the number of applicants and the volume of gifts.

Small enrollments may bestow some advantages; for example, more personalized attention from faculty and staff and closer bonds among the campus community. Financially, however, the end result frequently is declining enrollments at smaller HBCUs.

In the field of industrial organization economics, there is an adage, the "survivor principle," which asserts that if firms of a given size not only survive but expand their market shares over a long period, we can conclude that they are efficient—or, at least, more efficient than firms of a similar size whose market shares are dwindling. It is assumed that these prospering firms have met what is termed the "market test."

As applied to higher education, the survivor principle tells us that small HBCUs are inefficient because, as a group, they have been declining in size and losing market share. This is a severe judgment but (holding other things constant) one merited by the accumulated evidence. Viewing HBCUs in this context, one can see that without targeted additional government and private-sector foundation assistance, a dozen or more small, not-for-profit, independent-sector HBCUs are at risk of closing. Their failure would displace approximately 10,000 students, representing about 3 percent of total enrollments at America's HBCUs. Because this percentage is relatively small, some might be inclined to close their eyes as this "survival of the fittest" scenario plays out. However, there are factors other than financial ones to consider. The demise of ten to twenty small HBCUs would end the rich traditions of service to Black communities that most of these institutions have fostered over the years. They provide culture, entertainment, dignity, and employment as well as education. They often represent the very souls of their small towns and usually occupy a dominant economic role in their communities. "Our little town would dry up and blow away," one tenured woman HBCU faculty member lamented at the possibility that her institution might close became real to her.

Several supporters of smaller, endangered HBCUs told us they believe that some of the larger HBCUs covet their students and therefore will give no more than lip service to programs designed to ensure the survival of the smaller and weaker. Note that we do not reveal which are those larger institutions. Our goal is to enlighten readers about the circumstances of HBCUs, not promote personal or internecine battles.

MINI-CASE STUDY: KENTUCKY STATE UNIVERSITY AND THE BLACK LAND-GRANT UNIVERSITIES

Kentucky State University, founded in 1886, is the only HBCU in the state and a Black land-grant institution. The school offers a window on the existential challenges faced even by publicly supported HBCUs. Though Kentucky State is located in the capital city of Frankfort, its enrollment fell to 2,290 students in fall 2021, down from a high of 2,851 in fall 2011. It has not been greatly successful in serving the educational needs of state government; 62 percent of its students were nonresidents in fall 2021, and 40 percent of its undergraduate students were non-Black. The value of its endowment stood at only $21.9 million in mid-2021.

Kentucky State's status as a land-grant institution has meant relatively little in terms of programs or funding, as has been the case for nearly every Black land-grant institution. A recent informal study of the funding for seventeen such institutions concluded that their states have shortchanged them to the tune of $12.81 billion since 1987.[11] This estimate assumed that the Black land grants should have received the same amount per student as the PWI land grants, such as the University of Kentucky. The estimated funding deficits ranged from a gigantic $2.79 billion at North Carolina A&T University to no deficit at Delaware State University. Kentucky State's $1.66 million shortfall is relatively modest in this scenario.

Apart from land-grant funding, Kentucky State's recent history has been scarred by financial management problems and a November 2021 report from Kentucky's Council on Postsecondary Education, which documented a financial liquidity crisis so severe that supplementary funding of $23 million would be required for the university to make it through FY 2022.[12]

Kentucky State faces dilemmas that often confront HBCUs—should it emphasize its HBCU roots or focus on recruiting more non-Black students, especially state government employees? Can its land-grant status become meaningful? Given its financial position, how can it respond to the increased reliance on distance learning by many of today's students?

If Kentucky State were an independent-sector institution, it might be a candidate for merger or closure. Neither appears to be an option, and its future is uncertain.

3. For-Profit Private Institutions Have Cut Into HBCU Enrollments

The evidence in favor of this hypothesis is strong despite the efforts of the administration of President Barack Obama to rein in for-profits' ability to utilize the federal student loan program if their students had abysmal post-graduation employment experiences. The COVID-19 epidemic generated conditions conducive to enrollment in for-profit institutions—one reason being the great flexibility (some would argue excessive) they offer. IPEDS reports enrollment data for 1,322 degree-granting two-year and four-year institutions that are run on a for-profit basis. Only a minority of these institutions are accredited by a regional accrediting agency, but among them are Southern New Hampshire University (134,345 headcount students in fall 2020) and Grand Canyon University (103,427 in fall 2020). For-profit institutions collectively enroll three times as many students as HBCUs.

Further, Black students are more heavily represented at for-profit than other types of institutions. Approximately one in every four students at a for-profit is Black, whereas in higher education as a whole, that number is only one in eight. Hence, it is legitimate to conclude that for-profit institutions are siphoning off some HBCU enrollments and that this drain increased dramatically in the first half of the previous decade.

Once again, however, examining further details is productive. Figure 3.6 plots the enrollment of for-profit students by gender.

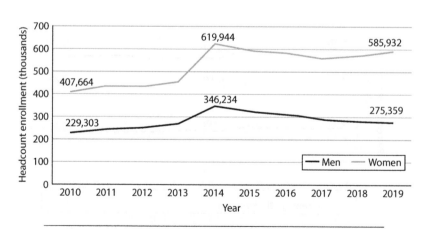

FIGURE 3.6 Percentage headcount enrollment by gender at 390 four-year for-profit institutions, fall 2010–fall 2019

Source: IPEDS.

In FY 2019, more than 73 percent of for-profit students were women, compared with about 63 percent at HBCUs and 56 percent in the remainder of higher education. Thus, the worry that for-profit institutions have strongly pulled from HBCUs the already scarce population of Black male college students does not appear to be valid. In reality, women are more drawn to for-profits than men.

Figure 3.7 shows the presence of Black students at for-profit institutions. One can see that the percentage has trended downward slowly for both Black men and women, although these percentages remain approximately double those in the not-for-profit sector.

For-profit institutions continue to be popular with Black students. In fall 2019, slightly more than 210,000 attended a four-year for-profit institution. That is only slightly smaller than the estimated 230,000 Black individuals attending HBCUs. Do the for-profits represent competition? Of course, but bear in mind

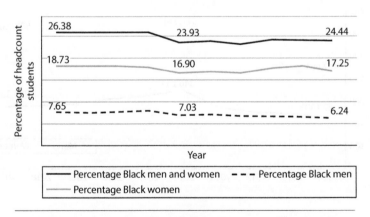

FIGURE 3.7 Percentage Black headcount enrollment at 390 four-year forprofit institutions, fall 2010–fall 2019

Source: IPEDS.

that differing programmatic mixes and admissions standards in these two sectors reduce any competitive overlap substantially.

That said, between fall 2010 and fall 2014, enrollment in for-profits grew by approximately 330,000 students, of whom more than 80,000 likely were Black. It is reasonable to assume that this tide of students had negative repercussions for enrollments at HBCUs. But it also is fair to assume that were those individuals to appear on HBCU campuses, their retention and graduation rates would be reduced.

4. PWIs' Increased Interest in Enrolling More Black Students Has Depressed HBCU Enrollment Levels

Figure 3.5 detailed the reality that public PWIs roughly maintained their market shares between fall 2010 and fall 2020. But competition for students with PWIs is always present. There are two ways to measure the impact of PWIs on Black enrollments at HBCUs. The first, a percentage effect, relates to the proportion of self-identified Black undergraduate students who enroll at PWIs. Figure 3.8, however, reveals that the percentage increases in the representation of Black students on many PWI campuses have been relatively modest, perhaps surprisingly so. Regional institutions led the way in terms of increases, followed by the metro leaders, with flagships trailing noticeably. Fewer than one in twenty undergraduate students at a flagship state university is Black.

But note that even if the percentages of Black students on each PWI campus remain constant, and given that PWI campus enrollments are growing, the end quantitative result will be more Black students on the growing PWI campuses. Empirically, this

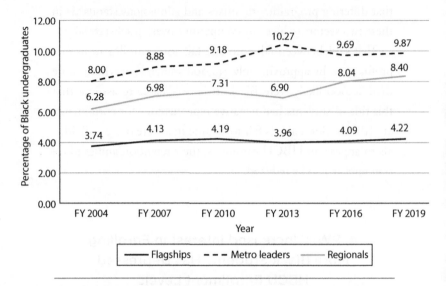

FIGURE 3.8 Percentage of Black undergraduates on campuses by institution type, fall 2004–fall 2019

Source: IPEDS.

effect has been accentuated because the overall number of students in American higher education has been declining. Thus, if the size of the typical PWI is increasing, that is likely to draw Black students away from HBCUs.

Table 3.2 estimates the total impact in FY 2019 on Black student enrollment at HBCUs in our sample of 186 PWIs due to increased enrollment of Black students at PWIs. Considering the percentages enrolled and size of institutions shown in table 3.1, we can estimate that the increased presence of Black students at PWIs may have reduced HBCU enrollments by 24,963 students. This large number provides some indication of how the increased interest in PWIs among Black students (and vice versa) has affected HBCUs.[13] We estimate that

TABLE 3.2 ESTIMATE OF THE IMPACT OF ADDITIONAL BLACK STUDENTS
AT PWIS ON HBCUS, FALL 2010–FALL 2019

Institution Type	Gain in headcount enrollment, FY 2010–2019	Percentage Black students	Projected annual growth in Black students, FY 2019–FY 2010	Number of institutions in category	Total FY 2019 impact (no. Black students)
Flagship	3,320	4.22%	140	76	10,648
Metro leader	2,311	9.87%	228	57	13,001
Regional	295	8.40%	25	53	1,313
Totals/averages	5,926	6.63%	393	186	24,963

Source: IPEDS and authors' calculations.

HBCU enrollments would have been 8.62 percent higher in
FY 2019 but for more Black students choosing PWIs. These
data suggest not only that PWIs have become more active in
courting Black students but also that some Black students
view some PWIs as more attractive places to attend college
than they did in previous years.

**MINI-CASE STUDY: OLD DOMINION UNIVERSITY AND
NORFOLK STATE UNIVERSITY**

Old Dominion University (ODU) and Norfolk State University (NSU) are public universities located just five miles apart in
Norfolk. ODU, a PWI, enrolled 24,286 headcount students in
fall 2019, while NSU, an HBCU, enrolled 5,457 students. Implic-
itly, they compete for some of the same Black students.

Norfolk is the traditional center of a metropolitan region of
about 1.7 million, 30 percent of whom are Black.[14] The world's
largest U.S. Navy base is located in there, and the city hosts the
fifth-largest port in the United States.

In the context of rich Olde Virginia's history, ODU and NSU are relative newcomers; ODU was founded as a division of the College of William and Mary in 1930, and NSU as a division of Virginia State University in 1946. Though they inhabit an urban area, both universities enjoy spacious, well-kept campuses and boast many new buildings.

NSU receives substantially more state-appropriated funds per student than ODU (about $12,300 per calendar year FTE student in 2018–19 compared with ODU's $7,700).[15] But ODU's endowment was valued at $261.7 million in June 2019 compared with NSU's $24.4 million.[16]

Among doctoral research institutions in Virginia, ODU offers a low-cost medical education and reported an average net price of $17,162 for an in-state, on-campus student in fall 2019. But NSU historically has underpriced ODU; its average net price for the same type of student was only $15,657. In the same year, 76 percent of NSU freshmen were Pell Grant recipients, while at ODU the number was 45 percent.[17]

The enrollment patterns at the two institutions are telling. The left-hand y axis of figure 3.9 plots the number of undergraduate students enrolled at NSU between FY 2004 and FY 2020. The right-hand y axis records the percentage of ODU undergraduates who self-identified as Black during the same period. It is easy to conclude that some (perhaps much) of the increased percentage of Black students at ODU came at the expense of NSU. The simple correlation coefficient between the two variables is -.633. Hence, if one knew nothing else about these institutions other than these two facts, one could explain 40.1 percent of the variability in NSU's undergraduate enrollment by looking at the percentage of Black undergraduate students at ODU.

A wide variety of factors ultimately determine which college a student decides to attend. Cost is an important consideration, and as noted, NSU consistently has underpriced ODU by a wide

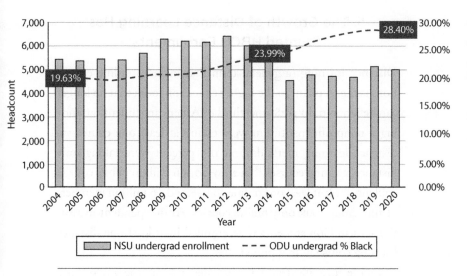

FIGURE 3.9 Headcount undergraduate enrollment at Norfolk State University and percentage of Old Dominion University undergraduate Black enrollments, fall 2004–fall 2019

Source: State Council of Higher Education for Virginia, https://research.schev.edu/info /Reports.Guide-to-the-Fall-Headcount-Enrollment-Reports.

margin. Nevertheless, large numbers of Black students have opted to attend ODU. Already in 2011, ODU was enrolling more Black students than NSU.

Although competitive situations in other states differ substantially, the example of these Virginia institutions suggests that in some situations, HBCUs will have steep hills to climb if they must compete with PWIs that are interested and actively engaged in enrolling more Black students. For a variety of reasons, some percentage of Black students may prefer to attend PWIs.

It remains to be seen whether recent events, such as the disturbing murder of George Floyd, ultimate will result in changed patterns of enrollment.

5. The Growth of Distance Learning Has Stunted HBCU Enrollments

Distance learning (a general term that includes online education) is the elephant in the higher education room that no longer can be ignored. In 2018, one-third of American students attending a nonprofit institution were taking at least one course via distance learning methods, and 11.9 percent were taking only distance learning courses.[18] In 2019–20, 4.6 million public college students took at least one online course, and 1.6 million members of this group took only online courses. At independent institutions, 1.1 million students were enrolled in at least one distance learning course in that period.

Figure 3.10 illustrates the gradual rise in the importance of distance learning in American higher education. Between fall 2012 and fall 2018, the percentage of students at PWIs not engaged in distance learning declined by 13 percent. This may

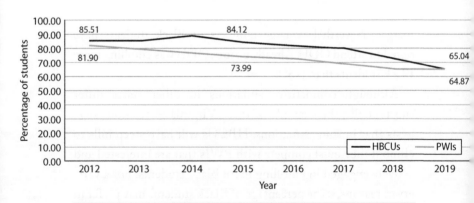

FIGURE 3.10 Median percentage of undergraduate students taking no distance learning courses: HBCUs and PWIs, fall 2012–fall 2019

Source: IPEDS.

not seem impressive, but that percentage at HBCUs in FY 2018 represents about 35,000 students.

Distance learning has been accelerated by the COVID-19 pandemic, which seemingly forced institutions to initiate or expand their efforts. Institutions have had to think strategically about distance learning. Among the questions each institution must answer are the following.

- Will we sponsor and produce our own distance learning courses?
- If we do, are we actively going to sell our courses to students outside our institution?
- Will we allow students to transfer credits from distance learning courses from other institutions, whether a nearby community college, state university, or Southern New Hampshire University, the latter of which enrolled almost 90,000 distance learning students in fall 2019?[19]

HBCUs have responded to these questions in a variety of ways. As figure 3.10 reveals, HBCUs collectively have become more active in the distance learning arena. They were late to the scene, but by at least one measure—the percentage of students taking no online courses—they have closed the gap and reached levels equal to PWIs. Still, in 2018–19, institutions including Fisk, Morehouse, Rust, Spelman, Virginia State, Virginia Union, and Wilberforce reported that none of their students had taken any distance learning courses. They are not alone in eschewing distance learning: the University of California, Berkeley reported that only 4 percent of its undergraduates were enrolled in an online course.[20]

Not offering distance learning represents a gamble on the part of these institutions. Will their students opt to take distance learning courses from other institutions, leading to reduced tuition revenue and ultimately the loss of students? Will actively supplying distance education require massive new expenditures and perhaps even damage the university's brand?

Whether or not it makes use of distance learning technologies, an HBCU must decide if it is going to accept transfer credits for distance learning courses from other regionally accredited institutions. If it does, will this open the proverbial floodgates and eventually wreak havoc with tuition collections? Should the institution "grin and bear it" (the language of a public university provost at a smaller institution) because this educational evolution increases student welfare and stimulates graduation rates?

Distance learning usually leads to substantial increases in the number of students transferring course credits from one institution to another. Before COVID-19, the Department of Education estimated that 35 percent of students attended multiple institutions within six years of starting their higher education careers. Among those who transferred, 68 percent did so only once, but 9 percent attended four or more institutions. There were only minor differences between public and private institutions.[21]

In almost 40 percent of transfer cases before COVID-19, no transfer credit was granted by the receiving institution, and the average transferring student received credit for only 56 percent of the credits accumulated. Approximately one-third of students were successful in transferring all their credits from the old to the new institution. This was most often the case when an individual transferred credit from a public community college to a public four-year institution in the same state. Transfers from community colleges were triple the number of transfers from public four-year colleges and five times the number from independent-sector institutions.[22]

The salient point is that the COVID-19 pandemic accelerated a growing long-term trend for multiple institutions to be involved in producing bachelor's degree recipients. "We imitate K-Mart or Target," ruefully commented a PWI administrator, who observed that students drop by, shop, buy what they want, and move on. This, of course, is a bit of an exaggeration, but one that underlines the changing nature of the higher education landscape. "We are damned if we do and damned if we don't," opined an exasperated administrator at a small, private HBCU. In the case of his institution, he saw only costs and headaches in the future for his campus, no matter how it chose to address the issue of distance learning.

It is apparent that some students are willing to take distance learning courses and, in fact, prefer to do so. The relevant question is, can a representative HBCU (or, for that matter, a PWI) compete with the likes of universities such as Arizona State, Grand Canyon, Liberty, Southern New Hampshire, Maryland's Global Campus, and Phoenix in providing distance learning coursework and muster the necessary support for it?

The six institutions just mentioned collectively enroll more distance learning students than total enrollment at all HBCUs combined. At those universities, proportions of their undergraduate enrollments of self-identified Black individuals are 7, 16, 10, 15, 26, and 22 percent, respectively. Hence, it is easy to conclude that the growth of these institutions has redirected students away from HBCUs. Regional HBCUs seem especially susceptible to competition from distance learning providers.

The existential question concerning distance learning and HBCUs is straightforward: should we attribute some portion of the decline in HBCU enrollments over the past decade to distance learning? The answer is yes. While distance learning may have attracted some new students into higher education, it also has redistributed students among institutions. Let's inspect the mathematics behind this assertion. Consider two primarily distance learning institutions, Grand Canyon University and the University of Phoenix. In fall 2019, 16 percent of Grand Canyon's 58,997 undergraduates were Black, and at Phoenix, 22 percent of its 72,485 undergraduates were Black.[23] Together, these institutions enrolled more than 25,300 Black students. In a typical year, about 10 percent of all Black students attend an HBCU. Hence, it is reasonable to conclude that these two institutions alone reduced HBCU enrollments by about 2,500 students.

Grand Canyon and Phoenix are only the tip of the iceberg. A half-dozen other distance learning giants exist, and all enroll healthy proportions of Black students, some of whom would have attended HBCUs but for the advent of distance learning. This is a new and unavoidable reality for HBCUs and, indeed, for all of higher education.

6. Falling Birth Rates and Unfavorable Demographics Have Damaged HBCU Enrollments

Birth rates have been declining in the United States, and ultimately this means fewer individuals might attend college. Figure 3.11 illustrates that the crude birth rate (number of births per 1,000 individuals) in the United States in 2019 was less than half what it was in 1960.

The birth rate in the 1990–2000 decade might presage the number of potential college students in 2020–30. In 1990 the rate was 16.7 and fell to 14.4 in 2000.[24] This represents a 13.7 percent decline, and some point to that decline as a reason headcount college enrollments shrank in 2010–20. Perhaps it is, but the number of public high school graduates nationally increased by 143,000 during the decade.[25] Figure 3.12 reveals that between FY

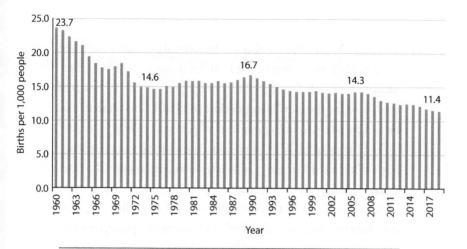

FIGURE 3.11 U.S. birth rates, 1960–2019

Source: Federal Reserve Bank of St. Louis Economic Data (FRED), "Crude Birth Rate for the United States," 2019, updated April 27, 2021, https://fred.stlouisfed.org/series /SPDYNCBRTINUSA.

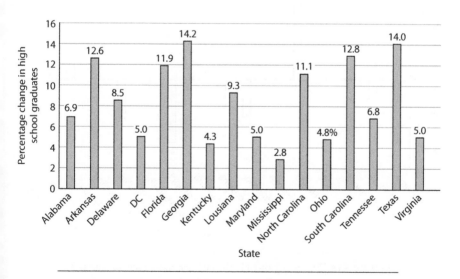

FIGURE 3.12 Growth in the number of high school graduates, selected states, 2014–19

Source: Western Interstate Commission for Higher Education, "Projections of High School Graduates" (2020), in *Knocking at the College Door*, https://knocking.wiche.edu /wp-content/uploads/sites/10/2020/12/All-Projections.pdf.

2012 and FY 2019, the number of high school graduates increased in every state where one of the HBCUs in our sample is located. Thus, there is only limited validity to the perception that much of the blame for the enrollment decline in HBCU enrollments can be attributed to declining numbers of potential college students.

The future of HBCU admissions, however, appears challenging, as illustrated in figure 3.13.[26] After increasing marginally from 3.144 million in 2010–11 to 3.287 million in 2020–21, the number of high school graduates nationally is slated to decline 10.4 percent between 2025 and 2037. Perhaps more to the point, between 2020 and 2030, the number of Black public high school graduates

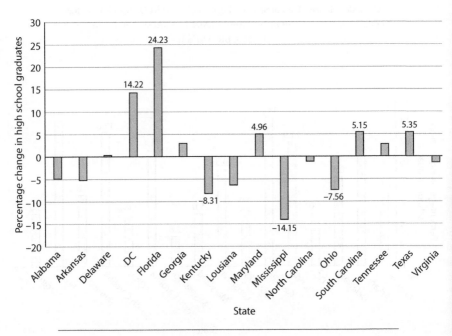

FIGURE 3.13 Projected growth in the number of high school graduates, selected states, 2019–34

Source: Western Interstate Commission for Higher Education, "Projections of High School Graduates"; and IPEDS.

is predicted to decline by 9.0 percent, following by another 8.0 percent decline between 2030 and 2036.[27] The most important demographic challenges for HBCUs are still on the horizon.

7. Rising Labor Force Participation by Blacks Has Reduced the Number Going to College

The assertion that Black individuals have taken jobs rather than attend college is substantially unfounded. For one thing, labor force participation rates for younger individuals generally have fallen over the past fifty years, as shown in figure 3.14. They have leveled out in recent years—except for Black males age 20 to 24; that rate continues to ease downward. This decline does not eliminate the possibility that some young men and women entered the labor force rather than attend college, but it tells us that this effect has been rather small. One of the mysteries of modern labor

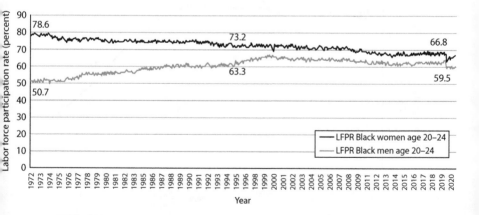

FIGURE 3.14 Labor force participation rates (LFPRs) for Black men and Black women, age 20–24, 1972–2021

economics is why labor participation rates for Black individuals are so low at the same time that their college-going rates are also low.

8. HBCUs Are Less Successful Than PWIs at Enrolling Male Students

Males make up approximately half the population of the United States but only 36.85 percent of the student bodies at 86 four-year not-for-profit HBCUs in FY 2019. This situation has worsened in recent years. As figure 3.15 reveals, the percentage of male students fell by 2.35 percent between FY 2015 and FY 2019 at those HBCUs. By contrast, in the rest of higher education, men constituted about 45.0 percent of headcount enrollments.

Men in general, and Black men in particular, have been abandoning higher education. It does appear, however, that Black

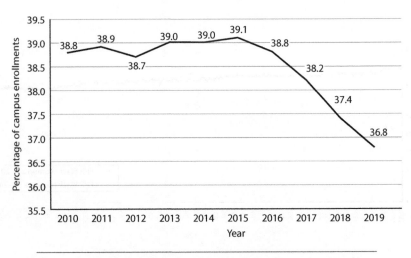

FIGURE 3.15 Percentage of HBCU enrollments of men,
86 four-year institutions, 2010–19

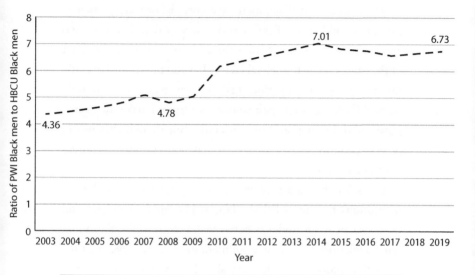

FIGURE 3.16 Ratio of Black men attending PWIs to
Black men attending HBCUs

Source: IPEDS.

men are more likely than Black women to choose a PWI. Consider figure 3.16, which reports the ratio of Black men attending a PWI to those attending an HBCU. One can see that the ratio rose substantially in the first decade of this century, topped out in 2014, and then then declined, though the 2019 ratio (6.73:1) is significantly higher than the 4.36:1 ratio that obtained in 2003. Could it be that Black women react more favorably to the nurturing and occasionally invasive service and care that HBCUs traditionally have provided? We cannot answer this question definitively, but PWIs (relatively speaking) seem to have more success than HBCUs in attracting and retaining male Black students. We are not aware of any explicit economic factors (for example, financial aid policies that might favor Black men over Black women) that might contribute to this difference.

The reasons that Black men have lower labor force participation rates and lower college attendance rates than Black women are many and complex. It will suffice for us to observe that most of the causes relate to societal factors beyond the control of institutions of higher education. HBCUs can and should actively recruit Black males for their student bodies and make their campuses more inviting and user-friendly. But though that would be very good for society at large, it may not represent a winning enrollment strategy.

Consider the data reported in table 3.3, which lists the ten institutions that recorded the largest percentage increases and decreases in male students between FY 2010 and FY 2019. A quick look informs us that enrollment increased in seven institutions that proportionately were shedding men but declined at eight institutions that proportionately were adding men. Further, those losing men tend to be larger than those adding men.

These are intriguing, though hardly definitive, results. They are sufficient, however, to question the notion that HBCU recruitment strategies focused on Black men will be as productive as those directed at women. Given that most recruitment pitches are gender-neutral, this observation may not have any practical significance. Nevertheless, the information presented here underlines that the paucity of Black men at most HBCUs remains and their overall presence continues to ebb. This could be a reason that HBCUs that have comparatively "male-heavy" enrollment have tended to experience larger enrollment declines than those with a greater presence of women.

We believe that the overall circumstances of young Black men in the United States constitutes nothing less than a national tragedy that is deserving of far more attention than we can give it here. The declining presence of Black men at HBCUs (and in higher education overall) is but one part of this phenomenon.

TABLE 3.3 HBCU MALE STUDENTS, INSTITUTIONAL GROWTH RATES AND TOTAL ENROLLMENT, FALL 2010-FALL 2020

Institution	Percentage change in male enrollment, FY 2010–FY 2019	Percentage growth in total enrollment, FY 2010–FYI 2019	FY 2019 headcount enrollment
Ten largest declines			
Huston-Tillotson U	-12.48	24.195	1,244
Central State U	-11.56	-8.260	2,033
Cheyney U of PA	-8.92	-70.618	616
Jarvis Christian Coll	-8.12	84.674	867
Lincoln U PA	-7.33	0.635	2,241
Alabama A & M U	-7.17	5.022	4,190
Fisk U	-7.10	34.483	874
Paul Quinn Coll	-6.24	143.363	2,451
Tuskegee U	-6.18	2.716	2,876
Savannah State U	-5.90	-0.074	3,668
Ten largest increases			
Simmons C of KY	49.76	133.333	209
Virginia U of Lynchburg	30.18	-46.306	270
Arkansas Baptist C	12.96	-53.083	531
Allen U	10.82	-12.382	817
Paine Coll	7.87	-49.297	448
Wiley Coll	4.94	-25.759	712
Saint Augustine's U	4.93	-49.138	899
Stillman Coll	3.54	-24.527	861
Talladega Coll	3.23	71.671	1,239
U of the Virgin Islands	3.03	-27.406	2,084

Source: IPEDS.

9. Changes in Federal Financial Aid Regulations Have Disadvantaged HBCUs

President Obama's administration fought pitched battles with for-profit institutions and instituted rules that restricted them and their students. Among the problems identified by the administration were very low graduation rates from programs at those institutions, high rates of borrowing by students, elevated loan default rates, and poor job market placement, leading to low salaries for graduates of for-profits.[28] Considerable evidence has accumulated that supports these generalizations.

The Trump administration revoked several of the rules instituted by Obama, but the Biden administration has restored several of them. The biggest issue relates to the "gainful employment" rule, which denies federal loans to students enrolled in programs that have exhibited very poor records of graduating students who obtain jobs related to their education and earn enough to enable them to pay off their loans.

What does this have to do with HBCUs? Two things. First, the application of the Obama administration rules put a crimp on for-profit institution enrollments (as figure 3.6 reveals), because students no longer could obtain loans for at least one thousand specific programs at the nation's for-profit institutions.[29] Second, in an effort to prevent students (and families of students) at for-profits from incurring excessive debt, in 2011, the administration tightened rules governing the government's Parent Plus loan program. This resulted in student/family loan applications being disapproved. The United Negro College Fund estimated that 28,000 HBCU students and families lost their Parent Plus loans in 2012–13 alone.[30]

Between FY 2010 and FY 2016, headcount enrollments at HBCUs declined almost 10 percent. It is reasonable to attribute some of this decrease to the changes in federal rules, which were aimed primarily at for-profit institutions. HBCUs turned out to be collateral damage.

SUMMING IT UP

Though the total number of individuals enrolled at the nation's HBCUs declined visibly during the most recent decade, that is only half the story. The HBCU share of the higher education enrollment market in the United States did not decline noticeably, even in the face of powerful new threats that included a decline in the percentage of Black individuals in higher education, burgeoning distance learning, and a long-delayed determination by PWIs to recruit more Black students.

From the standpoint of society as a whole, the advent of distance learning has been a propitious development despite accompanying limitations and hiccups. Similarly, the new-found interest of non-HBCU institutions in recruiting and financing more Black students is a net positive for society. Further, cracking down on the sometimes predatory practices of for-profit institutions represents a step forward for society. Each of these developments, however, made life more difficult for HBCUs and increased already considerable enrollment pressures on them. These changes have forced HBCUs to up their game, and by and large, most have taken steps to do so.

Lurking in the future, however, is a fifteen-year-long decline in the number of high school graduates in all but a few states. Historically, high school graduates rather than more mature students and graduate students have been the enrollment bread and butter of HBCUs. As this traditional source of students begins to wither, adjustments in outlook and approach will be required on the part of HBCUs. They would do well to begin to reorient themselves now to this emerging new world.

4

THE SAMPLE AND THE DATA

If you torture the data long enough, they will confess to anything.

—A perhaps apocryphal statement attributed to the
Nobel Laureate economist Ronald Coase

Since the aim of this book is to remove the veil that has obscured many aspects of HBCU performance, it is necessary to present and interpret ample amounts of data. One of the hallmarks of quality data-driven research is that it must be replicable. That is, other researchers need to be able, using the same sources, to find, organize, and analyze the data and generate the same results. Serendipitously, this may lead them to embark on new directions and thereby extend scholarly horizons.

While some readers may be inclined to sprint ahead to succeeding chapters that present our policy recommendations, in some ways the material in this chapter is essential. Though it is the equivalent of the plumbing and heating hidden inside a structure, we believe that one should be able to delve into it, even if the data are from sources that cannot be accessed and whose definitions are not precise, and from statistical findings that cannot be reproduced.

We acknowledge that we approach the issues relating to HBCUs with experiential baggage. One author spent fifteen years as the president of two public predominantly white institutions (the University of Montana and Old Dominion University). The other author is an undergraduate product of an HBCU (Florida A&M University) and currently chairs the Department of Economics at a large, well-regarded HBCU (Howard University). Both authors earned PhDs in economics at highly regarded private PWIs (Northwestern University and Duke University). These and other of our life experiences influence how we identify issues and interpret evidence. Perhaps they affect even our decisions to collect and use certain data. It certainly has influenced our choice of the questions to pursue.

We recognize fully that in the current societal milieu, some of the topics we broach in this book qualify as touchy. Nonetheless, the pursuit of knowledge—indeed, the search for truth—should be unfettered. We should not avoid coming to grips with topics that are vital but perhaps controversial.

Therefore, we take pains to explain how we are dealing with the issues addressed and the assumptions that underpin our analysis. Doubtless, some readers will find fault with our approaches and how we choose to address issues, especially when we joust with what might be viewed as the conventional wisdom concerning HBCUs.

We attempt to steer a sometimes slippery middle road as we take a sympathetic but honest look at many aspects of HBCU performance. We anticipate that our work will inspire both critical commentary and additional empirical work, both of which we welcome. From this give and take, however, should emerge a clarified picture of the position(s) that HBCUs occupy in American society.

THE SAMPLE

Our sample includes 50 HBCUs (30 public, 20 private), 81 public flagship institutions, 46 large metropolitan leader public institutions, and 60 primarily regional institutions. The non-HBCUs supply valuable perspective for our analysis; for example, when we discuss administrative and athletic expenditures. Appendix A lists the HBCU institutions in our sample.

The largest single source of data we utilize is IPEDS, the Integrated Postsecondary Education Data System, fed and maintained by the National Center for Education Statistics of the U.S. Department of Education. For FY 2020, IPEDS reported headcount enrollment for 102 HBCUs, of which 20 were two-year institutions. Of the 82 four-year HBCUs, our 50 accounted for 79.2 percent of the fiscal year FTE student enrollment. Figure 4.1 shows the locations of those 50 institutions.

We believe our sample is representative of the core HBCU universe. The primary reason for excluding institutions was the absence of critical enrollment or financial data. Pennsylvania's Cheyney State University and Arkansas' Philander Smith University are examples. A secondary reason for omitting an institution was that its student body has become overwhelmingly white. Bluefield State College and West Virginia State University fall into this category, as they enroll only 10 percent and 9 percent Black students, respectively.

Our basic observational unit is an individual campus, such as Central State University in Ohio. This unit may be a member of a university system; for example the University of Maryland Eastern Shore is a constituent of the University System of Maryland. Such a system in turn might be part of a larger statewide higher education conglomeration; the University of Massachusetts campuses are part of the Massachusetts System of Higher Education.

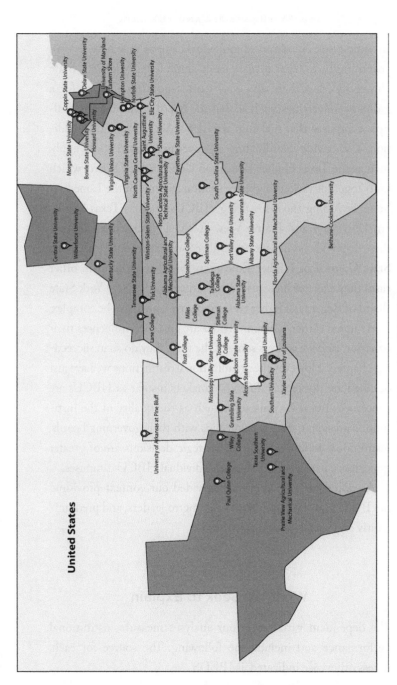

FIGURE 4.1 Locations of the 50 HBCUs in our sample

Credit: Faisal Mahmud.

In some cases, our observed individual campus may have its own governing board that focuses on it alone (e.g., Michigan State University), but there also may exist a governing board for a group of universities, such as that the board governing the multiple campuses that make up the Texas A&M system. In addition, a statewide coordinating or governing board could apply, such as the Texas Higher Education Coordinating Board, which knits together various higher education systems in the Lone Star State, including those involving HBCUs, such as Texas Southern University and Prairie View A&M University. Sometimes these statewide bodies are primarily coordinating enterprises (the State Council of Higher Education for Virginia), but in other cases they exercise final governing authority (the New York State Board of Regents). Higher education governance can be complex.

As noted earlier, how universities are governed influences their behavior,[1] and we address some of the ways they do so in succeeding chapters. However, the organizational distinctions we have just outlined are not crucial difference makers insofar as HBCUs are concerned. Local circumstances such as the quality of the institution's president, their relationships with their governing boards, institutional funding, and local strategic decisions are of greater importance in the performance of individual HBCU campuses.

As noted earlier, we have subdivided our context-providing 186 PWIs into flagship institutions, metro leaders, and predominantly regional institutions.

What We Seek to Explain

The dependent variables in our analyses measure institutional performance and include the following. The source for each, unless otherwise indicated, is IPEDS.

ENR = Calendar year full-time equivalent (FTE) institutional enrollment.

CHGENR = Percentage change in calendar year full-time institutional enrollment.

RETENT = Freshman to sophomore year retention rate for first-time full-time undergraduate students.

GRAD = Six-year graduation rate for first-time full-time freshmen students

INSTRUCT = Annual expenditures on instruction as a percentage of expenditures on the sum of instruction + academic support + student services + research + institutional support.

INSTITUTSUPP = Annual expenditures on institutional support as a percentage of expenditures on the sum of instruction + academic support + student services + research + institutional support.

ENDOW = Annual rate of change in the value of the institution's endowment, measured from July 1 to July 1 (source: National Association of Collegiate and University Business Officers).[2]

MOBILITY = Opportunity Insights' mobility coefficient times 100. This coefficient measures the percentage of students at an institution who came from a household ranked in the lowest income quintile and, after leaving the institution, subsequently rise to the highest income quintile. Opportunity Insights weights this percentage by the percentage of students each institution admits from the lowest income quintile. Hence, this is a measure of the overall quantitative impact an institution has on mobility rather than its success with what can be a rather small proportion of lower-income students (source: Opportunity Insights).

INCGRADS = Average midcareer annual earnings of this institutions' graduates (source: Brookings).

Explanatory Influences

We divide our independent explanatory variables into three groups: influences that are primarily external to the institution and over which it has little or no control, factors over which the institution has some influence and in theory can adjust over time, and variables that classify the institution.

EXOGENOUS INFLUENCES

These are the conditions over which the institution has little or no control:

> UNEMP = Average annual rate of unemployment in the institution's home state (source: FRED).[3]
>
> HHINC = Average national percentile for the annual incomes of the students' household (source: Opportunity Insights).
>
> POP = Average annual population of the institution's home state (source: FRED).
>
> POPAREA = Average annual population of the metropolitan area in which the institution is located, or the average annual population of its county if it is not located in a metropolitan area (source: FRED).
>
> NHSGRADS = Annual number of public high graduates in the institution's home state (source: Department of Education).[4]
>
> STATEBLACK = Absolute number of individuals in the institution's home state who self-identify as Black or African American (source: FRED).
>
> STATEAPP = Real annual state appropriation per annual FTE student (source: IPEDS).

INSTITUTIONAL DECISION VARIABLES

Conditions over which the institution has some degree of control, at least in the long run are the following. Source is IPEDS unless otherwise noted.

ENR: Calendar year FTE student enrollment.

PCTWHITE = Percentage of the institution's student body composed of individuals who self-identify as white.

PCTBLACK = Percentage of the student body composed of individuals who self-identify as non-Hispanic, Black/African American.

PCTHISPANIC = Percentage of the student body composed of individuals who self-identify as Hispanic or Latino.

PCTASIAN = Percentage of the student body composed of individuals who self-identify as Asian.

PCT25+ = Percentage of the student body composed of individuals age 25 years or older.

RETENT = Freshman to sophomore year retention rate for first-time full-time undergraduate students.

GRAD = Six-year graduation rate for first-time full-time freshman students.

HHINC = National percentile ranking of the income of the student's household (source: Opportunity Insights).

PELLPCT = Percentage of undergraduates receiving a Pell Grant.

PELLEVERPCT = Percentage of undergraduates who ever have received a Pell Grant.

AVEDEBT = Average student debt held by former students, whether or not graduates (source: College Scorecard).

MOBLITY = Opportunity Insights' mobility coefficient times 100 (see previous explanation; Source: Opportunity Insights).

KIDS/PAR = Kids' income percentile divided by parents' income percentile (source: Opportunity Insights).

ENDOW = Annual rate of change in the real value of the institution's endowment, measured from July 1 to July 1 (source: NACUBO).[5]

INSTRUCTEXPEND = Annual expenditures on instruction as a percentage of expenditures on the sum of instruction + academic support + student services + research + institutional support.

STUDSERVEXPEND = Annual expenditures on student services as a percentage of expenditures on the sum of instruction + academic support + student services + research + institutional support.

INSTITUTSUPPEXEND = Annual expenditures on institutional support as a percentage of expenditures on the sum of instruction + academic support + student services + research + institutional support.

SAT = Midpoint between the 25th and 75th percentile SAT scores for entering freshmen, with ACT scores converted to SAT scores (source: College Scorecard).[6]

NODISTANCE = Percentage of undergraduate students who are not taking any course via distance learning.

PRESIDENTEXPER = Average number of years of service as president at this institution for the current president and the preceding president, not counting interim presidents (source: individual college websites).

ATHLEXPEND = Real total annual expenditures on intercollegiate athletics (source: Department of Education, Equity in Athletics Data Analysis).[7]

PRIVATE = 0,1 dummy variable with 1 = private (independent) institution.

FBS = 0,1 dummy variable where 1 = the institution fields an NCAA FBS division ("big-time") football team (source: National Collegiate Athletic Association [NCAA]).[8]

FCS = 0,1 dummy variable where 1 = institution fields an NCAA FCS division football team (source: NCAA).

LOWERDIV = 0,1 dummy variable where 1 = institution fields an NCAA Division II or III football team, or a team in the National Association of Intercollegiate Athletics outside the NCAA (source: NCAA).

NOFB = 0,1 dummy variable with 1 = institutions that do not field a football team (source: NCAA).

INSTITUTIONAL CLASSIFICATIONS
Variables that classify institutions are as follows.

> FLAGSHIP = Institution is designed as a flagship public university (0,1 dummy variable where 1 = flagship).
>
> METROLEADER = Large, typically influential non-flagship public universities located in metropolitan areas (0,1 dummy variable where 1 = metropolitan leader institution).
>
> REGIONAL = Institutions, public or private, whose student bodies and reach are predominantly regional (0,1 dummy variable where 1 = predominantly regional institution).
>
> HBCU = Historically Black College or University (0,1 dummy variable where 1 = HBCU).

Table 4.1 summarizes critical characteristics for each of these groups. The data supply us with a contextual picture of the typical HBCU.

The median HBCU is about one-ninth the size of the median public flagship institution, and private HBCUs are less than one-twentieth the size of the median public flagship university. This is relevant because of the substantial economies of scale that exist in university operations. No HBCU is sufficiently large to be able to realize the available economies of scale. Most are so small that their unit costs are substantially higher than those of the median PWI. The absence of economies of scale is a major contributor to the differences we observe between HBCUs and PWIs.

Between FY 2010 and FY 2018, while the median flagship gained 7.8 percent in FTE student enrollment, the median HBCU lost 9.9 percent of its enrollment. Highly regarded HBCUs suffered enrollment declines as well: Florida A&M University, –21.6 percent; Hampton University, –14.7 percent; Howard University, –19.2 percent; Morehouse College, –14.1 percent;

TABLE 4.1 COMPARISON OF MEDIAN INSTITUTIONAL CHARACTERISTICS OF THE INSTITUTIONS IN THE SAMPLE AND THEIR STANDARD DEVIATIONS, FY 2018

Characteristic	HBCU (N = 50)	HBCU Public (N = 30)	HBCU Private (N = 20)	Flagship (N = 76)	Metro Leader (I = 55)	Regional (N = 58)
Calendar year FTE enrollment	3,015 (2,669)	4,706 (2,624)	1,305 (2,153)	28,016 (12,387)	22,487 (10,478)	22,486 (10,199)
Enrollment change, FY 2010–FY 2018	-9.9% (56.0)	-5.9% (30.6)	-12.0% (85.3)	7.8% (15.2)	9.9% (17.0)	9.5% (17.2)
Enrollment change, FY 2004–FY 2018	-10.2% (41.5)	-9.4% (40.7)	-14.6% (44.1)	24.5% (21.6)	30.6% (22.7)	28.1% (22.8)
Percentage Black undergraduates	86.0% (10.4)	84.0% (11.2)	90.4% (7.7)	4.3% (9.6)	9.5% (15.9)	7.8% (8.1)
Percentage white undergraduates	2.26% (5.65)	3.46% (6.56)	1.2% (1.5)	66.1% (15.7)	54.7% (22.3)	66.49% (15.6)
Percentage Hispanic undergraduates	1.49% (3.70)	2.32% (2.46)	0.8% (5.0)	6.5% (11.7)	12.1% (20.0)	5.8% (14.3)
Percentage Asian undergraduates	0.37% (1.20)	0.64% (.71)	0.5% (1.7)	5.2% (11.3)	4.4% (14.1)	1.9% (3.5)
Percentage women undergraduates	60.3% (12.6)	60.9% (6.4)	57.8% (18.4)	51.5% (5.0)	55.5% (4.2)	57.9% (8.0)
SAT midpoint	934 (109)	945 (81.8)	920 (145.4)	1235 (88.5)	1144 (68.6)	1124 (92.6)
Midcareer salary 2015	$70,900 (8,316)	$70,900 (8,315)	n.a.	$78,550 (11,796)	$77,900 (11,613)	$75,400 (9,300)

average net price if aid	$13,483 (6,878)	$12,712 (3,636)	$16,450 (8,524)	$16,258 (2,924)	$13,906 (3,321)	$14,099 (3,048)
Average net price $0–$30K	$13,705 (7,737)	$12,252 (4,480)	$15,840 (9,070)	$11,131 (3,253)	$10,999 (3,142)	$11,894 (5,018)
Percentage expend. on instruction	46.5% (11.5)	44.6% (10.4)	48.6% (8.8)	42.5% (7.36)	51.2% (7.8)	54.8% (8.7)
Percentage expend. on institutional support	26.5% (10.3)	20.8% (7.0)	35.3% (8.9)	9.67% (4.38)	12.9% (5.5)	15.6% (4.5)
Full professor average salary	$96,827 (15,823)	$87,771 (11,473)	n.a.	$102,184 (22,445)	$112,687 (21,992)	$91,561 (18,162)
Student-faculty ratio	16 (3.65)	16 (3.03)	n.a.	17 (2.37)	19 (3.8)	17 (3.0)
State appropriation per FTE student	n.a.	$9,317 (5,105)	n.a.	$8,050 (4,171)	$6,049 (2,501)	$5,506 (3,717)
Percentage undergraduates Pell Grants	67.5% (12.9)	65% (8.9)	76% (17.1)	25% (7.1)	36% (10.3)	36% (9.9)
Household income percentile	40.3 (11.3)	40.6 (4.2)	40.0 (11.6)	70.6 (6.0)	61.9 (6.9)	63.0 (8.3)
Mobility coefficient	2.94 (.98)	2.93 (.85)	3.10 (1.22)	1.48 (1.47)	2.16 (1.7)	1.61 (1.49)
Former student debt	$17,490 (3,943)	$18,750 (3,252)	$16,250 (4,676)	$15,625 (2,548)	$14,750 (2,984)	$15,647 (2,930)
Total annual expend. on intercollegiate athletics (000,000s)	$4.52 (4.73)	$7.73 (3.86)	$1.86 (5.27)	$87.66 (47.37)	$30.72 (20.55)	$16.92 (17.85)

Sources: U.S. Department of Education, Integrated Postsecondary Data System, (https://nces.ed.gov/ipeds), for all except the estimates of midcareer salary (Jonathan Rothwell and Siddharth Kulkarni, "Beyond College Rankings: A Value-Added Approach to Assessing Two- and Four-Year Schools" [Washington, DC: The Brookings Institution, 2015]), professorial salaries, student debt (U.S. Department of Education, College Scorecard, https://collegescorecard.ed.gov), household income percentiles and mobility coefficients (Opportunity Insights), and presidential experience (individual institutional websites).

and Spelman College, −9.9 percent. Enrollment-wise, 2010–20 was a difficult decade for some HBCUs.

Despite suggestions to the contrary and recent advances, the median PWI does not enroll large proportions of Black students. However, the median metro leader enrolls twice as many Black students proportionately as the median flagship institution. Regional PWIs fall in between.

The median HBCU enrolls only very small proportions of self-identified white, Hispanic/Latino, and Asian students. While the latter two segments have been growing slowly on the typical HBCU campus, the proportion of white students has declined over time.

HBCU undergraduate student bodies are more heavily female than is true at the median PWI. Male students continue to be much sought after but not so frequently enrolled at HBCUs. While HBCUs cannot by themselves significantly alter the societal conditions that have caused many Black males to avoid postsecondary education, they represent a major unexploited source of additional HBCU students in the future. The National Center for Education Statistics reported that in fall 2018, only 33 percent of Black males age eighteen to twenty-four were attending any form of college, compared with 41 percent of Black women.[9]

There is not much difference between the median average net price HBCUs offer their lowest-income students and their average student. This means that the median HBCU does not heavily engage in redistributive price discrimination, whereby more wealthy students effectively make it possible for the institution to offer lower net prices to lower-income students. By contrast, PWIs engage in considerably more of this type of redistribution.

Because PWIs engage in more price discrimination and redistribution in the variety of net prices they charge undergraduate students, often they underprice nearby HBCUs in the same state for very low-income students.

The median HBCU spends a smaller proportion of its budget on instruction than the median PWI in any institutional classification but a larger proportion on institutional support (administration) than the median PWI. Indeed, the median regional PWI (whose size matches that of HBCUs more than either flagships or metros) spends 8.3 percent more on instruction than does the median HBCU.

As noted, in FY 2019, the median public HBCU received more state appropriation funding per FTE student than any classification of PWI institution, including the public flagship universities. Times have changed, but it will take some years of generous funding to overcome a century or more of deliberate underfunding.

At the median HBCU, students come from households whose incomes are significantly lower than those of students at a PWI in any classification. For example, the household incomes of students at the median flagship institutions are thirty percentiles higher than those at the median HBCU. Viewed another way, the median percentage of Pell Grant recipients at HBCUs is 69 percent, whereas it is only 23 percent at flagships, 36 percent at metro leaders, and 30 percent at regionals. These income differentials have a significant impact on both student and institutional performance at the HBCUs and must be considered in the multivariate analyses we present in the next chapter.

HBCUs excel at raising the economic mobility of significant proportions of their students. Our computed mobility coefficient for HBCUs is almost double that for flagship institutions. The latter usually do well for their lower-income students, but increasingly their student bodies are income stratified and include only small proportions of lower-income students. Thus, flagships' total impact in upward economic mobility is surprisingly modest.

Median presidential experience (measured by the mean number of years of service of the incumbent and prior president but excluding interim presidents) is lower at the representative HBCU than at any PWI. Presidential turnover is particularly high at public HBCUs, where the median number of years of service of both the current and previous president is only 4.50. Contrast this to the 6.0-year median at flagship institutions and 7.25-year median at the metro leaders. If experience counts, then the typical HBCU president and their institution operate at a disadvantage.[10]

The impact of intercollegiate athletics in general and football in particular on HBCU performance has often been noted but largely escaped empirical analysis. Table 4.2 looks at two enrollment-based performance variables and focuses on how they differ depending on the relationship of a campus to intercollegiate football. These results are intriguing and suggest that operating an FCS Division football program is important with regard to HBCU enrollment. While it is important not to attribute cause and effect to the data reported in table 4.2, it is apparent that HBCUs that operate larger, more expansive football programs not only are considerably larger than those that have none but also grew their calendar year FTE enrollments between FY 2010 and FY 2018, even while such enrollments plummeted at institutions with less ambitious football programs or no program at all. Of course, there could be many additional causes of the enrollment differentials we observe in table 4.2, and we address these possibilities in succeeding chapters as we perform multivariate analyses.

It also seems likely that bidirectional causality is in evidence in table 4.2. A plausible hypothesis is that grander football

TABLE 4.2 COMPARISON OF MEDIAN ENROLLMENT METRICS FOR THE INSTITUTIONS IN THE SAMPLE, FOOTBALL PROGRAMS, FY 2018

	PWI FBS Division program (N = 103)	PWI FCS Division program (N = 46)	HBCU FCS program (N = 20)	HBCU Division II or III program (N = 21)	HBCU any football program (N = 41)	HBCU no football program (N = 9)
Calendar year FTE enrollment, FY 2018	26,241 (12,152)	11,071 (7,223)	5,329 (2,546)	1,613 (1,760)	4,202 (2,781)	946 (884)
Enrollment change, FY 2010–FY 2018	11.4%	-4.8%	6.1%	-42.9%	+6.2%	-17.4%

Sources: IPEDS.

programs attract students; however, if a campus is small, it may not have the financial means to do so. Hence, FCS-level football may positively affect institutional size, but size could influence whether or not a campus can launch FCS-level football.

HBCU Presidential Leadership

HBCUs often have powerful presidents who may affectionately be called the "boss" or less favorably denigrated as a "dictator." The legendary Dr. Benjamin Mays once lamented, "in all too many Negro colleges authoritarianism takes the place of democracy.".[11]

Skillful, charismatic presidents such as Hampton University's William Harvey (whose tenure lasted forty-two years) became known for the control they exercised over all aspects of campus life. Such leaders dominate and even select the members of their governing boards.

On some HBCU campuses, however, the opposite holds true. Some HBCU governing boards exhibit a penchant for micromanagement and frequently venture beyond overseeing policy making into daily administrative actions. This came to a head several years ago on the campus of Texas Southern University, whose Board of Regents terminated its sitting president with minimal explanation. This prompted the highly regarded former president of Dillard University, Walter Kimbrough, to lash out at Texas Southern's board in a precedent-setting opinion piece in *Diverse Education*.[12] Kimbrough described the situation on that campus as "micromanaged misery" and offered a blunt piece of advice for prospective future candidates for the presidential mantle at Texas Southern: "Don't." It is highly unusual for a president at one institution to comment on affairs at another institution and subsequently tell candidates to steer clear.

On occasion, some HBCU presidents have been known to overstep their bounds. But this is not unique to HBCUs (nor is governing board micromanagement). Nevertheless, when such things do occur, they often result in unseemly public tiffs between the board and the president. The result is bad publicity, which discredits the institutions involved and usually forces another presidential search. Episodes during the past decade at Florida A & M University, Jackson State University, and Texas Southern University demonstrate this scenario. As one HBCU president said to us, "We sometimes hang out our dirty laundry for everyone to see."

Of course, the same situations sometimes occur at flagship PWIs. Witness the contretemps surrounding an abortive presidential firing at the University of Virginia a decade ago, and the 2021 revelations concerning sexual harassment and intercollegiate athletic activities at Louisiana State University that seeped over to Oregon State University and led to a presidential resignation there.

There is an occasional tendency for HBCUs to "recycle" presidents who have been terminated at other HBCUs.[13] HBCU communities often are very forgiving, and they prize individuals with experience who have graduated from the "school of hard knocks." Such hires are risky, and the recycled individuals may bring bad habits along with them. Much depends on the lessons they have learned.

Whether the president is new or recycled, however, HBCU campus constituents are reluctant to accept leaders who they believe might not understand them. On occasion, this might include a variety of non-Black individuals, especially whites. There are historical reasons why this is occurs.

Hence, with regard to HBCUs, some qualified personnel at non-HBCU institutions hesitate to compete for the position of president, as evidenced by the paucity of white applicants in most HBCU presidential searches. Experienced white administrators, of whom there are many in American higher education, may believe it is useless to apply for an HBCU presidency because they will not be selected; even if selected, they would find it difficult to be accepted on campus and in the surrounding Black community. To the extent this is true, it represents an interesting turnabout, given that historically, this perspective is often attributed to Black applicants.

There was an era when many HBCUs—especially those founded by whites—had white presidents. This practice has disappeared in the last fifty years. The final HBCU to hire its first Black president was the University of the District of Columbia in 1977.[14] Today, HBCUs hire a fair number of white employees, especially faculty, and on occasion even appoint white head

TABLE 4.3 MEDIAN YEARS OF TENURE OF THE CURRENT PRESIDENT, HBCUS AND OTHER INSTITUTIONS, 2021

	Flagships	Metro leaders	Regionals	HBCUs	HBCUs public	HBCUs private
Median completed tenure	7.50 years (4.26)	8.00 years (7.35)	7.00 years (5.02)	5.00 years (8.51)	5.00 years (5.66)	5.00 years (11.38)

Sources: Individual university websites. Interim presidents are not considered. Standard deviations are in parentheses.

football[15] and basketball coaches. But HBCU presidents who are not Black are like proverbial hens' teeth.

There is somewhat dated evidence that HBCU presidents serve shorter terms than PWI presidents.[16] As table 4.3 reveals, the median tenure of sitting HBCU presidents in 2021 was noticeably shorter than that of flagship, metro leader, or regional presidents.

The data in table 4.3 are interesting, but the salient question is straightforward: Do these things matter with regard to HBCU performance? Our data set includes information on presidential tenures, and we will use it in our empirical work in succeeding chapters.

> "We hire more whites than you hire Black individuals," a sitting HBCU president remarked to one of the authors. This is true with respect to faculty. In FY 2019, in our 236-institution sample, the faculties of the 50 HBCUs were 22.05 percent white, whereas the faculties of the 186 PWIs were only 3.77 percent Black. Only 1.70 percent of PWI faculty were Black men.

5

ENROLLMENT, RETENTION, AND GRADUATION

Black diversity made a great playground for great debate and banter. It was truly a sharpening iron for us all. I wouldn't be the man I am today if it weren't for South Carolina State.

—Darrell Dial, a South Carolina State University alumnus[1]

Colleges and universities are complex organizations, considerably more difficult to understand than uninitiated observers may perceive. Economically speaking, they are multiple-product enterprises offering not only credit hours and graduates but also research, public service, entertainment, housing, food, and sundry other things. They are unusual in that they sell many of their most visible products at a financial loss. Thus, what they charge students does not cover the cost of educating those students. This is a recipe for bankruptcy outside the halls of academe.

Higher education institutions stand out because they exhibit the remarkable ability to convince former consumers (their graduates) to send them money. A corporate giant such as Microsoft can only wish that Office 365 buyers will remain so strongly attached to that software that they voluntarily send the company periodic checks for the rest of their lives. Not even the most loyal fans of the Los Angeles Dodgers or the New England Patriots willingly send money to these franchises unless they are purchasing tickets or merchandise.

Complicating things on a typical campus are a variety of public-private partnerships and foundations that are connected to the institution but just disconnected enough that they do not have to satisfy its usual spending and transparency rules. Approximately seventy-five campuses nationally operate medical schools, which transports them into a complex world replete with a plethora of funding sources, expenditure targets, compulsory charitable endeavors, and ubiquitous regulations.

Virtually every institution engages in pervasive cross-subsidization. The one hundred students in a Psychology 101 course effectively subsidize the ten students registered for a North American archeology class. Freshmen typically subsidize seniors, who tend to have schedules that involve smaller classes and laboratory courses. Commuter students tend to subsidize residential students, as commuters do not participate in as many on-campus activities. In general, students subsidize intercollegiate athletes.

Universities engage in "price discrimination" when they offer Jane a different net price than the one they offer John, who may be sitting in the same row of the same classroom. On occasion they also sometimes charge Jane and John the same price even if the two are receiving remarkably different products.

The complexity of campus operations often astonishes even seasoned business executives, who, on joining an institution's governing board, believe that their business experience will translate readily to the campus. That does not always hold true; some of the business world's logic and best practices transfer easily to the academic world, but others do not. For example, it is wise for campuses to run their auxiliary enterprises, such as food services, as a business, but they cannot apply the same business-like approach to the activities and curriculum of the Department of English.

For nearly every institution, power and authority are broadly diffused. Shared governance reigns on university campuses, which means that most legislatures and governing boards long ago assigned significant authority to campus groups as various as department curriculum committees and faculty senates. Hence, even though a university president is the chief executive of a campus, she often bears greater resemblance to a politician seeking votes and attempting to find consensus. Coalitions must be assembled and a degree of consent achieved lest the institution fall apart.

On a typical twenty-first-century American campus, a variety of faculty and staff groups possess the ability to frustrate or block action on proposals they do not favor. Depending on the school, these groups include those representing women, Black individuals, and LGBTQ communities, but on some campuses, Hispanics, Asians, and those with military connections exercise similar influence because they have the ability to publicize and embarrass.

Members of campus governing boards sometimes are taken aback when they confront the diffusion of power at their institution and realize that campus parties who share authority ultimately are not responsible for the recommendations and decisions they make. Faculty senators who demand more money for student scholarships or propose that the number of faculty sabbaticals be doubled can go home, put their feet up, and hoist their favorite libation, because they are not responsible for operating the institution or funding or implementing their choices.

A fundamental principle of management is that those who bear responsibility for an action should be the ones entrusted with making the decision to do so. As noted, this is rarely the case on American campuses. Trustees of governing boards may grumble that such a situation is like "letting the inmates run the asylum" (the comment of a one-time board member to one of the authors). This remark is a provocative exaggeration, but the underlying sentiment may be on target. Campuses often are surprisingly complicated places that dance to tunes at variance with the remainder of society.

At the same time that we acknowledge campus foibles, however, we also recognize that despite sometimes Byzantine operations, U.S. institutions hold most of the top rankings in virtually every list of the best universities in the world. The substantial net flow of foreign students into the United States each year (at least until the onset of COVID-19) is a vivid testament to the high regard with which American universities are held. Somehow or another, it all seems to come together and work tolerably well.

Bear that in mind as we move on to examine six measures of campus performance: enrollment, graduation rates, student retention, student-faculty ratios, institutional support, and student debt. Each metric represents an important aspect of HBCU performance, but we do not assert that they reflect everything HBCUs do or that these measures necessarily capture the many important long-term civic tasks that HBCUs perform.

Let's begin our empirical journey by focusing on the determinants of annual HBCU campus enrollments.

OUR GENERAL STATISTICAL MODEL

In presenting our core empirical evidence, we have banished the tables containing it to the appendices and reserve the main text for discussing our findings and their significance for HBCUs in particular and higher education in general.

The centerpiece of our statistical evidence is a set of semi-logarithmic regressions in which the dependent variable is the logarithm of the variable we wish to explain. Some readers may feel inclined to turn the page because they are not conversant with the statistical niceties behind this statement. We therefore provide a more intuitive explanation.

One of the aspects of HBCU performance we wish to explain is enrollments. What factors plausibly influence them? It is not difficult to produce a list of possibilities, including factors such as the price of attending an HBCU, how many Black individuals reside in the institution's home state, how wealthy the state is, and so forth.

Conventionally, we would say the variable we want to explain (HBCU enrollments) is the dependent variable and assign it the letter Y, then assign the letter X to the factors that we believe can explain the variations we observe in HBCU enrollments. A simple mathematical way to express this is $Y = f(X)$, (in other words, "Y depends on X"), where Y is what we wish to explain and X represents the things we think will explain Y.

With 50 HBCUs in our sample plus a diverse group of 186 PWIs, we are able to provide meaningful comparisons. Some of the relationships in which we are interested develop slowly (for example, PWIs beginning to enroll more Black students), so it is important that we trace changes over time. We have annual observations of each of the campuses beginning in FY 2004 and extending through FY 2019, a total of sixteen years.

Let's consider a single observation. In FY 2010, the average net price paid by an in-state Texas student attending Prairie View A&M University was $7,636. We have similar information for each year for each institution in our sample and end up with more than 100,000 individual observations describing these and other data regarding their status.

We generate our statistical results by relying on a widely utilized statistical technique known as linear regression analysis.[2] Readers who wish to know more about this technique may consult a standard textbook on the topic.[3] However, it is not necessary for readers to know the ins and outs of regression analysis to understand the evidence we present or the issues we pose.

HBCU ENROLLMENT

Initially, we will look at the factors determining enrollments at all HBCUs and then separately focus on those in the public and the independent sector.

HBCU Campus Enrollments

One of the most fundamental characteristics of a college or university is its enrollment. In this section, we explain the calendar year full-time equivalent (FTE) student enrollments in our sample. FTE student measures are more valuable than headcount metrics because they more accurately reflect the size of the resource demands that enrolled students place on institutions.

In our examination of HBCU enrollments, we utilize three kinds of variables in our regression analyses:

> *External economic/demographic factors.* We account for the number of high school graduates in the institution's home state, the number of Black residents of that state, the state's rate of

unemployment, and the population of the metropolitan region or county in which the campus is located.

Campus demographics. These variables include the percentages within student bodies that are white, Black, women, men, 25+ years of age, and Pell Grant recipients.

Campus characteristics. These variables include average student SAT scores, students' average household income percentile, net tuition and fees per FTE student, success of this campus in promoting upward economic mobility, percentages of major expenditures on instruction and student services, graduation rate, level of the institution's football program (if any), the institution's total expenditures on intercollegiate athletics, and whether the institution is private or public.

Appendix table C.1 reports the precise statistical results[4] for our HBCU-only sample. Let's delve into several of our more interesting findings.

Somewhat to our surprise, several of the external economic and demographic factors that we thought would have substantial impacts on campus enrollments did not prove to be as important as we anticipated. Of the four external conditions variables, only the rate of unemployment and the number of Black individuals in the institution's home state emerged as statistically significant predictors of HBCU enrollments across all estimates.

The underlying economics motivating the relationship of enrollments to the rate of unemployment is driven by common sense: when unemployment rises and prospective students do not have jobs, the opportunity cost associated with higher education declines because they have less to forfeit if they attend college.

With respect to the Black population variable, the reality is that about three-quarters of all students at HBCUs are Black.

This means that the number of Black citizens in a state is a measure of a significant potential source of students.

To be more precise about these relationships, we find that a 1.0 percent increase in the rate of unemployment in an institution's home state increases the enrollment of a typical institution by 2.23–5.44 percent. A 1.0 million increase in the number of Black individuals in a state generates a 5.87–15.07 percent increase in enrollments for the typical HBCU. Table 5.1 records these and related estimates.

TABLE 5.1 ESTIMATED IMPACT OF STRATEGIC CHANGES ON HBCU CAMPUS ENROLLMENT

Variable	Change in variable	Change in enrollment
Number of Black individuals in state	+1.0 million Black individuals in home state	5.87%–15.07% increase
State unemployment rate (from eqs. 1, 2, 3, 4, and 5 of table C.1)	+1.0% increase	2.23%–5.44% increase
Percentage Undergraduates 25+ Years	+1.0% increase	0.32%–0.77% increase
Net tuition and fees per FTE student	+$1,000 annual increase	1.34%–3.23% decrease
Percentage women students	+1.0% increase	0.89%–1.86% increase
Household income percentile	+5 percentile increase	2.19%–4.90% increase
Percentage doing no distance learning	+1.0% increase	0.26% decrease
Annual expenditures on athletics	+$1.0 million annual increase	3.09% increase
FCS Division football	Having an FCS Division football program vs. no football program	25.4%–134.8% increase
NCAA Division II or Division III football	Having an NCAA Division II or Division III football program vs. no football program	5.95–20.0% decrease

An immediate institutional and administrative policy implication arises from the preceding analysis. While unemployment rates and Black population influence enrollments, the actions many college administrators take, more so than they may perceive, usually are more influential in determining their long-term enrollments than external economic and demographic conditions.

An example of a critical campus decision variable is the effective price that students must pay to attend. We capture a portion of the price phenomenon by means of variables that record each institution's net tuition and fee collection per FTE student after institutional grants and scholarships have been deducted. The finding that emerges is straightforward: holding other things constant, students shy away from higher-priced institutions. We estimate that a $1,000 increase in the net tuition and fees is associated with a decline in enrollment that ranges from 1.34 percent to 3.23 percent.

The negative relationship we have found between high price and low enrollment conforms to what is taught in economics. However, the recent college admissions scandal seemingly

---

Elizabeth City State University, an HBCU located in northeast North Carolina, offers an illustration that HBCU students are price-sensitive. The North Carolina Promise Program reduced Elizabeth City's in-state tuition and fees to $500 per student per semester and to $2,500 for out-of-state students. Since the Promise Program was implemented in 2017, the university's enrollment has increased approximately 40 percent. Lower income students are price sensitive.

Sarah Brown, "Model or Fluke?" *Chronicle of Higher Education*, January 13, 2022, https://www.chronicle.com/article/model-or-fluke.

provided evidence that some students and families, far from objecting to paying higher prices, derive satisfaction from it and let others know they are doing so.[5] Harvey Leibenstein recognized this phenomenon almost seventy-five years ago when he coined the terms "snob effects" and "Veblen effects" to describe this behavior.[6] Some may associate the higher prices with better quality and believe their friends and neighbors do the same. In this milieu, sending one's child to a high-priced private institution serves the same function as buying a Mercedes and parking it for all to see in your driveway. Do high tuition rates at HBCUs send such signals? We aver that only a few (perhaps Hampton, Howard, Morehouse, and Spelman) might do so, but most HBCUs do not, as our results confirm.

Household incomes are statistically significant positive predictors of HBCU enrollments. Higher family incomes[7] reduce the possibility that students will drop out because of financial problems. Specifically, we estimate that a ten-percentile climb in the incomes of student households (for example, from the 40th to the 50th percentile nationally) will produce an increase in enrollment ranging from 21.9 percent to 49.0 percent (holding other factors constant).

We find SAT scores to be positively related to campus enrollment, although their quantitative impact is small. A one-hundred-point increase in HBCU students' average SAT score is associated with less than a 0.2 percent increase in enrollment.

It seems likely that the small enrollment effect we discovered with respect to SAT scores reflects the complicated nature of their impact on HBCU campuses. If self-identified Black students dominate HBCU enrollments, and they bring with them standardized test scores lower than the national average, elevated SAT admissions requirements not only will reduce the size of HBCU admissions pools but also put them in direct competition with PWIs for high-scoring students. The competitive problem that develops is that PWIs may have the ability to offer Black applicants with high scores attractive financial packages. In recent years, highly regarded HBCUs (that also draw high-scoring students) such as Florida A&M, Hampton, Howard, Morehouse, and Spelman have experienced declining FTE enrollments. It is reasonable to assume that these institutions are losing some of their traditional clientele to PWIs, both public and private. Elevated SAT scores, then, may seem a noble goal but represent a mixed blessing.

Campuses develop reputations concerning the importance of academic work and instruction. One indicator of campus academic values is the proportion of major expenditures for instruction.[8] We find that a 1.0 percent absolute increase in major expenditures devoted to instruction is associated with a 0.67 percent to 1.28 percent increase in enrollment.

Our results also encourage the notion that institutions with student bodies more heavily weighted toward women and older students fare better in the enrollment wars. Women are more likely to attend college and less likely to drop out. The same often is true for more mature students. Thus, even though young Black males represent a major untapped market for HBCUs, the enrollment "bread and butter" continues to be women students. While our estimates are somewhat variable, it appears that a 1.0 percent increase in the proportion of women in an undergraduate student body is associated with an increase of 0.89–1.86 percent in enrollment.

Roughly two of every five undergraduate students in the United States are age 25 or older. They represent a market that many HBCUs have neglected. In FY 2018, the median percentage of undergraduate students 25 years or older was 23.7 percent at PWIs but only 19.1 percent at HBCUs. Strategically, it would benefit the typical HBCU to focus on this demographic because we estimate that each 1.0 percent absolute increment in more mature students (25+ years) results in as much as a 0.46 percent to 0.77 percent increase in campus enrollment.

Ceteris paribus, HBCU students do not appear to be paying much attention to the racial makeup of their student bodies. In particular, we find no evidence to support the notion that greater proportions of white students on HBCU campuses would result in larger total campus enrollments.[9] However, statistical relationships such as this assume that other factors that plausibly influence enrollments do not deviate far from their average values. Suppose instead that a campus is especially attractive, or that it offers distinctive high-demand programs, or is located in a high crime rate area, or that it might be fighting for accreditation. Then, the two variable "other things held constant" enrollment relationship we have just cited might not hold. Hence, *ceteris paribus* effectively means "given the current situation, this is the relationship between these two variables."

Nor do we find any evidence that institutional graduation rates have any statistical connection to HBCU enrollments. Given that HBCUs generally have low six-year graduation rates, marginal differences in rates on these campuses do not make an impression on prospective students or serve as a differentiating factor.

We have already noted the increasing importance of distance learning and that as late as FY 2018, no students at several HBCUs (e.g., Dillard, Lane, Morehouse, Rust, Spelman, Tougaloo, Virginia State, Virginia Union, and Wilberforce) were enrolled in any online courses. But the effect of distance learning on enrollment is modest; we estimate that a 1.0 percent increase in the number of students not taking distance learning courses results in only a 0.26 percent decline in enrollment. (We hazard that were current data available that reflect the COVID-19 pandemic, our estimate would be substantially larger.) Today's students can "vote" with their eyes and feet. HBCUs that do not satisfy students' demand for distance learning risk forfeiting enrollments to institutions such as Southern New Hampshire University, which in fall 2019 enrolled more than 113,000 headcount students.[10]

Intercollegiate athletic programs have a large, positive, and thought-provoking influence on HBCU enrollments. Perhaps the highest-impact program on a typical HBCU campus is football, because it often is accompanied by storied marching bands, homecoming festivities, parades, and the like. Our estimate is that fielding an FCS division football program is worth a 25.4–134.8 percent increase in enrollment. Operating a Division II or III program does not generate similar benefits. Indeed, fielding no football team at all typically results in 13.4–20.0 percent higher enrollment than fielding a Division II or III team.

Shifting the focus from football specifically to intercollegiate athletic expenditures overall, one finds a positive connection between intercollegiate athletics and HBCU enrollments. Our estimate is that a $1.0 million increase in athletic spending drives a 3.09 percent increase in enrollment at the representative HBCU. To place this in context, the median annual expenditure by an HBCU on intercollegiate athletics was $4.52 million in FY 2018 but $87.66 million at the median flagship institution. The largest annual HBCU expenditure that year was Howard's $16.89 million.

Finally, we examined the impact of an institution's mission and sector on enrollment. Our estimating equations controlled for several factors, such as price, that are related to independent rather than public status. We estimate that the typical independent-sector HBCU has a 42.0 percent lower enrollment than a public-sector HBCU (all other things being equal).

The results in table 5.1 enable us to draw several fact-based conclusions and suggest actionable strategies for HBCU administrators and governing boards.

(1) Encourage women students to apply. They continue to be a primary differentiating factor in HBCU undergraduate enrollments.

(2) Place additional emphasis on serving older students.

(3) Resist the temptation to raise the net price of attendance, when it is practical to do so.

(4) Maintain or increase, perhaps gradually, the percentage of institutional expenditures on instruction (which implies spending less on administrative overhead and other areas).

(5) Increase the institution's commitment to distance learning.

(6) Exhibit skepticism concerning the notion that increased recruitment of white students represents a cost-efficient solution to enrollment challenges.

(7) Consider the ways and means by which intercollegiate athletic programs might generate more students.

(8) Recognize that adverse economic conditions ordinarily are good rather than bad for HBCU enrollments (though the same logic does not apply to retention and graduation rates).

(9) Take necessary steps to ensure the continued existence of independent-sector HBCUs, which can be exceedingly perilous.

Narrowing Our Focus to Public-Sector HBCUs

In this section, we take into account the public nature of thirty of our fifty HBCUs, which receive appropriations from their respective state governments. We report our regression results in appendix table C.2.

We found a statistically significantly negative relationship between calendar year FTE student enrollment and the real (price-adjusted) state appropriation that each public institution receives annually for those students. This may seem a counterintuitive result, but the negative relationship is consistent with reality. Between FY 2004 and FY 2019, even while the median FTE student enrollment at a public institution in our sample rose 20.97 percent, the real state appropriation per student was declining 16.25 percent.[11] The typical public institution during this period was forced to make do with less. Thus, the absolute size of public institutions during this period was not directly tied to funding per FTE student but, rather, to other factors, some of which are controlled by the institutions. We noted some of these factors previously; for example, increasing institutional focus on instruction, augmenting institutional focus on older students, and providing distance learning opportunities.

Our statistical results for public institutions support those we found when we looked solely at HBCUs. Enrollments there were somewhat less sensitive to price; the estimated negative impact in enrollment due to a $1,000 increase in net tuition and fees per FTE declined from 1.34–3.23 percent of calendar year FTE student enrollment to 0.56–0.58 percent. Our expectation had been the opposite, because a $1,000 increase in net tuition and fee collections at a public institution likely is proportionately larger than the same increase would be at an independent institution. An explanation offered by HBCU administrators for this decrease is that independent-sector HBCU students have greater financial need than public HBCU students and are at the limit of their ability to pay even without an increase. There is some evidence supporting this proposition; in FY 2018, the median percentage of Pell Grant recipients at independent-sector HBCUs was 79.5 percent, whereas the comparable median was only 65.0 percent at public HBCUs.[12] This finding reminds us that HBCU student bodies are diverse and the market positions of small, independent-sector HBCUs (such as Lane College and Saint Augustine's University) may differ significantly from those of larger public HBCUs (e.g., North Carolina A&T University and Prairie View A&M University).

In conducting this analysis of public-sector universities, we examined institution type; that is, whether an institution was a flagship, metro leader, regional, or an HBCU. We asked, "What differences in enrollment can we attribute to institution type as opposed to other factors, such as economic conditions and campus demographics?

HBCU status was accompanied by what amounts to an enrollment penalty, which we estimated to be 36.3 percent lower than enrollment at a representative regional PWI. This is a rough measure of the apparent aversion that some students (especially white students) may have to attending an HBCU. It informs us that if we are comparing an HBCU with an otherwise similar regional PWI, we should expect the HBCU's calendar year FTE student count to be about three-eighths the size of that at the PWI. A similar enrollment scenario applies to flagship institutions: holding other factors constant, our results tell us that we should expect a flagship to be 80.6 percent larger than a regional.

Our data do not enable us to differentiate between individual Black students and students of other races, but it seems likely that some of the reluctance to attend HBCUs also exists among Black collegians. As one observer put it in *TeenVogue*, "Some HBCU students have issues with Black students attending PWIs and some PWI students look down on HBCUs, which causes a sort of divide in the Black community."[13]

Our analysis of public colleges and universities also revealed that students at public PWIs do not value FCS-level football teams as highly as do HBCU students. Fielding a team merited only a 34.2 percent increase in enrollment among our broader sample of PWI institutions (holding other things constant) versus the 99.0–134.0 percent enrollment bonus we found at HBCUs. Once again, however, we found that in terms of enrollment impact, not fielding any football team was superior to sponsoring an NCAA Division II or Division III team. Our estimate indicates that we should expect the "football-free" institution to have a 23.7 percent higher enrollment than one that fields an NCAA Division II or III team (again, holding all other things constant).

Private-Sector Considerations

Of our fifty HBCUs, twenty are independent (private, nonprofit) institutions. Even after holding constant a host of variables such as the level of net tuition and fees per FTE student, we found a 54.4 percent enrollment penalty associated with being an independent HBCU as opposed to a regional PWI. True, public institutions have struggled to maintain the price-adjusted value of their state appropriations, but independent HBCUs seldom, if ever, have access to such revenue sources. This curtailment of their revenues affects the quality of their physical plants and reduces their offerings. The COVID-19 epidemic only added to these challenges, and it is fair to say some small HBCUs now face the prospect of closure.

A much-publicized recent book, *The College Stress Test*,[14] though not addressing HBCUs, provides a methodology that enables one to identify at-risk institutions. More than a few HBCUs have been so identified. The Department of Education (DOE), which tracks the financial status of institutions, places problematic institutions either on its "heightened cash monitoring 1" list or its even more endangered "heightened cash monitoring 2" list. Nine HBCUs were on the 1 list in March 2021, three of which are part of our fifty-institution sample. None of the HBCUs in our sample was on the "2" list.[15]

Inclusion on such at-risk lists is not something to be disregarded as irrelevant. Between 1997 and 2019, fifteen HBCUs closed their doors.[16] It is reasonable to say that 10 percent or more of HBCUs are considered by reputable external authorities to be at risk. This class of institution is underrepresented in our sample. We would have included more of them had we any data, which is itself a telling circumstance. Institutions facing the possibility of closure often do not place a high priority on sending information to the federal government.

Paul Quinn College, located in Dallas, Texas, is an innovative 150-year-old HBCU affiliated with the African Methodist Episcopal Church. The college, whose calendar year FTE student enrollment grew 338 percent between FY 2010 and FY 2019, demonstrates how HBCUs can offer students a distinctive experience that they will value. Its stated goal is for its students to graduate with less than $10,000 in loan debt. An important part of this program is Paul Quinn's status as a "work college"— an institution where undergraduates are expected to hold jobs while studying. The college says it strives to prepare students for lives that combine character and financial freedom. Financial help from the federal government helps make this a reality. Paul Quinn also is unusual because it admits families—students can bring up to two non-student family members to campus when they come to study.

GRADUATION RATES

The most-cited graduation rate measures the percentage of first-time full-time freshmen who graduate within six years of matriculation. Even as we present our statistical analysis, we assert that this rate receives much more attention than it deserves. To begin, in fall 2020, 35.3 percent of students at public four-year institutions were part-timers and therefore not covered.[17] Further, more than 40.0 percent of students attending public institutions today are age 25 or older.[18] They are less likely to start their college careers as first-time full-time freshmen. A 2015 report found that 48.0 percent of all undergraduate students began their careers at a community college and that 37.0 percent of all students transferred from one institution to another during the six years after they matriculated.[19] Which institution(s) should receive credit (or criticism) for their performance?

These enrollment realities tell us that the first-time full-time graduation rate is a less useful metric than it might at first appear. It may miss the realities facing half or more of current undergraduates. Nonetheless, despite its deficiencies, first-time full-time six-year graduation rates are cited frequently by the media, rating agencies, legislators, students, and parents. We bow to this usage even while we ask readers to bear in mind the caveats we have cited.

Let's give our attention to the FY 2018 graduation rates at various types of institutions in our sample. Huge differences exist among the institutional types with regard to retention and graduation rates. As table 5.2 reveals, graduation rates are 13.8 percent to 33.3 percent higher at PWIs than at HBCUs. However, once one controls for two factors—SAT score and household income—these differences not only disappear but, in most instances, reverse themselves. As we show, HBCUs perform very

TABLE 5.2 GRADUATION RATES ON SIX TYPES
OF CAMPUSES, FY 2018

Institution type	Percentage of first-time full-time freshmen who graduate within six years
HBCU	34.1
HBCU public	33.5
HBCU private	35.4
Flagship	68.7
Metro leader	53.5
Regional	49.2

Sources: For retention rates, U.S. Department of Education, Integrated Postsecondary Data System, https://nces.ed.gov/ipeds; for graduation rates, U.S. Department of Education, College Scorecard, https://collegescorecard.ed.gov/data.

well given the academic preparation and economic status of the students they enroll. Indeed, the typical HBCU outperforms the typical PWI once we take these other factors into account.

We are not the first researchers to examine HBCU graduation rates,[20] but until recently, there has been more discussion about rates at HBCUs than hard analysis. Fryer and Greenstone and Price et al.[21] touched on the topic a decade ago even as they focused primarily on the incomes earned by HBCU graduates. More recently, however, Gordon et al.[22] utilized rigorous methods to focus on HBCU graduation rates. We roughly imitate the approach of Gordon et al. by using control groups, which enables us to place HBCU graduation performance in context.

We rely here on the same basic statistical model that we utilized to investigate HBCU enrollment. In this case, the dependent variable is the six-year graduation rate for first-time full-time students. Our regression analyses relative to graduation rates are found in appendix table c.3. Table 5.3 summarizes how graduation rates are affected by changes in key variables.

We estimate that the six-year graduation rate at the representative HBCU will be 10.67 percent higher than at the typical

TABLE 5.3 ESTIMATED IMPACT OF STRATEGIC CHANGES ON GRADUATION RATES AT HBCUS AND OTHER TYPES OF INSTITUTIONS

Variable	Change in variable	Change in graduation rate
Institutional size in FTE students	1,000-FTE student calendar year increase	0.25%–0.53% increase
Percentage undergraduates 25+ years	+1.0% increase	0.46% decrease
SAT midpoint score	+50-point increase	7.0%–8.5% increase
Pell Grant percentage	+5.00 increase	1.40%–2.75% increase
Net tuition and fees per FTE	+$1,000 increase	0.34%–1.41% decrease
Percentage expenditures on instruction	+1.0% increase	0.32% increase
Percentage expenditures on student services	+1.0% increase	0.37% decrease
Flagship status (from eq. 1 of table C.2)	Being a flagship rather than a primarily regional institution	5.25%–7.95% increase
HBCU status (from eq. 1 of table C.2)	Being an HBCU rather than a primarily regional institution	2.99%–11.26% increase
FCS	Fielding an FCS-level football team vs. NCAA Division II or II team	4.89% increase
NOFB	Having no football team vs. having an NCAA Division II or II team	4.79% increase

regional PWI after we have accounted for six explanatory factors: SAT scores, the percentage of Pell Grant recipients, household income, the number of Black individuals in the institution's home state, net tuition and fee collections, and the size of the institution.[23] If we rely on more complicated models with additional factors that might influence graduation rates (such as net price), our estimate changes only slightly, but the superiority of HBCUs over regional institutions could be reduced to 2.99 percent. Nonetheless, our results reveal that an undergraduate student is more likely to graduate from an HBCU than a similarly situated student at a primarily regional PWI institution.

The typical flagship university also outperforms a representative regional institution in terms of graduation rates: 5.25 percent versus 7.95 percent. Metro leader institutions and regionals perform approximately on a par with each other.

How do factors such as SAT score and income affect graduation rates? With respect to SAT scores, we estimate that a fifty-point increase in average scores is associated with a 7.0 percent increase in a campus' graduation rate.

The connection between graduation rate and income emerges most clearly when we focus on the percentage of undergraduates who are Pell Grant recipients. We estimate that a 5.0 percent absolute increase in the percentage of undergraduate Pell Grant recipients will result in a 1.40–2.75 percent reduction in an institution's graduation rate. This finding helps to explain why many ratings-conscious campuses enroll such small numbers of Pell Grant recipients. If they were to enroll more, their graduation rates likely would decline, and so would their ratings. With pay packages tied to graduation rates, what university president would want to preside over an institution whose ratings are in decline, even if the decline was accompanied by increased access for lower-income students?

Within our sample, the median percentage of Pell Grant undergraduates is 68.0 percent on HBCU campuses but only 24.0 percent at flagship institutions. Among flagships , the University of Virginia recorded the lowest Pell Grant percentage in FY 2019: 12.93 percent. Contrast this to the 89.0 percent of undergraduates receiving Pell Grants at Talladega College or 88.0 percent at Lane College, both HBCUs.

It is ridiculous to assume that comparisons of graduation rates that fail to account for the income disparities we have just identified are very informative. In fact, raw comparisons of graduation rates without the kinds of controls we utilize in appendix table c.3 are deceptive and fail to identify which institutions are achieving the most, given their circumstances. Public policy should not be built on the basis of data that may be accurate but nonetheless powerfully misleading.

Does campus size make a difference? One of the most consistent findings in our work dealing with graduation rates is that holding other factors constant, larger institutions do a better job graduating students than smaller institutions. We estimate that an incremental 1,000 FTE students is associated with 0.25–0.53 percent higher graduation rates. Likely this increase is possible due to the greater availability of resources that are used to track and support students. This fact is useful in explaining some of the elevated student attrition rates on HBCU campuses.

Groundbreaking work by respected observers such as Astin[24] and Tinto[25] points to the importance of integrated, targeted, generously supported student services for improving institutional performance. Their thesis was straightforward: both students and universities benefit when challenged, satisfied students persist to reach goals such as graduation, and quality student services are an important tool for success. Their message resonated in academe. As figure 5.1 indicates, the typical public

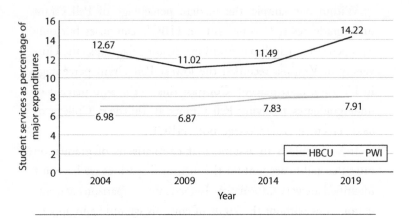

FIGURE 5.1 Percentage of major expenditures on student services, HBCUs and PWIs, FY 2004–FY 2019

Source: IPEDS.

university has "walked the walk" in recent years and made generous additional investments in student services even during difficult economic times.

Nevertheless, we do not find evidence of a statistical connection between student services spending and graduation rates; indeed, we find the opposite. Our estimates suggest that a 1.0 percent absolute increase in the share of expenditures on student services *reduces* graduation rates by about 0.37 percent. We caution that student services expenditures sometimes include intercollegiate athletics and that they frequently include admission and recruiting expenses. Thus, the expenditure data we have are not as clean as we would prefer, which cautions us to avoid making too much of this finding. However, the results are consistent with earlier work by Gansemer-Topf and Schuh.[26]

Not surprisingly, student services professionals find such conclusions difficult to accept and fervently believe they are doing positive things. We carry no brief about student services activities and expenditures, but sufficient evidence has accumulated to raise legitimate questions about their impact. Rigorous evaluation of HBCU student services, however, will require that they generate measurable metrics that will assist institutions in evaluating their student services activities more rigorously. That evaluation will require a change in culture on campuses where student affairs personnel have been resistant to attempts to measure their output. Not everything that is important can be measured, but it seems reasonable to ask student affairs personnel to keep track of which students access which campus activities and what happens to them. This information is absolutely essential for evaluating the effectiveness of student affairs programs.

Note in table 5.3 that our graduation rate analysis did not account for either the quality of an institution's facilities or the amount of money each campus spends per student.[27] Measuring the quality of facilities is beyond the scope of the work we report here; however, as noted earlier, the advantage that flagships have enjoyed in state funding per FTE student has diminished visibly in recent years.

Nevertheless, flagships' funding sources other than from states (for example, from their related foundations) vastly exceed those on which regional institutions rely. National Association of College and University Business Officers (NACUBO) data reveal that the average value of a flagship's endowment on July 1, 2018, was $1.503 billion, whereas the comparable value at the regional institutions in our sample was only $97.27 million.[28] Thus, the typical flagship had fifteen times more in related foundation resources to utilize. Were we able to include these factors in our analysis, the graduation rate performance superiority of HBCUs would increase.

RETENTION RATES

There is abundant evidence that large economic losses result when students drop out of college before graduating. In a review of the evidence, Oreopoulos and Petronijevic concluded that the average college dropout earns not much more than the average high school graduate.[29] Whether an academic program confers a certificate, associate degree, or bachelor's degree, there are substantial financial benefits attached to completing it.

The median retention rate among HBCU institutions is well below that of PWIs (see figure 5.2). The problem is sufficiently severe that the United Negro College Fund launched an initiative in 2021 to bring four thousand dropout students back to their HBCUs. The organization noted that more than five million Black Americans age 25 and older have attended college but not earned a degree.[30] Hence, retention rates are vitally important for HBCUs.

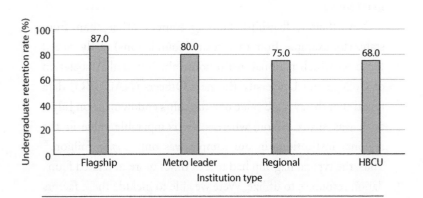

FIGURE 5.2 Median retention rates for first-time full-time freshmen, by institution type, FY 2019

Source: IPEDS.

Are the factors that explain HBCU student retention rates similar to those that pertain to graduation rates? That is, once we control for SAT score and household income, are HBCU retention rates as good as or better than those at PWIs? That is largely the case, though these relationships are complicated where HBCUs are concerned. Appendix table c.4 contains our statistical work on this topic.

By "retention" we refer to the rate at which first-time full-time freshmen remain at their institution and through their sophomore year. Clearly, such a rate misses a swath of today's students but nevertheless is frequently cited as a measure of institutional effectiveness. Reality, as noted earlier, is that 35.3 percent of all undergraduate students were part-timers in Fall 2019, while more than 40 percent were 22 or more years of age. Thus, retention statistics that focus on 18- to 21-year-old individuals who attend college full-time are much less informative than many might initially assume.

We suspect that some reporting lags exist in determining retention rates. This year's retention of sophomores depends partly on their experiences as freshmen, and so we introduce several single-year lags in our predictive equations.

The implications of retention in relation to SAT score and household income are less clear than when we were considering graduation rates. We provisionally estimate that a fifty-point increase in the average SAT score at an institution is associated with a 0.75 percent increase in its retention rate, because this relationship disappears when we utilize alternative statistical methods. The impact of household income and student Pell Grant status is similarly unclear.

Larger institutions exhibit higher retention rates, all else being equal, but the size of this advantage is not huge. A increase of one thousand FTE students in a model institution's calendar year student body will increase that institution's retention rate by only 0.23–1.45 percent.

The role of intercollegiate athletics in retention is not clear. One of our estimating equations, however, did suggest that having no football team at all has a negative impact on retention. This conclusion is worthy of additional research.

In general, our retention rate analyses yielded less definitive results than our findings about graduation rates. We do estimate, however, that HBCUs' performance is superior to that of all PWIs. All things being equal, we estimate that HBCUs outperform PWIs by 6.67 percent with regard to retention rates. This estimate represents the net effect of HBCUs on retention after we have taken account of fifteen explanatory factors.

The large average difference in earnings between college dropouts and graduates raises interesting questions. Is the large financial bonus that college graduates realize due to their gaining knowledge and skills that are invaluable in labor markets, or is this earnings reward the result of "signaling"—employers can be more confident that a college graduate possesses a certain level of skills, meets deadlines, shows up on time, communicates, get along, and so on? Do employers use a college diploma as a filter that narrows their applicant pool rather than expecting the degree to indicate specific skills that can be used on the job? In *The Case Against Education: Why the Education System Is a Waste of Time and Money* (Princeton, NJ: Princeton University Press, 2018) Bryan Caplan makes a not-to-be ignored case for the signaling interpretation. He concludes that it is very important and that many of the resources society currently expends on sending individuals to college ultimately are unnecessary and therefore wasted.

STUDENT-FACULTY RATIOS

The student-faculty ratio is the proverbial coin with two sides. On one side, this ratio often is used as a measure of educational quality, with a low ratio indicating better quality, and many higher education ranking systems use some variation of them to determine quality level. On the other side, student-faculty ratio is sometimes used as a measure of efficiency; institutions with higher ratios either objectively are or can be viewed as more efficient. Legislators who are critical of how public institutions are utilizing their resources sometimes use student-faculty ratios to buttress their perception that faculty may not be working hard enough. Typically, lawmakers then comment that reliance on technology could enable institutions to serve more students with the same or even a smaller number of faculty.

Table 5.4 reports estimated median student-faculty ratios for a variety of institutional types in FY 2012 and FY 2018. We emphasize the label "estimated" here because the data are based on calendar year FTE student enrollments, including part-time

TABLE 5.4 ESTIMATED MEDIAN STUDENT-FACULTY RATIOS, FY 2012 AND FY 2018, BY INSTITUTION TYPE

Institution type	Estimated student-faculty ratio FY 2012	Estimated student-faculty ratio FY 2018
HBCUs	17.14	17.35
Flagships	19.21	17.87
Metro leaders	22.70	20.95
Regionals	14.90	13.93

Source: IEPDS.

faculty, who frequently are excluded from the student-faculty ratios that institutions publicize. We regard the numbers in table 5.4 as more realistic measures of activity in higher education today than the ratios published by IPEDS.[31]

It is apparent from the table that except for HBCUs, student-faculty ratios fell in public higher education between FY 2012 and FY 2018. But they drifted upward by 1.2 percent at HBCUs during this period. Why? Some PWIs (for example, the metro leader institutions) increased their use of part-time faculty—individuals who typically teach more than full-time faculty—but this was not generally true, and in any case, the percentage of part-time faculty at HBCUs also trended upward by 2.0 percent as well during this period.

Student-faculty ratios are susceptible to multiple interpretations and must be interpreted with care. These ratios do not exist in a vacuum; ultimately, they reflect a variety of choices made throughout an institution. Student-faculty ratios are sensitive to the internal resource allocation choices that HBCUs make across their campuses, as well as to economies of scale. Tobler's First Law of Geography reminds us that "Everything is related to everything else."[32] Thus, the inability of most, if not all, HBCU campuses to benefit from potentially available economies of scale impacts multiple aspects of their performance, and student-faculty ratios provide but one example.

Holding constant approximately a dozen possible influences on student-faculty ratios, including SAT score and income, the "adjusted" ratio of the representative HBCU is 28.26 percent lower than found at a typical regional institution (see appendix table c.5). Arguably, these lower student-faculty ratios are an important part of the personalized attention and concern that HBCUs believe sets them apart from the usual PWI.

INSTITUTIONAL SUPPORT AND
ADMINISTRATIVE COSTS

Let's now talk about institutional support, which many observers classify as "administration" because it includes expenditures to fund areas, such as the payroll office, that are necessary to keep the institution operating but do not directly generate any credit hours. Some refer to institutional support expenditures as overhead, but there are many other aspects within a university that also might be considered overhead (for example, a dean's office) but typically are not included in the institutional support category.

The primary difference between HBCUs and PWIs in the institutional support arena is that HBCUs spend proportionately more. Table 5.5 reveals that the median percentage of major expenditures per FTE student devoted to institutional support at HBCUs[33] is almost triple the percentage at a flagship. Further, the HBCU proportion grew 1.8 percent between FY 2012 and FY 2018.

Figure 5.3 provides a visual representation of the relationship between institutional support expenditures per FTE student and institution size, as measured by each campus' calendar year FTE student enrollment. Institutional support expenditures are subject to significant economies of scale. No HBCU today is large enough to realize the available economies of scale that can come from spreading an institution's fixed costs over additional students. This problem has been exacerbated by falling HBCU enrollments. Many HBCUs have been moving upward on their cost curves rather than downward. Growing institutions have the potential to realize economies of scale and devote greater proportions of their expenditures to instruction. Unfortunately, this has not been the world that HBCUs have inhabited during the past decade.

HBCUs as a group have a reputation for being administratively top-heavy. One can see in table 5.5 and figure 5.3

TABLE 5.5 MEDIAN PERCENTAGE OF MAJOR EXPENDITURES ON INSTITUTIONAL SUPPORT BY INSTITUTION TYPE, FY 2018

Institution type	Median percentage of major expenditures per FTE student for institutional support	Median calendar year FTE student enrollment
HBCUs	26.5%	3,015
HBCU public	20.8%	4,706
HBCU private	35.3%	1,305
Flagship	9.6%	28,016
Metro leader	12.9%	22,487
Regional	15.6%	22,486

Source: IPEDS.

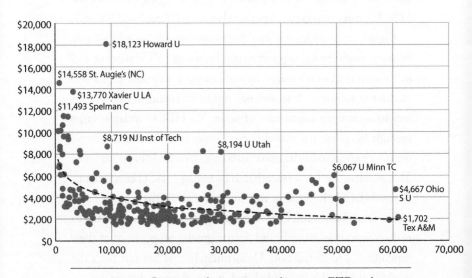

FIGURE 5.3 Institutional support expenditures per FTE student, by institution size, FY 2019

Source: IPEDS.

that there is empirical evidence to back this perception. Is this result a function of smaller institutional size or prevailing campus culture? We cannot supply a definitive answer, but we can observe that the absence of economics of scale eventually affects a wide variety of services and activities offered at HBCUs. These are economic realities on which any campus culture must build.

STUDENT DEBT

HBCU student bodies are generally less wealthy than those at PWIs. Figure 5.4 reveals that the average household of a student attending an HBCU ranked in the 40.18th percentile in the national income distribution for households in 2015. Compare

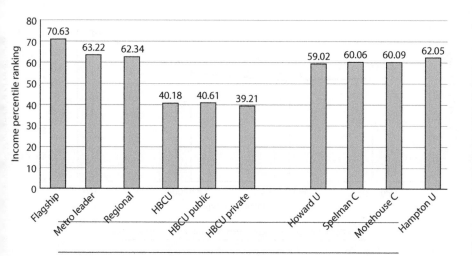

FIGURE 5.4 Students' household income percentile ranking in the national household income distribution, by institution type, FY 2015

Source: Opportunity Insights.

this with the 70.63rd percentile ranking of students attending flagship institutions.

But there are notable exceptions. The figure also shows that the income percentile ranking of students attending Hampton University was 62.05. Howard University, Morehouse College, and Spelman College all recorded percentiles above 59.0. These rankings may not seem remarkable until one compares them with the 40.18th percentile ranking of all HBCUs.

Hampton, Howard, Morehouse, and Spelman are independent institutions. Despite their more elevated rankings, the HBCU independent-sector institutions in our sample recorded only a 39.21st percentile ranking. This tells us that some small independent HBCUs enroll students with very limited financial means.

The preceding income numbers are background for figure 5.5, which displays the median federal student debt owed by graduates

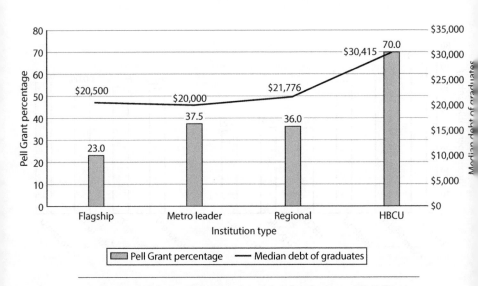

FIGURE 5.5 Median federal student debt of graduates and Pell Grant percentages, by institution Type, FY 2019

Source: IPEDS.

of various types of institutions. The $30,415 debt value for HBCU graduates is 39.7 percent higher than that of regional PWI graduates. Further, remember that these data do not include private student loan debt nor does it include Parent Plus federal debt incurred by parents and guardians. In FY 2019, the median value of the latter for students at HBCUs was $12,583 per family.[34]

Thus, the typical HBCU student exhibits significant financial need. One indicator is that 75 percent of HBCU students were eligible for Pell Grants in FY 2019,[35] more than triple the percentage of Pell Grant students at flagship institutions.

Indebted students and graduates do not start families, buy automobiles, purchase homes, leave home, launch businesses, or even get married as often as those without debt.[36] Alas, what many student debtors do not understand is that student debt ordinarily cannot be discharged in personal bankruptcy. Thus, those who fail to pay their student loans will carry a black mark on their credit records for the rest of their lives.

In FY 2017, 9.7 percent of all student loans were in default status three years after entering the repayment phase, whether or not they earned a degree. This number rose to 14.7 percent at for-profit institutions.[37] Student debt in the United States has particular relevance in the case of HBCUs because their students not only take on more debt but also are more likely to default on it—which has serious consequences.[38] It is not an exaggeration to say that student debt constitutes a drag on the economy at large as well as on individuals.

Table 5.6 reports federal student loan default rates for selected institutions in two states with a substantial number of HBCUs (Alabama and Georgia). With the exception of Spelman College, it is apparent that loan default rates at HBCUs are several multiples higher than those at the PWIs in our sample from those states.

The essential facts in table 5.6 are grim. The salient question (to paraphrase Lenin!), is, What is to be done about this? Some observers and elected officials believe that some or all student debt should be canceled.[39] Such forgiveness would have

TABLE 5.6 FY 2017 COHORT DEFAULT RATES ON FEDERAL STUDENT LOANS (THREE YEARS AFTER EXIT), SELECTED INSTITUTIONS, ALABAMA AND GEORGIA

Institution	FY 2017 default rate, in percent (three years after exit)
Alabama	
Alabama A&M University	19.8
Alabama State University	21.1
Miles College	11.25
Stillman College	22.9
Talladega College	32.0
Auburn University	3.0
Jacksonville State University	11.8
Troy University	10.4
University of Alabama Birmingham	5.9
University of Alabama Tuscaloosa	5.2
Georgia	
Albany State University	14.1
Fort Valley State University	14.2
Morehouse College	13.4
Savannah State University	18.5
Spelman College	5.0
Georgia Institute of Technology	1.2
Georgia State University	9.6
Georgia Southern University	6.4
University of Georgia	2.4

Source: U.S. Department of Education, Federal Student Aid, "Official Cohort Default Rates for Schools," https://www2.ed.gov/offices/OSFAP/defaultmanagement /cdr.html.

a positive impact on HBCU students. However, reasonable arguments can be made against forgiving large amounts of student debt. One is that it would be very expensive to do so. The Brookings Institution estimates that forgiving all student debt would exceed the total combined cost of individual federal programs such as unemployment insurance, the Earned Income Tax Credit, and food stamps.[40]

Further, there is general agreement that among the major beneficiaries of student debt forgiveness would be middle- and upper-income students and their families.[41] This means that loan forgiveness would represent a large transfer of funds from all taxpayers to students and households, many of whom arguably need these dollars the least.[42] There also is a related incentive problem. If a student and family saved for college and did not incur any debt, what benefit would they receive from loan forgiveness? The apparent answer is nothing, other than implicit encouragement to not scrimp and save in future.

Loan forgiveness presents a moral hazard for some individuals because it provides them with an incentive to transfer the costs of their actions to others. Affected individuals might well conclude, "I don't really need to save for college because they are going to find a way to forgive my student debt."

The optimal solution to the challenges involving student debt has three parts. First, there is an overwhelming need to reduce the rate of increase in the cost of attending college. It is well known that even after the value of grants and scholarships is deducted from colleges' posted costs, the net cost of attending has increased much more rapidly than the Consumer Price Index. The College Board reports that the net cost of attending a four-year public institution increased annually an average of 1.20 percent more rapidly than the CPI between 2006–7 and 2019–20. For four-year not-for-profit independent colleges, the comparable increase in excess of the CPI was 0.71 percent.[43]

Though a variety of justifications have been offered for these excesses, none is capable of explaining the college pricing behavior we have observed since the turn of the century. Blame accrues in a variety of quarters.[44] What is unmistakable, however, is that these cost increases have priced many Americans out of higher education.

Second, society must support more generous financial aid programs that directly address the needs of students. It does not suffice for elite institutions to announce with fanfare that they meet 100 percent of the financial needs of their lower-income students if they admit hardly any of these students.

Third, student loan procedures and policies need to be reformed and should, for example, make greater use of income-based student loan repayment programs. Multiple parts of the student loan system either are broken or in need of change. We will have more to say about this in chapter 7.

The notion of a mismatch between students and colleges has received considerable acceptance in the discipline of economics. The hypothesis is that some talented but financially disadvantaged students could have succeeded at a more prestigious and selective institution than the one they attended and that this choice carries a lifelong financial penalty. Had they experienced success at a more selective institution, they would have earned a higher income. Harry J. Holzer and Sandy Baum, in *Making College Work: Pathways to Success for Disadvantaged Students* (Washington, DC: Brookings, 2017), make this case and cite a bevy of studies that support it. This theory has profound implications for HBCUs because it implies that many talented Black students should be directed away from HBCUs to more selective PWI institutions.

It will suffice here to observe that current financial aid policies strike particularly hard at HBCUs because those institutions enroll so many students with significant financial need. To some extent, the lower retention and graduation rates posted by HBCUs relate to inadequacy of the financial aid system that exists in higher education. We have attempted to recognize and control for the relationship between the ability to pay and graduation rates by employing a metric that reflects household incomes. But there is a need for more refined ways to calculate the financial needs of campuses that increasingly are made up of older, part-time, and financially independent students. HBCUs have more at stake here than the typical PWI.

FINAL THOUGHTS

The focus of this chapter has been on oft-cited and -referenced measures of college and university activity such as enrollment, retention and graduation rates, administrative expenditures, and student debt. In general, HBCUs perform as well as or better than PWIs once one understands and controls for their specific circumstances. Graduation rates provide the most obvious example. After accounting for student SAT scores and household incomes, one can see that the typical HBCU's adjusted graduation rate exceeds that of the typical PWI.

A major exception to HBCUs' superior performance is expenditures on institutional support, which typically are several times higher than at PWIs on a calendar year FTE student basis. This is a financial affliction common to institutions with smaller enrollments, and the reality is that the median calendar year FTE student enrollment of the HBCUs in our sample was less than one-sixth of the median PWI in FY 2018.[45] Consequently, most PWIs have the potential to experience economies of scale that are out of reach for the typical HBCU.

But the HBCU story with respect to administrative costs is not a reflection solely of institution size. Sometimes elevated administrative costs at HBCUs reflect deliberate choices and traditions. Witness Howard University, whose FY 2019 average institutional support expenditure was $18,123 per calendar year FTE student—almost four times the comparable expenditure at Ohio State University, though Ohio State was 6.67 times larger than Howard.[46] Howard might be perceived as an unusual case because of its federal funding sources, but expansive expenditures on institutional support are common to well-regarded HBCUs of many sizes. The FY 2019 average institutional support expenditures per calendar year FTE student were $6,116 at Morgan State University, $9,211 at Morehouse College, $11,286 at Spelman College, and $13,522 at Xavier University in Louisiana.[47] A school's ability to incur institutional support costs, and its taste for doing so, appear to matter as much as the size of its student body.

6

A DEEPER DIVE INTO
HBCU DYNAMICS

*At [predominantly white institutions], Black people are
ignorant until they prove that they're smart. At an HBCU,
Black people are smart until they prove that they're ignorant.*

—Julianne Malveaux, Bennett College president, 2007–12

American colleges and universities are complex, many-faceted operations. HBCUs are no exception and, if anything, provide interesting new facets to consider and understand. We have observed some of this distinctiveness, including the ability of HBCUs both to inspire and graduate students who might fall along the wayside at a PWI and the substantial role that intercollegiate athletics plays on HBCU campuses.

We now extend our reach and consider multiple additional aspects of HBCU performance, including admissions yield, the differences between the performance of male and female students, endowment values, and the ability of HBCUs to provide economic mobility.

ADMISSIONS YIELD

Campus student recruitment frequently is conducted in three distinct phases. The first focuses on the need for institutions to generate applications and typically involves visiting locations such as high schools, hosting visits to campus by prospective students, using alumni as advocates, and advertising extensively. Second, campuses must decide which applicants to admit.[1] Third, their major challenge becomes turning those who are admitted into enrollees.

The end product, enrollment, reflects the cumulative effects of a variety of factors over time. Let us focus on the third phase of the enrollment process: turning those admitted into enrollees. The label usually attached to the percentage of admitted individuals who later enroll is "yield." We want to know if campus characteristics and policies influence yield and, in particular, how they play out at HBCUs.

One can see in figure 6.1 that yield rates are considerably lower at HBCUs than at PWIs. Why is this so? The two most likely reasons are that some prospective HBCUs students discover they cannot afford to attend college, and/or they opt to attend a PWI.

In FY 2019, yield rates at our selection of HBCU institutions varied from a low of 8.80 percent at Rust College to a high of 43.94 percent at the University of Arkansas Pine Bluff.[2] Converting admitted students into enrolled students is an annual existential struggle at some HBCUs. If prospective students in an institution's pipeline do not register in sufficient numbers, the institution may be forced to close or, at the very least, lay off employees and freeze many expenditures. When campuses conspicuously fail to meet the enrollment targets on which they have based their budgets, the consequences usually are budget

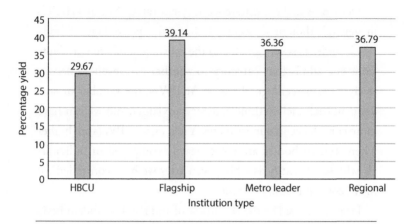

FIGURE 6.1 Median campus yield rates

Source: IPEDS

cuts, abandoned programs, terminations, canceled plans, falling morale, and disruptive finger-pointing. By contrast, improved admissions yields lead to expanded programs, new hires, salary increases, rising morale, and optimism. Hence, there are abundant reasons to examine admissions yields.

Do patterns exist that determine campus yield percentages? We present a variety of regression specifications in appendix table c.6 that address this question.

An initial noteworthy finding is that, holding other things constant, institution size does not appear to confer any advantages with respect to yield. This is an important finding for HBCUs for two reasons. First, most HBCUs are smaller than most PWIs, and if size disadvantages existed in this area, it would hurt them. Second, as we have already seen, larger institution size does confer some advantages in areas, such as enrollment and graduation rates, even though the benefit does not extend to admissions yield.

Does race make a difference in yield rates? Not at HBCUs in general, though at some of them, the percentage of non-Black students is very small and the movement of a few students from one admissions category to another can result in deceptively large percentage changes. At PWIs, the number of students in each racial/ethnic category are larger, and we can have more confidence in our estimates. Yield rates at PWIs are higher when student bodies are more heavily composed of individuals who self-identify as white, even after we have controlled for SAT score and family income.

Is yield affected by the Blackness of an HBCU's student body or faculty? We inserted variables into our explanatory equation that represented the percentage of undergraduates and faculty on a campus who self-identify as Black. We could not find general statistical evidence to support the hypothesis that either factor is connected to an institution's admissions yield. If anything, the statistical relationship between these measures of institutional Blackness and admissions yield may be negative. The evidence suggests that many prospective Black students who are shopping the higher education market are not heavily swayed by the Blackness of a campus when deciding where to attend college. This is an interesting and perhaps even controversial finding, in that many students at HBCUs clearly state that they are there because it is an HBCU and the student body is mostly Black.[3]

Both those seeking a Black experience and those who are not can exist and thrive within the diverse world of higher education in the United States. The future prosperity of HBCUs, however, depends in part on the existence of a large, viable proportion of Black individuals who seek a Black collegiate experience. Our statistical evidence does not support the view that the Blackness of a campus matters to large numbers of prospective students.

An example of a talented Black woman with options who chose
to attend an HBCU (in this case, Spelman College) is Corinne
Amany, who notes that her mother graduated from an HBCU and
that she wanted to experience a predominantly Black institution.
Amany believes that "Spelman prepared me, as a woman and a
Black woman, to face the world. . . . Spelman laid down the foundation for me to understand what I was going up against in this
world and to always carry myself with dignity and respect." High
praise indeed. Jaweed Kaleem and Kurtis Lee, "We Asked for Your
Experiences at Historically Black Colleges. These Are Your Stories," *Los Angeles Times*, April 22, 2019, https://www.latimes.com
/nation/la-na-hbcu-reader-experiences-20190422-story.html.

Not surprisingly, the prices that students pay influence yield.
For our HBCUs, a $2,000 increase in an institution's average
net price per FTE student drives a 0.6–1.0 percent decline in
an institution's yield. This is not a huge effect, but it cannot be
ignored.

With regard to the roles that intercollegiate athletic programs play at HBCUs, we examined whether the extent of an
institution's commitments to intercollegiate athletics affect its
admission yield. Our statistical results indicate that sponsoring an FCS football team (and everything that comes with it)
makes a huge difference in yield; holding other things constant,
the predicted campus admissions yield is 48.46 percent higher
at institutions that have FCS football teams. Yet, at the same
time, we find that fielding no football team at all also hikes the
admissions yield. This means that the least beneficial action
for a generic HBCU to take with regard to admissions yield is

to compete at the NCAA Division II or III level in football. (NCAA Division II institutions can grant the equivalent of thirty-eight full athletic scholarships annually, while but Division III institutions cannot grant any athletic scholarships.) Our results suggest "go big or not at all."

Is the typical HBCU's admission yield sensitive to the ways it spends its money; for example, the emphasis on either instruction or student services? We find only minimal evidence that changes in yield are tied to expenditures in either area. Over a space of five or six years, the emphasis a campus places on either instruction or student services may make a difference in overall enrollment, but neither appears to have a consistent impact on yield.

MALE AND FEMALE GRADUATION RATES AT HBCUS

We argued earlier that excessive attention is paid to first-time full-time six-year graduation rates, given that these rates reflect no more than half of the undergraduate students on today's campuses, and those rates continue to receive a great deal of attention. *U.S. News and World Report*, for example, assigned a weight of 17.6 percent to graduation rates in its 2021 institutional rating scale.[4] Thus, like it or not, graduation rates may have some relevance in the case of freshmen who enter college as full-time students soon after graduating from high school.

It is no secret that first-time full-time six-year graduation rates (which we shorten to "GRADRATE") are lower at HBCUs than at other institutions. Figure 6.2 reports GRADRATE data for institutions overall, including separate rates for men and women. GRADRATEs are approximately two times

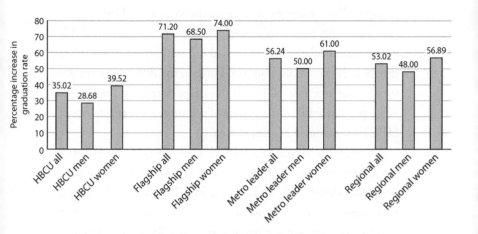

FIGURE 6.2 Median first-time full-time six-year graduation rates, by institution Type, FY 2020

Source: IPEDS.

higher at flagship institutions than at HBCUs, and HBCU GRADRATEs are roughly 15 to 20 percent lower than comparable rates at metro leader and regional institutions. If we restrict our focus to HBCUs, we observe that GRADRATEs for women are about 1.5 times higher than for men.

We have made the case that when one controls for SAT score and household income, the GRADRATE differences between HBCUs and PWI's vanish. We now sharpen this focus in two ways. First, we shine a spotlight on the persistent GRADRATE differences between men and women at HBCUs. Second, when we subdivide PWI institutions into our usual three institution types (flagships, metro leaders, and regionals), this reveals that HBCUs' GRADRATE outperforms those some but not all types of PWIs.

Suppose we estimate separate predictive regressions for men and women students at HBCUs (see appendix table c.7 for the details). What emerges is a sharp dichotomy in HBCU performance with regard to gender: HBCUs underperform PWIs where male students are concerned but outperform them when the focus is on female students. Further, the differences are not small—our estimate of HBCU underperformance for men is −6.49 percent, while our estimate of the superior performance of HBCUs for women is +8.23 percent.

Comparatively speaking, HBCUs are doing a much better job for women than men, even after SAT score and income have been considered. This finding is a step beyond simply noting that men's graduation rates are lower than women's; we assert as well that men are not being served as effectively as females. This important finding has significant implications for HBCU administrators, faculty, and staff.

A Black administrator at an HBCU told us, "We don't enroll as many men as women and when the men come, somehow we are not serving them as well." Perhaps the same observation might be made about American society at large. Black men, especially young men, often fall through policy cracks, especially when the issues are economic in nature. The plight of young Black males in American society is well documented but complex. Whether the lower graduation rates of Black males that we have found are due to the often trying circumstances that Black males confront or can be attributed to the institutions themselves, or some combination of both, is not something we are able to illuminate with this data set. The topic is a fertile area for future research.

When we compare HBCU and PWI graduation rates, does the type of non-HBCU institution make any difference? Yes. Once SAT score, household income, and institution size are accounted for, HBCUs outperform metro leaders and regionals but lag behind graduation rates at flagships. The typical HBCU outperforms the GRADRATE of the typical regional institution (all of which are PWIs in our analysis) by 4.75 percent.

In summary, after we control for the variables SAT score, household income, and institution size, we find that although HBCUs perform well overall, they are not doing as well as some might think with respect to their male students. Flagship institutions appear to be doing a better job in this area, possibly because flagships engage in "cream-skimming" to recruit talented and motivated Black men. However, family characteristics and attitude may differentiate Black students who attend flagships and other PWIs from those who attend HBCUs. This is yet another interesting area for future research.

Our results can be used in interesting ways; for example, to help explain the differences in graduation rates we observe between specific institutions. They tell us that a 100-point increase in the average SAT score of a student body is associated with a 20 percent increase in its predicted graduation rate. Consider Coppin State University, whose first-time full-time graduation rate was 24.48 percent in FY 2018. Compare that with Morehouse College's comparable graduation rate, which was 55.24 percent that year. Morehouse's average midpoint SAT score, however, was 1050, while that at Coppin was 930. What difference did this make? A big one. The difference in graduation rates between the two institutions would be wiped out if the two institutions enrolled students with the same SAT scores.

The comparison of Coppin with Morehouse is useful, though simplistic. These institutions differ in many ways besides their students' SAT scores, including location, physical plant, and family income. What our analysis demonstrates, however, is that a substantial proportion of the performance differences we observe can be attributed to differences in the SAT scores and incomes of their student bodies. Thus, differences in graduation rates may not signify that one institution is better or more productive than another; rather, the differences indicate that they enroll difference kinds of student bodies and therefore end up performing different tasks. The institutions may not be comparable in many respects.

ENDOWMENT VALUES

University endowment values always are of great interest to those connected to higher education because to some observers, endowments are symbols of endurance, stability, and success. The thought is that campuses doing really good things will receive bountiful contributions from grateful alumni, appreciative citizens, foundations, and businesses that assign them high grades for their activities. To some, endowment values serve as a thermometer that records institutional health.

Though this view of endowments has its critics, our experience suggests it has some empirical validity. Individuals and organizations are not likely to give gifts to failing campuses or those that appear to be badly managed. They do give gifts to campuses they that perceive to be able to make productive use of those gifts. These attitudes have not always worked to the advantage of HBCUs, especially when they have been dealing with prospective donors from the white-dominated establishment.

Currently, the general perception of HBCUs is more favorable than it has been for many years (perhaps forever), and several HBCUs have received financial gifts and support from major corporations and foundations that previously ignored them. Still, providing scholarship funds for inner-city Black individuals (or Appalachian whites) often is not as attractive to many donors as naming a football practice field, endowing a named chair in the medical school, or placing one's name on a respectable business school. The larger social and economic missions that HBCUs fulfill remain hazy or unknown to a significant proportion of Americans who have the financial ability to make a difference on HBCU campuses.

The average value of HBCU endowments was $59.91 million on June 30, 2020. But we hasten to point out that this average is based on only 18 of our 50 institutions.[5] The other 32 either did not have endowments large enough to rank them within the top 717 institutions in the United States in this regard or they chose not to report.

The largest HBCU endowment in mid-2020 was Howard University's $688.6 million, and this ranked it 162nd largest in the nation. Howard's endowment prowess is an unusual circumstance among HBCUs and reflects its distinctive history and location. The typical HBCU's situation is quite different. We surmise that the median HBCU endowment value may be in the area of only $25 million, which underlines the extent to which nearly all HBCUs with similarly modest endowments are tuition-driven institutions. They live and die on their net tuition collections and can count on little help from their endowments if and when financial crises emerge.

Given the small number of HBCUs for which we have foundation and giving data, we added them to our larger sample to analyze them. We focus on June 30, 2018, endowment values because requisite data were not available for either 2019 or 2020. Appendix table c.8 supplies our regression results, which focus on explaining the size of these endowments at the end of the 2018 fiscal year.

The financial status of each institution's graduates is a very important determinant of the size of its endowment. A 10-percentile upward movement in the national income distribution by an institution's graduates is associated with a $34 million increase in the value of its endowment. On the other hand, a 10-percent increase in the percentage of Pell Grant students at an institution translates to an $11.5 million decline in its endowment value. We find modest evidence that endowment value is positively related to the proportion of graduates who earned a degree in science, technology, engineering, or mathematics (STEM). To the extent that this finding is meaningful, HBCUs are at a disadvantage, because their curricula may be less STEM-heavy than those at PWIs.

Flagship institution status by itself is worth an incremental $49.5 million in endowment value. Metro leader status is a neutral factor with regard to endowment value, and (for our limited sample) HBCUs appear to hold a fundraising advantage over regional PWIs.

We find evidence that athletic directors often tout their intercollegiate athletic programs to promote fundraising. Even taking into consideration the incomes of graduates and the nature of the institution, we estimate that the existence of an FBS-level football program boosts endowment value by $49.3 million. We did not find similar evidence for FCS-level or NCAA Division II- and III-level programs. Note that no HBCU fields an FBS-level football team.

Even after we have held a host of other factors such as alumni incomes constant, institution size confers an advantage: larger institutions have larger endowments, presumably because they have more alumni. But this effect is very modest and amounts to no more than $1 million at a flagship and a pittance at the typical HBCU.

In a nutshell, though our sample size is limited, we find that HBCUs fundraising performance is superior to that of regional institutions, similar to that of metro leader institutions, and inferior to that of flagships. Recall that we are using only a nonrandom sample of 18 HBCUs in this endowment subsample, so these estimates must be viewed as less precise than others we have presented.

ECONOMIC MOBILITY

Anecdotes often are used to assert that HBCUs excel at providing students with upward economic mobility. In chapter 1 we cited individuals such as Oprah Winfrey as evidence of HBCUs' success in this regard. The Opportunity Insights project provided grist for this mill by publishing data that enable one to find the probability of a former student moving upward or downward in the income distribution relative to their parents. For example, 13.4 percent of Grambling State University students who were born between 1980 and 1991 and came to the campus from a household in the lowest income quintile moved up to the highest quintile in 2015.

HBCUs excel when economic mobility metrics are applied because there is so much room for upward movement in the incomes of their students. The data in table 6.1, which provides median mobility index values for various types of institutions, bear this out. Among the institutions in our sample, the median income percentile of the parents of students on an HBCU campus was only 40.7, while it was 70.6 at the flagships.

Using Opportunity Insights data, we compiled an index that tracks the percentage of students who come to a campus from the bottom 20 percent of the income distribution and end up in the top 20 percent in 2015. For example, at Virginia Tech, 47.5 percent of students born between 1980 and 1991 who came to its Blacksburg campus from the lowest income quintile ended up in the highest income quintile in 2015.

Opportunity Insights takes this a step further and weights Virginia Tech's 47.5 percent by the percentage of its student body from the lowest income quintile. Such individuals accounted for only 2.84 percent of its student body, signifying that only about one in every thirty-five students came from the lowest income quintile. Opportunity Insights multiplies the weighting by the student body (0.475 × 0.0284), resulting in an index of 0.0184. We multiply this value by 100 to give us an index of 1.84 (see table 6.1). Note that the median index value for HBCUs, 2.85, is larger than any PWI institutional classification and almost twice the flagship index value. Only the urban metro leader institutions can hold a candle to HBCUs in enabling upward economic mobility for its students.

Other researchers have found similar results, including Espinosa, Kelchen, and Taylor[6] for the American Council on Education, and the team of Nathenson, Samayoa, and Gasman at the Rutgers Center for Minority Serving Institutions.[7] Both studies relied on Opportunity Insights data. Espinosa et al. provided estimates of the economic mobility opportunities of several categories of minority-serving institutions. They found that the typical HBCU outperformed the typical PWI in accelerating upward movement in students' incomes after leaving school. However, HBCUs did not perform quite as well as Hispanic-serving institutions, those serving large Asian-American populations, or non-HBCU campuses that predominantly serve Blacks (often referred to as BSIs). The star performers in their analyses were non-flagship, usually urban institutions such as the City University of New York's Baruch College, City College, and Lehman College; California State University, Los Angeles; and what is now called the University of Texas Rio Grande Valley.

Nathenson et al. used a similar methodology but packaged their results in a different fashion, emphasizing upward economic movement from any household income quintile to any higher household income quintile, rather than concentrating only on movement from the lowest to the highest quintile. For example, they reported that 11.21 percent of students came from households in the second income quintile and then tracked those students over time to observe that 69.04 percent of them ended up in one of the top three income quintiles in 2015. The authors relied on a 50-HBCU sample (as we do) and compared the performance of these HBCUs with that of PWIs collectively.

Though interesting, the studies just cited do not tell us why one kind of institution excels over another in terms of mobility besides showing that it helps an institution to enroll a lower-income student body. Rigorous large-sample studies addressing this question are few in number. Among those that have pushed the ball forward with regard to HBCUs is work by Fryer and Greenstone[8] and Price, Spriggs, and Swinton,[9] though their conclusions differed as to whether HBCUs excelled at helping their students achieve upward economic mobility. Our evidence, drawn from a sample different from either of those studies, strongly suggests that HBCUs do.

We provide more definitive answers in table 6.1, where we report the magnitude, labeled "KID/PAR," for each of the 236 institutions in our sample. KID/PAR is the ratio of the kids' income percentile in 2015 divided by the parents' income percentile when the kids entered college. ("Kids" is Opportunity Insights terminology for children who grow up, attend college, and subsequently earn incomes.)

Our regression analysis focuses on campuses as the observational unit rather than individual students (see appendix table c.9). Individual students have been assigned to the institutions most responsible for their higher education. The work we report also differs from previous studies in that we hold many other

TABLE 6.1 ECONOMIC MOBILITY MEASURES
BY INSTITUTION TYPE, FY 2015

Institution Type	Median parents' income percentile	Median Opportunity Insights income mobility coefficient	Median KID/PAR*
Flagships	70.6	1.48	.93
Metro leaders	61.9	2.60	.98
Regionals	64.3	1.60	.98
HBCUs	40.7	2.85	1.29

*KID/PAR = kid's income percentile divided by parents' income percentile.
Source: Opportunity Insights.

variables constant in evaluating the mobility performance of HBCUs versus PWIs.

Though table 6.1 shows that HBCUs outperform PWIs in providing upward economic mobility, what are the sources of this advantage? Our analysis tells us that the primary advantage of HBCUs is that they typically enroll lower-income students. Simply put, they willingly provide opportunities. The median percentage of students coming to the HBCUs in our sample from the lowest income quintile was 24.72. Compare this with the PWI median of 6.83 percent, the College of William and Mary's 1.35 percent, or the University of Delaware's 2.23 percent. Such institutions are not providing many opportunities for individuals at the very lowest levels to move upward.

A representative campus's income mobility is enhanced when it has a higher proportion of women in its student body. There are two apparent reasons for this. First, women as a group are less well off financially than men and therefore have more to gain financially from higher education. Second, women are more likely to graduate than men, again resulting in larger financial gains.

By contrast, campuses that enroll larger percentages of older students tend to record lower income mobility scores. The reason might be that the older students' financial circumstances often are marginally better than younger students' and, holding other things constant, they graduate at lower rates than younger students because their needs and goals differ.

Internal resource allocations (how much campuses spend on instruction, student services, and intercollegiate athletics) do not tell us very much. SAT scores are also not a factor in explaining KIDPAR.

In order to win in the KID/PAR derby, an institution must enroll a substantial proportion of lower-income students. This ability, accompanied by campus programs that address students' financial circumstances, is what enables schools to record attractive economic mobility scores. All but a few HBCUs enroll lower-income student bodies and so most exhibit high KID/PAR scores.[10] However, PWI campuses such as the City College of New York and California State University at Los Angeles are similar to HBCUs in this respect and have enabled students to move upward (economically speaking) when they graduate.

A potential shortcoming of the KID/PAR upward mobility metric is that it is much easier for institutions with low-income student bodies to show greater relative improvement than it is for institutions whose student bodies already are higher income. We allowed for this possibility by fashioning a new relative KID/PAR variable based on how an institution performed given its possibilities. This empirical approach did not yield any new insights, and the explanatory power of the equation deteriorated substantially.

7

A ROADMAP FOR THE FUTURE

Not everything that is faced can be changed,
but nothing can be changed until it is faced.

—James Baldwin, in "As Much Truth as One Can Bear,"
New York Times Book Review, January 14, 1962

Race often dichotomizes information and understanding about HBCUs. Many non-Black individuals do not know much of substance about America's HBCUs and, further, may not care to learn, because to them, HBCUs do not matter. They did not attend an HBCU and don't know anyone who did so. Residents of Los Angeles, for example, live more than a thousand miles from the nearest HBCU, so those institutions likely are not on their radar.

Who better to demonstrate this relative lack of information than former U.S. Secretary of Education Betsy Devos, who, in 2017 told a surprised audience of HBCU presidents that HBCUs were "real pioneers when it comes to school choice."[1] Senator Claire McCaskill of Missouri acerbically responded that DeVos's view was "totally nuts" because HBCUs in the

South were founded on a racial basis and were designed explicitly to cement an absence of choice, not to provide choice.

"Hazy" is a good word to describe the knowledge that the 86 percent of Americans who are not Black have about HBCUs. Campuses such as Florida A&M University, Grambling State University, and Howard University have some name recognition among that 86 percent but primarily because of the sometime athletic achievements of Florida A&M and Grambling State and the prominence of Howard graduates. But fame can be fleeting. When an HBCU such as Norfolk State University or Texas Southern University scores an upset victory in the NCAA men's basketball tournament (and both did so in 2021), it makes newscasts and earns newspaper headlines, but this institutional celebrity recedes. What occurs is an HBCU version of Andy Warhol's "famous for 15 minutes."

Therefore, if one initiates a discussion of HBCU policies and procedures that might improve their circumstances and those of their students, one must recognize that this will plow new ground for many non-Black Americans. Their knowledge of HBCUs likely is fragmentary, and the distinctive needs of HBCUs and their students do not register as a high-priority concern.[2]

We seek to improve this situation but harbor no illusions that non-Blacks will read this book and then energetically swing into action. Change on major social issues often occurs slowly and incrementally in the United States, except when major social upheavals or disruptions intrude, such as wars and economic depressions, which forcefully reorient societies even as they introduce new circumstances and values. COVID-19 bodes well to fit into this category because it has triggered numerous changes in behavior and attitudes.

It remains to be seen if the increased degree of racial awareness surrounding a series of racist events that have included the murder of George Floyd will reorient American society to a similar degree. The gap between intention and action on racial issues often is immense. However, we do sense increasing willingness among non-Black citizens to confront issues involving race. By extension, they also may be more receptive to considering the distinctive circumstances relating to America's HBCUs. We believe now is the time of possibility for HBCUs. It also may be the time for Black individuals to learn more about HBCUs and acquire more accurate information about their performance.

OUR FINDINGS

This section summarizes what we have learned about HBCUs.

Relying on empirical evidence from a large sample, we have reaffirmed that HBCUs continue to fulfill vital societal purposes. Even though most PWIs recently have demonstrated much more interest in recruiting and retaining Black students, it is apparent that many Black individuals continue to find HBCUs to be comfortable, reassuring, personally productive places to attend college. That this holds true is demonstrated by the data: a representative Black student with a given SAT/ACT score and a given family income is more likely to graduate from an HBCU than from a PWI. If they graduate, by midcareer they will be earning more than had they graduated from a representative PWI. Further, on average, Black HBCU students report being more satisfied with their collegiate experiences.

HBCUs generally perform better than PWIs in terms of generating upward economic and social mobility for their graduates. Economic mobility is a somewhat slippery measure because relatively speaking, one cannot move upward in the economic distribution if one already ranks close to the top—a mathematical reality that afflicts many elite institutions. That said, if we account for SAT score and family income, HBCUs move more individuals farther up the economic distribution than does the typical PWI flagship institution or elite independent campus.

HBCUs continue to supply American society with impressive numbers of high-performing individuals. While PWIs' increasing interest in recruiting Black students could change matters, there is no dispute that HBCUs are the primary original source of highly skilled Black professionals in the United States today, including medical doctors, attorneys, laboratory scientists, social workers, and college professors. This impressive performance must continue and expand because it represents one of many steps that must be taken to reduce long-standing economic and social inequalities in American society. If W. E. B . DuBois were alive today, likely he would be pleased, though not satisfied, with the progress that has been made.

We reaffirmed that HBCU student bodies are composed predominantly of individuals from lower-income households. This comes as no surprise given that in 2019, the median income of households headed by self-identified Black people was 35.6 percent below that for self-identified white householders.[3]

Almost two-thirds of HBCU undergraduate students are women and that the proportion of male students at HBCUs has fallen significantly in recent years. Further, evidence suggests some Black men find some PWIs more attractive than HBCUs.

After a century or more of deliberate financial starvation, public HBCUs in several states (Maryland, South Carolina, Texas, and Virginia) now receive more funding per FTE student than comparably situated PWIs. Even so, we note that one reason for these higher levels of funding per FTE student at HBCUs is that

The distinctive case of Tennessee State University is worthy of mention. Because it is a land-grant institution, it was supposed to have received support in the form of matching funds from the state and the federal government. For some five decades, Tennessee State did not receive its financial due and might have been shortchanged by as much as $544 million. The other Tennessee land-grant institution, the University of Tennessee, was not similarly disadvantaged. State legislators have acknowledged the problem and seem prepared to do something about it, though paying the entire funding shortfall seems unlikely. Sara Weissman, "A Debt Long Overdue," *Inside Higher Education*, April 26, 2021, https://www.insidehighered.com/news/2021/04/26/tennessee-state-fights-chronic-underfunding.

student enrollment at several of these institutions has declined and their state funding has not been reduced accordingly. Ironically, it has taken tough times (at least in terms of enrollments) for some public HBCUs to receive more generous funding from their states.

Public HBCUs' current financial stresses often relate less to a shortage of operating funds and more to the quality of their buildings and equipment, which often are old, reflect long-term neglect, and in need of rehabilitation or replacement. Startling disparities between HBCUs and PWIs in some Deep South states continue to exist in the area of capital building and maintenance.[4]

For a century or more, intercollegiate athletic programs have occupied an astonishingly large role in American higher education, at least if one compares their importance in the United States with the more limited role sports plays at universities in other countries. This emphasis on athletic programs is typical at HBCUs. Despite the reality that no HBCU fields a "big-time" NCAA FBS football program, the median HBCU that supports an FCS division football program spends substantially more per FTE student on intercollegiate athletics annually than do PWIs that sponsor either type of program.[5] However, it may pay off. Our "holding other things constant" lower bound estimate is that HBCUs that field an NCAA FCS-level football program enjoy on average at least a 25.4 percent larger enrollment.

Attracting students to an HBCU with an intercollegiate athletic program is not the same as retaining or graduating them. There is little evidence that operating a significant football program or spending additional money on intercollegiate athletics improves either retention or graduation performance. Indeed, sponsoring no football program at all often appears to be helpful for graduation and retention.

On the private side of the higher education ledger, we found that the representative independent HBCU usually has immense capital needs. A former HBCU president told us that she worried that a basic system (such as heating) might break down in one of her campus buildings because she knew there were insufficient liquid funds to pay for the needed repair. Even Howard University, well-heeled in terms of the size of its endowment and the recipient of more than $200 million annually from the federal government, must deal with a surprisingly large number of outmoded, inefficient, unattractive campus buildings. These examples demonstrate that it is important to differentiate operating budget needs from those relating to an institution's physical plant.

As a group, HBCUs have been losing enrollment. However, they have succeeded in roughly maintaining their market share. Further, overall HBCU enrollment declines will be difficult to avoid because during most years between now and 2035, the absolute size of high school graduating classes will decline in most states. That decrease in high school graduation rates has been compounded by falling college attendance rates, especially among men who might attend HBCUs. These demographic realities tell us that absent new external financial assistance, as many as a dozen HBCUs (all small, all independent, and nearly always located in a rural area) will be forced to close their doors. This is a sad prediction that has a degree of tragic inevitability about it—if nothing is done.

The shuttering of HBCUs will wreak economic devastation on the small communities where they reside, because in nearly every case, the campus is the largest industry in town. Further, it seems likely that closures will reduce the total enrollment market share of HBCUs, as some of the students who attend these campuses will not end up transferring to another HBCU and/or may drop out of higher education. A well-designed program of financial assistance to HBCUs and their students would avert this disaster.

Declining HBCU enrollments are also related to our finding that every HBCU is too small to take full advantage of economies of scale that are available to campuses with at least 15,000 fiscal year FTE students. In our sample of HBCUs, the median campus size was about 3,100 fiscal FTE, with the minimum about 500 and the maximum approximately 11,200 (FY 2019 data). HBCUs' smaller sizes indicate that they have higher unit costs than larger institutions, a majority of which are public, and can spread their fixed costs over greater numbers of students. The typical HBCU today is inefficiently small, with the disadvantage of an average cost per student that seems likely to be exacerbated in the future because of generally declining enrollments. This economic reality is substantially unavoidable.

Though definitions of what constitutes an administrative expenditure often differ among institutions, HBCUs usually spend more on administration on a per student basis than PWIs. Institutional support expenditures are an imperfect measure of administrative expenditures but often are used as a proxy. We found that institutional support expenditures per FTE student were noticeably higher at HBCUs than at any major classification of PWIs and that even after we controlled for campus size, those expenditures were higher at a representative HBCU. This is not a distinction to be relished. Though the reasons for their apparent administrative heft require further investigation, institutions such as Howard University spend four times more per FTE student on institutional support than flagship universities such as Ohio State. The word on many HBCU campuses is that they are administratively top-heavy.

Evidence indicates that HBCUs that spend larger proportions on instruction exhibit higher graduation and retention rates (holding other things constant). We also found more persuasive evidence that graduation and retention performance on campuses deteriorates when institutions spend larger proportions of their budgets on student services. We note these findings with caution because many HBCU campuses maintain that their student services operations are a key to their success. We do not doubt that they can make positive contributions, but expenditures on student affairs may be subject to diminishing returns. Additional investments in student services may not be productive. Doubling expenditures on student affairs, for example, is unlikely to double measures of performance.

HBCUs as a group operate at a huge disadvantage in terms of the value of their endowments. Whereas the median institution in our sample of institutions boasted an endowment valued at $117.0 million at the end of June 2019, the comparable number for HBCUs was only $24.5 million ($22.3 million for independent-sector HBCUs and $24.8 million for public-sector campuses).

HBCUs suffered even in comparison with regional public institutions, whose median endowment was valued at $117.0 million.[6] Thus, endowments seldom offer financial salvation for today's typical HBCU. If an HBCU with a median endowment of $24.5 million spends 4.0 percent of it each year this will generate only $980,000. No doubt that money will be put to good use, but it seldom is a game changer. That these numbers hold true is a commentary on philanthropic giving patterns in the United States.

Approximately three-quarters of the students enrolled at HBCUs are Black, and they tend to come from households with lower earned incomes than students who are enrolled at PWIs. In 2019, the median household income of self-identified whites was $73,105, while it was only $46,698 for self-identified Black individuals.[7] Only 12.35 percent of white households had incomes that placed them below the poverty level that year, but this percentage rose to 25.65 for Black households.[8] These data tell us that very large proportions of HBCU students are candidates for financial aid and that their ability to access such aid—especially via Pell Grants or federal student loans—is crucial in determining whether they enroll, persist, and graduate. Alas, these programs exhibit a variety of inefficiencies, and funding for Pell Grants, for example, has declined significantly in real terms over the past decade.

Students at a representative HBCU take on more debt to pay for their higher education than do students at a typical PWI. Thus, they are more dependent on Pell Grants, federal student loan programs, and state need-based financial aid programs than are students at PWIs. Unfortunately, as we will see below, the real value of funds the federal government devotes to Pell Grants has declined significantly, federal student loan programs are complicated and difficult to access for many students, and many state financial aid programs are not based on students' financial need.

ASSESSING THE CRITICAL ROLE
OF THE FEDERAL GOVERNMENT

Federal financial aid to students is the most important way the U.S. government influences and helps HBCUs. That aid falls into three major categories: Pell Grants, student loans, and tax credits. While each is valuable, there is room to quarrel with their specifics and considerable room for improvement.

Pell Grants

Pell Grants are the foundation of federal financial aid programs. They have existed for about fifty years and are designed to increase low- and moderate-income students' access to college. Pell Grants focus entirely on a student's financial need, do not have to be repaid, and can be used for the equivalent of twelve full-time semesters.

In FY 2021, the government expended about $26 billion in Pell Grants to students. The maximum grant to an individual in that year was $6,345, insufficient to pay for a year's education but large enough to make a difference in enrollment, retention, and graduation. Unfortunately, because of inflation, the spending power of Pell grants shrank by 38.5 percent between FY 2011 and FY 2021.

It is easy to conclude that the U.S. Congress has not placed a high priority on Pell Grants despite the critical role they play in enabling lower-income individuals to attend college. A mitigating factor relative to this reduced real support is that the total number of individuals attending college has been declining.

The data in figure 7.1 reflect what we regard as a serious dereliction of duty and loss of purpose on the part of the federal government if it is truly interested in promoting an

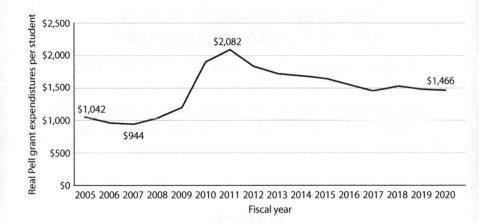

FIGURE 7.1 Real Pell Grant expenditures per student, FY 2006–FY 2020

Sources: For Pell Grant expenditures (2020 prices), Statistica, "Total Expenditure on Federal Pell Grant Awards in the United States from 1990/81 to 2020/21," https://www .statista.com/statistics/235374/expenditure-on-federal-pell-grants-in-the-us. For enrollments, U.S. Department of Education, Digest of Educational Statistics, table 303.25, "Total Fall Enrollment in Degree-Granting Postsecondary Institutions, by Control and Level of Institution: 1970 through 2018."

opportunity-based society in which all citizens have a shot at improving their status. More than any other financial tool utilized by the government, Pell Grants enable individuals to attend college without accumulating excessive debt.

We believe the evidence supports restoring Pell Grants to the peak inflation-adjusted value they had in FY 2011. Reputable studies reveal that these Grants positively affect graduation rates and the subsequent earnings of students who receive them. Further, these gains are sufficiently large that they overcome the substantial costs of the grants, which are recouped within ten years.[9] Here is a program that works.

There is no doubt that restoring the real value of Pell Grants on a per-student basis would have a salutary effect on HBCUs. In our sample, the median percentage of Pell Grant recipients among HBCUs' first-time full-time freshmen was 75.1 in FY 2019. This has little in common with the world of elite public institutions such as the College of William and Mary, where the comparable statistic hovered around 10.0 percent, or Georgia Tech, where it has been about 11.0 percent.[10]

But it does not have to be this way. Other fine institutions have excelled at providing opportunities: 47 percent of undergraduate students at the University of California-Riverside received Pell Grants in 2019–20, while the comparable number at the University of California-Davis (one of *U.S. News and World Report's* top 25 public universities) was 33 percent.[11]

We believe some proportion of federal financial support for institutions should be based on their meeting certain Pell Grant representation minima, perhaps 20 percent. Meeting that criterion would represent a firm and meaningful movement toward establishing and maintaining an opportunity-oriented society rather than reinforcing one that is socially and economically sclerotic.

We found in mining Opportunity Insights data dealing with income mobility that HBCUs as a group performed very well after we controlled for average student SAT score and household income. The value-added of HBCUs in this area was substantial and documentable. Public policy should capitalize on this finding by doing two things: first, restore the price-adjusted federal funding of Pell Grants to the FY 2011 level and, second, require institutions to meet minimum standards in terms of the proportion of undergraduate student bodies that receive Pell Grants. There is no doubt that in addition to benefiting HBCUs and

Black students, these initiatives would make higher education an important part of the process of reducing societal inequities. We do not believe that higher education is responsible for all society's ills, but in our view, colleges and universities have become an agency that tends to reinforce the status quo rather than providing opportunity and increasing social mobility. HBCUs are positioned to occupy a central role in restoring an opportunity-oriented society; refashioning the Pell Grant process is an excellent place to start.

Federal Loans and the FAFSA

Is there a polite way to state that the current federal student loan process is messed up and needs work? In this section, we provide a window on this less-than-ideal situation and offer recommendations for improvement.

The Department of Education (DOE) offers low-interest loans to help students meet their educational financial needs. These loans either are subsidized (DOE pays the interest that accrues on the loan while the recipient is in school and for six months thereafter) or unsubsidized (the recipient is responsible for all interest payments). Both are commonly referred to as "Stafford loans."

Currently, while institutions exercise considerable authority over how much a student may borrow, the DOE imposes overall limits. A financially dependent third-year student, for example, can borrow $7,500 annually, but no more than $5,500 can be via subsidized loans. Limits for financially independent students are higher. Overall, there is a $57,500 limit for undergraduate students, and no more than $23,000 of that amount can consist of subsidized loans. Limits for graduate students are higher. The maximum period in which one might receive a subsidized loan is six years. As of this writing, the interest rate being charged to undergraduate borrowers is 3.73 percent, but it is 5.28 percent for graduate students. In addition, a loan fee is charged to all recipients of direct loans. As of this writing, the loan fee (which is deducted from each disbursement) was 1.057 percent.[12]

Other federal student loan programs (FFEL and Perkins primarily) enable students to borrow money. In aggregate, their loans total about one-fifth the amount offered in direct loans. PLUS loans also exist and are available to graduate students and the parents of dependent undergraduate students. These loans ordinarily carry higher interest rates than Stafford loans.

Nothing we have described thus far applies to loans that students and parents might take out with private lenders. In early 2021, Americans owed private lenders $132 billion related to college attendance.[13] Interest rates on these loans are market-driven and consistently higher than government rates.

We provide these details to emphasize some of the complexity involved in the federal direct loan process. To receive a federal loan, one must have completed the Free Application Form for Federal Student aid (FAFSA), which for some can be a daunting process. The FAFSA requires one to have available social security numbers; tax returns; current information on any untaxed income, savings accounts, and investments including stocks, bonds, and real estate (excluding one's home); and perhaps evidence that the applicant really is a financial dependent.[14] Though the FAFSA application has been simplified over time, it remains sufficiently burdensome that it deters prospective students from completing it and therefore prevents them from enrolling in college.[15] In 2018, more than two-fifths of all students did not complete a FAFSA, meaning that not only could they not receive federal financial assistance, but also that the institutions they attended were unlikely to give them any.[16]

When student borrowers finish college (regardless of whether they earned a degree), they are automatically assigned to a repayment plan that amortizes the loan principal and accrued interest over a ten-year period. Most borrowers, however, can select a repayment plan based on their income after leaving college.

If borrowers later default on repaying their loans, this adverse information is turned over to credit agencies. Further, defaulted federal student loan balances ordinarily cannot be discharged in a bankruptcy proceeding, and therefore the destructive consequences of a default could follow the student for the rest of their lives and ruin their chances of buying a house or an automobile. The federal government is a tough creditor and may utilize garnishee arrangements that remove money from an individual's salary without their consent. The government also may turn the defaulted account over to a private credit agency, which will hound the borrower for repayment. We applaud the Wells Fargo Foundation's 2021 decision to commit $5.6 million to improving financial literacy and habits of students at six HBCUs.[17] This action may prevent future disasters.

The picture we are painting is one of complexity coupled with some confusion, replete with barriers that result in frustration among students and parents over federal student loan policies and procedures. Others have written extensively about these circumstances, and we will not replicate those discussions here. We do, however, adjudge that these circumstances have been bad news for HBCUs. Reducing the complexity, barriers, and frustrations associated with student financial aid would result in greater benefits for HBCUs because the financial circumstances of their students (and their financial experience) likely differ from those of students attending other institutions. As we noted earlier, much larger proportions of HBCU students receive Pell Grants, indicative of financial need.

Our prescription for what ails the federal student loan system includes the following.

- Simplify the FAFSA so the only two factors that really matter are family size and family income.[18]
- Eliminate the need to guess what interest rates will be charged.
- Automatically enroll borrowers in repayment programs based on their incomes (imitate Australia here).[19]
- Unless a borrower requests otherwise, make the repayment time period twenty-five years (again, like the Australians).
- Enable loan repayment via payroll deduction.
- Widen the circumstances under which unpaid loan balances can be reduced for public service employment.
- Either cease turning over the collection of defaulted loans to private loan collectors or regulate and supervise their behavior.
- Reward colleges and universities that increase their costs less than the increase in the Consumer Price Index (a longer-term solution).
- Devote resources to publicizing federal loan processes and subsidizing financial literacy efforts on campuses.

Tax Credits

Via the Internal Revenue Service, the federal government provides support for college attendance through a series of tax credits. Two tax credits relate to expenditures for higher education expenses. The American Opportunity Credit allows an individual to claim up to $2,500 per student per year for the first four years of undergraduate study. The Lifetime Learning Credit allows an individual to claim up to $2,000 per student per year for tuition and fees, books, and supplies and equipment required for coursework, provided they were purchased at the student's college. This benefit gradually phases out as the taxpayer's income grows.

These tax credits are generous and, by 2016, totaled more than $30 billion, an amount roughly two-thirds of government spending on Pell Grants that year.[20] The problem is that there is no evidence that the tax credits have made a difference in college attendance. The reason for this lack of connection appears to be that the credits are taken primarily by middle- and upper-income taxpayers who would have sent their children to college even if the tax credit did not exist. Practically speaking, not as many lower-income Black families benefit from these tax credits compared with members of other racial/ethnic groups. By extension, HBCUs typically benefit less than PWIs. This is another example of an ostensibly racially neutral policy that turns out to produce racially tinged results.

Higher education tax credits represent an expensive use of funds that produces minimal results. They constitute what economists label a "welfare transfer"—a movement of funds from one segment of society to another without producing any corresponding productivity or value. These scarce dollars could be more productively employed to support Pell Grants, a reallocation that would benefit HBCUs and Black students and underline a commitment to an opportunity-based society.

We doubt the constitutional validity of tax credits, and funding formulas in general, that are based on race and do not advocate for them here. But we question the wisdom of policies that appear to invoke racially neutral criteria but neither turn out to be racially neutral in practice nor appear to be generating the forecasted benefits. In general, we assign low marks to policies that result in one segment of society gaining at the expense of others without seeing any redeeming documentable justification.

Summing Up Our Federal Observations

While the rate of increase in the cost of attending college has moderated recently, it remains true that over the past thirty years, the inflation-adjusted net cost, even after scholarships and grants have been taken into consideration, increased 197.0 percent at four-year public institutions; 97.0 percent at four-year, not-for-profit independent institutions; and 65.0 percent at public two-year institutions. Meanwhile, inflation-adjusted median household income increased only 20.6 percent over the same period.[21]

Quite simply, the growth in college costs has outstripped the ability of many students and families to pay, and among the results have been declining college enrollments (though other causes for this decline also exist), rising student debt, and reduced upward economic mobility in our society. HBCUs especially have been damaged by these events for a variety of reasons, prime among which is that HBCU student bodies predominantly are composed of individuals coming from lower-income households. Need-based financial aid has not kept up with rising college costs, and as a result, students are incurring such large debts that they find it difficult to pay them off—compounded by the fact that the real value of need-based federally financed Pell Grants has declined significantly over the past decade. At HBCUs, students are dropping out because of financial pressures, which ultimately has generated elevated rates of loan default.

It might be overly critical to label the complex federal student financial aid system a mess, but as noted earlier, there are numerous reasonable and mostly uncontroversial improvements that can be made, beginning with a simplification of the FAFSA application, which remains the key to unlocking financial aid for most students. Federal student loan repayment should be based on the incomes students earn after they leave college, the loan repayment period lengthened to twenty-five years, and opportunities broadened for individuals to reduce their outstanding loan balances by working in occupations connected to the public good. Such changes would yield particular benefits for HBCUs and Black students.

In general, we believe more emphasis should be placed on need-based student financial aid programs, a prescription that would diminish or eliminate expensive non-need-based programs such as tax credits that do not appear to be generating forecasted results. Once again, HBCUs and Black students as a group would profit.

It almost goes without saying that the fates of colleges and their students would improve if governments increased rather than decreased funding for higher education in general. However, in our estimation, prospects are not bright, and therefore the welfare of HBCUs more likely is going to be determined by targeted inflows of funding from the federal government and sympathetic states, along with some of the reforms noted earlier. It remains to be seen if the increased attention that HBCUs have received recently ultimately will translate into changes that are financially concrete.

ACTIVITIES OF STATES

State Financing of Higher Education

Most states have eased away from their financial support of higher education.[22] Robust economic conditions typically bring increased state funding, but recession carries with it cuts in support.

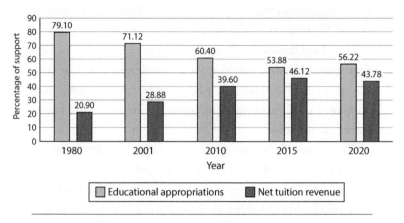

FIGURE 7.2 Change in the relative size of states' financial contributions versus net tuition revenue, FY 1980–FY 2020

Source: State Higher Education Executive Officers Association, "State Higher Education Finance, FY 2020," table 2.1, SHEF FY 2020.

One can see in figure 7.2, however, that if we focus only on state appropriations plus tuition and fees, state contributions to higher education declined from 79.10 percent of the sum of appropriations plus tuition and fees to only in FY 1980 to 56.22 percent in FY 2020. HBCUs, however, fared better than the typical four-year public institution in this regard. In FY 2005, states supplied 60.40 percent of HBCUs' major revenues (state support plus net tuition and fees). That contribution rose to 64.35 percent in FY 2020. That is, states were supplying relatively more fiscal sustenance to HBCUs in FY 2020 than in FY 2005.[23]

Such was not the case at PWIs. The portion of their major revenues from state appropriations declined from 59.35 percent in FY 2005 to 43.59 percent in FY 2020. This reduction reflected two things. First, the price-adjusted value of state appropriation fell 19.0 percent at the PWI institutions in our sample during this period, but they compensated for the dip by raising their tuition and fee charges. Net tuition and fee revenue (after grants and scholarships) rose 53.1 percent at our PWIs during the same period. Compare this with the 2.3 percent increase that occurred at HBCUs. Historically, many PWIs have been able to increase their prices without suffering great enrollment loss. The same cannot be said of HBCUs, whose student bodies have been composed predominantly of individuals who come from lower-income households.

We do not doubt that some universities have the ability to increase prices without suffering noticeable enrollment losses or that some have endowments and accumulated fund balances that enable them to ride out fiscal storms. We do not believe very many HBCUs fall into these categories. Langston University, for example, is not at the same level as the University of Oklahoma financially speaking. Central State University is not Ohio State University.

As figure 7.3 reveals, the combination of rising costs and a relative decline in state support for higher education have

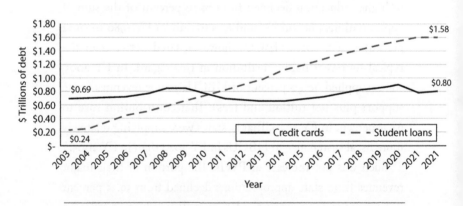

FIGURE 7.3 Growth of student loan debt versus credit card debt, United States, 2003–21 ($ trillions)

Source: Federal Reserve Bank of New York, Center for Microeconomic Data, "Household Debt and Credit," https://www.newyorkfed.org/microeconomics/hhdc/background.

resulted in college students taking on more debt, which reached an almost staggering $1.58 trillion in 2021. HBCUs and their students have turned out to be particularly vulnerable in this world. First, more Black than non-Black students go into debt (50.8 percent versus 40.2 percent).[24] Second, Black students borrow larger sums.[25] Third, their situation deteriorates over time: four years after graduation, Black graduates have $25,000 more debt than white graduates, roughly triple the amount they incurred by the time they graduated.[26] Fourth, they default on their loans at higher rates.[27] Finally, defaulting reduces the probability that debtor students will purchase an automobile or property but increases the probability that they will remain semi-dependent and remain living with their parents.[28]

States' budgetary actions have not had a neutral impact on their institutions and students. When state governments take money out of higher education, they inflict particular injury on Black students and HBCUs. In recognition, some states have cut funds for HBCUs to a lesser degree than for PWIs. Given the evidence, we think this is the right thing to do.

In some states, independent-sector HBCUs have a financial stake in these discussions because they benefit significantly from tuition grant programs. Virginia's Tuition Assistance Grant (TAG) program is the national model in this regard. In 2021–22, an estimated 23,000 Virginians who attended one of the state's independent-sector institutions received a non-need-based TAG grant worth $2,000 if they were undergraduates and $2,200 if they were a graduate student in the health professions. Hampton University students claimed 704 of these grants in fall 2018, while Virginia Union University students received 505. One of these grants effectively lowered Virginia Union's net price by about 10 percent for about one-quarter of its undergraduate student body.

Governing Boards

Governing boards are legally in charge of colleges and universities. Terrance M. McAdoo, in his interesting 2018 look at HBCU governing boards, commented that "HBCU Boards [are] unlike other Boards." He attributed much of the difference to "flaws" in the way board members are selected and leadership is determined.[29] In particular, he argued that HBCU boards were overweighted with business leaders and underweighted with experienced educational leaders and experts.

McAdoo's sample of institutions consisted of the ten largest HBCUs in the country at the time: Florida A&M University, Howard University, Jackson State University, Morgan State University, North Carolina A&T University, North Carolina Central University, Prairie View A&M University, Southern University, Tennessee State University, and Texas Southern University. He found that 75.0 percent of the members of these boards were men, 46.5 percent were business owners or executives, and 13.2 percent were attorneys. Individuals he classified as educators constituted only 16.4 percent of board membership. He observed that while the governing boards in other professional areas (such as accounting or law) were composed almost exclusively of individuals from those professions, that model was not pursued in higher education. He inferred that the heavy weighting of business backgrounds among HBCU board members might be a cause of the high rate of turnover in presidencies.

State legislatures nearly always exercise constitutional authority over public colleges and universities and often hold latent powers over independent-sector institutions. However, legislatures have long since transferred their most significant powers to governing boards. A major problem associated with this transfer of authority is that it seldom has been accompanied by guidance, goals, objectives, or criteria.

Consider this part of the *Code of Virginia* with respect to HBCU Virginia State University: "The board of visitors of Virginia State University (the board) is a corporation under the name and style of 'The Visitors of Virginia State University' and has, in addition to its other powers, all the corporate powers given to corporations by the provisions of Title 13.1 except those powers that are confined to corporations created pursuant to Title 13.1. The board shall at all times be under the control of the General Assembly."[30] Subsequently, the code advises that Virginia State's board "shall appoint all professors, teachers, and agents and [fix] their salaries and generally direct the affairs of the university," and states that "the board may confer degrees."

These statutes clearly confer power on Virginia State's governing board but, notably, fail to provide it with guidance about what it should be doing. Nothing is said, for example, about producing an educated citizenry or providing generous student access at the lowest feasible cost. Nor is anything said about producing critical thinkers, graduates who can pass licensure exams, or individuals who can function as literate citizens. Absent is mention of intercollegiate athletics or auxiliary enterprises, which turn out to be very big businesses on many campuses. State constitutions and statutes typically do not say much about establishing the responsibilities of independent college governing boards. The upshot is that virtually everything on campuses is left up to the changing memberships of their governing boards.

As a matter of practice, governing boards nearly always assign much of their power to campus governance bodies, the most meaningful of which are faculty senates or equivalents. This power transfer is recorded in the form of a faculty handbook or union contract that has legal standing. Thus, while board

members ultimately may vote to approve the appointment, pro-
motion, and tenure of faculty members as well as curricula, effectively they delegate their decision-making power on such items
to faculty. It is a well understood (though perhaps not univer-
sally accepted) principle that on academic matters, members of
governing boards should not attempt to substitute their judgment for that of faculty.

Practically speaking, board members seldom seriously discuss
the composition of their campus' liberal education program or
inquire if there is any evidence that students emerge better able
to think critically or write effectively. Topics such as pre- and
post-testing to obtain some notion of students' abilities when
they begin and end their education are seldom, if ever, discussed.
These are vital topics at HBCUs because nonnegligible numbers
of students arrive on campus with mixed academic preparation.

Our experience tells us that only some HBCU trustees (the
title most commonly accorded a member of a governing board)
pose respectful questions that penetrate the usually well-orches-
trated administrative presentations, which are skillfully couched
as a campus narrative and often accompanied by a video about
the image the institution thinks it has (or aspires to have).[31]
These narratives present the institution the way its administration wants others to see it and consequently could be divorced
from reality. In any case, many trustees end up being co-opted
by administrators, especially the institution's president, if that
person is charismatic. Board members then may permit shaky
assumptions to go unexamined and neglect to require evidence.
If the president is talented and appropriately motivated (an
important consideration), the institution may perform well in
terms of the usual metrics that are applied: enrollment growth,
fund-raising, rankings, and so on.

But are the HBCU and its president focused on providing opportunities? Do trustees have more than passing knowledge about how successful (or unsuccessful) their institution is in terms of providing its students upward economic mobility? Are they aware if its financial aid policies focus on lower-income students or instead reward those who produce higher standardized test scores? Do they know how athletic expenditures on their campus compare with others and what percentage of their athletes graduate? Do they have a sense of how military veterans are treated on campus? Have they seen any large-sample evidence that students actually are learning or that their critical thinking abilities have been enhanced?

These are among the serious, important questions that too frequently get derailed at HBCU board meetings because they are crowded out by administrative "show and tell" sessions that highlight successes and minimize difficulties. The preferred campus narrative too often shunts vital considerations to the sideline. While it is true that board members usually enjoy meeting the members of the victorious men's basketball team, getting to know the staff member who imitates Mother Teresa, or sampling the menu at the faculty club, these activities may not represent the best use of their limited time.

We believe the most telling neglect of governing board trustees at HBCUs (and PWIs) may be the contract they offer the president and that administrator's subsequent evaluation. Ultimately, presidents do what boards instruct them to do if the board backs this up by means of evaluation and compensation. In practice, most boards choose to reward presidents who grow enrollments, bring in major gifts, do well with the legislature, generate increases in research funding, and, depending on the institution, improve institutional rankings according to *U.S.*

News and World Report or whatever other source provides the most favorable positioning.

It is not that these aspects of institutional and presidential performance are irrelevant; they have obvious importance. However, they must be leavened by metrics that reveal whether the institution truly is making a difference in the lives of its students and connected communities. In other words, the evaluation and subsequent compensation must not fail to focus on the questions noted earlier.

As a practical matter, governing board members usually need assistance in assessing their president. Here is a tale to consider: a real-world HBCU governing board incentivized its president by promising that individual a sizable financial bonus if she was able to increase the institution's headcount enrollment by 10 percent. The results of this exercise probably were predictable. The president lowered admissions standards, transferred funds from other locations on campus (even from the library) into admissions activities, and hired more personnel in the admission area. And voila! This HBCU's headcount enrollment (though not its FTE) increased more than 10 percent. The president left the institution with bonus in hand before the board figured out what had gone down.

The fundamental lesson to take from this episode is that HBCU boards need to pay attention to the nature of any presidential incentives they offer. Further, rewards should be held in escrow and not be paid out immediately. An additional lesson is that most boards are well advised to employ experienced outsiders who are familiar with the range of campus games that can be played, what questions to ask, and where to find information. Even on small HBCU campuses, finances are complicated by foundations, public-private partnerships, student fees, federal COVID-19 relief dollars, auxiliary services, and intercollegiate athletics. We understand that utilizing knowledgeable outsiders will be costly, but ordinarily it is money well spent.

Are there more incentive and evaluation challenges for HBCUs than for PWIs? The answer is not clear. We do observe that some HBCU trustees overtly admire the considerable power and authority the president of their small institution exercise over campus events and conversations about those events. The campus influence and power wielded by some HBCU presidents is exceptional with regard to their educational programs. Not infrequently, these administrators dominate their boards and effectively determine both membership and officers.

Nevertheless, the universe of HBCUs is full of variety, and sometimes we observe quite the opposite paradigm among governing boards. Some engage in unproductive micromanagement and interfere in circumstances that should be none of their business. Marybeth Gasman noted that this dynamic seemed to occur during the last decade at respected HBCUs such as Florida A&M University and Morehouse College, even though those institutions had experienced, seemingly popular presidents.[32] Along these lines, we wince when we read that Texas Southern University's Board of Regents gave themselves the power to fire any campus employee, "even down to the janitor."[33] We do not quarrel with their right to do so, but the firing of janitors should not occupy the attention of board members.

The bottom line is that HBCU board members must prioritize the use of their time and the questions they ask. They should accord their president considerable respect, because that is the only individual who has the potential to see the institution as a whole and truly understand how one portion relates to another. Further, they should avoid micromanagement. Yet, board members must not shrink from asking the president and

administrators appropriately grounded questions, or from examining assumptions, requiring evidence, deciding that more information is essential, or opting to delay decisions. Most important,
they must present the president with clearly derived goals and
incentives that flow from the institution's mission and reflect a
realistic assessment of its strengths, weaknesses, and needs.

APPOINTING, TRAINING, AND EVALUATING BOARD MEMBERS

In the typical case, the members of the governing board of a
public HBCU are nominated by the state governor but must be
confirmed by one or both houses of the legislature. In the five
states that host the most HBCUs (Alabama, Georgia, Louisiana, Mississippi, and Texas), a statewide governing or coordinating body exercises power over the recommendations that come
from a campus. Several of these states have boards with student,
faculty, or staff members, but those individuals seldom have the
right to vote. In Alabama, both Alabama A&M University and
Alabama State University have committees that recommend
prospective board members to the governor, who sits on both of
their boards as an ex-officio member.

Appointments to college governing boards typically are much
sought by a variety of prospective trustees and are useful political "plums" for governors and legislators to dispense as either
rewards or inducements. In some states, it is widely accepted that
either one supports the governor and powerful political figures
with checks of an appropriate size, or one does not get appointed.

Therein resides a potential problem. Not all individuals who
have political connections or wealth are positioned to serve in
a fiduciary capacity as trustees. They may come to their board
membership with a specific interest they wish to promote or
an issue they seek to advance. For some, it is an athletic team

or a stadium. For others, it may be the engineering program or student services. It may be difficult to know before a member is appointed or elected what motivates that person. It can be a gradual process that turns into a "show and tell," a former HBCU president told us.

Most board members—and HBCUs are no exception—require training and orientation if they are to serve effectively. This is likely to hold true especially when non-Black individuals join the board of an HBCU. They must acquire knowledge and sensitivities and perhaps venture outside what had been their comfort zone.

It is not uncommon for board members—especially those new to the task—to focus their attention on a dashboard indicator, such as enrollment, to the exclusion of the other important matters. Of course, enrollment is important, but are the students who enroll learning anything of consequence? What do reputable data sources such as Opportunity Insights and the College Scorecard have to say about the degree to which the campus generates upward economic mobility for its graduates? These are examples of questions that experienced, properly motivated board members also ask.

The bottom line is that HBCU board members require training and orientation, though such a requirement seldom is written into state statutes. Further, in recent years, because of the advent of distance learning and COVID-19, circumstances on campuses have been evolving so rapidly that the training process needs to be repeated so boards can keep up with the changes. Our experience tells us that some trustees participate only begrudgingly (or not at all) in training and orientation sessions.

The margin for error by governing boards is smaller on many HBCU campuses, especially those that are independent rather than public. Many HBCUs operate on very thin financial margins. Thus, a major mistake might result in the demise of the institution. Hence, on such campuses, the identities, abilities, and attitudes of board members are critical.

We believe state statutes for public colleges and universities should establish that trustees are fiduciaries who hold a trust for students and citizens. In addition, the statutes also should mandate training for board members, and those who are unwilling to fulfill that requirement in a timely fashion should be prohibited from service.

State Student Financial Aid

The College Board reported that in 2019–20, the average state provided $980 in financial aid per FTE student to undergraduates.[34] This constituted 5.1 percent of the average cost of attendance at a four-year public institution.[35] However, in more than one-quarter of the states, less than half of this financial aid for meeting student's financial need. Georgia was notable both for supplying the most financial aid per FTE student ($2,480) and not dispensing any of those funds on the basis of financial need.[36]

What proportion of state student financial aid that should be devoted to student's financial need is not set in stone, but we believe that at least half of each state's allocation ought to address that need. Georgia's situation is instructive; it sponsors several popular publicly funded scholarship programs that reward students who have excelled academically in high school. We center our attention on two: the HOPE Scholarship Program and the Zell Miller Scholarship Program.

A HOPE Scholarship recipient must graduate from high school with a minimum 3.00 grade point average (as calculated by the Georgia State Finance Commission) and maintain a minimum 3.00 cumulative postsecondary GPA to remain eligible. In 2021, the scholarship paid 76 percent of the tuition cost of each student credit hour up to fifteen credit hours at nearly every accredited two-year and four-year college in Georgia. This list included all seven of its public HBCUs and three of its independent HBCUs: Clark Atlanta University, Morehouse College, and Spelman College.

The Zell Miller Scholarship is similar to the HOPE Scholarship but applies more stringent academic requirements. A recipient must graduate from high school with a minimum 3.70 GPA combined with a minimum SAT score of 1200 on the math and reading portions, or present a minimum composite ACT score of 26 and maintain a minimum 3.30 cumulative postsecondary GPA to remain eligible.

In contrast to grant programs that reduce tuition and fees, which benefit all students (regardless of race), only some students effectively can access the HOPE and Zell Miller scholarship programs. Figure 7.4 reveals that white college students are more likely to hold a HOPE scholarship than Black students and more than seven times more likely than a Black student to receive a Zell Miller scholarship. Further, 31 percent of all students households with an annual income of $120,000 or more received a Zell Miller scholarship, whereas only 7 percent of those whose household incomes were $15,000 or below were recipients. Hence, these well-intentioned scholarship program have not turned out to be race-neutral.

All funds to support the HOPE and Zell Miller scholarships come from the Georgia Lottery. It is well established that lotteries are regressive in nature; that is, they collect a higher proportion of the income of lower-income households than from the wealthy. Thus, the net effect of these two scholarship programs is to redistribute income from lower-income

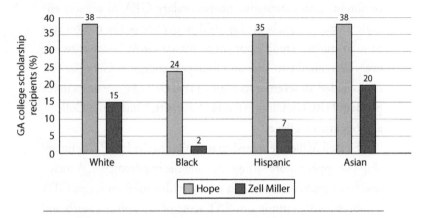

FIGURE 7.4 Percentage of Georgia college students of various races who received a HOPE or Zell Miller Scholarship, fall 2018

Source: Jennifer Lee, "Moving HOPE Forward Into the 21st Century," Georgia Budget & Policy Institute, September 14, 2020, https://gbpi.org/moving-hope-forward-into-the-21st-century/.

to upper-income households. That was not the goal, but it has nonetheless occurred.

The assembled research on these programs, especially the Zell Miller scholarship, suggests that financial assistance is frequently provided to individuals who would have been able to attend college anyway. In our view, that reduces the societal impact of these awards.

In FY 2021, Georgia spent about $890 million on the HOPE and Zell Miller scholarship programs.[37] Would some of these dollars have had a larger impact if they had been dispensed in the form of need-based scholarships? We believe so, primarily because scholarships based on financial need would increase the number of individuals going to college, including Black students as well as HBCUs. We are not the first to make this point. Early on, Rubenstein and Scafidi revealed the income-regressive nature of funding for these programs and how they are awarded.[38] Lee's more recent analysis[39] reveals this situation has not changed, and in *Inside Higher Education*, Whitford went so far as to refer to it as the "dark side" of lottery-funded scholarships.[40]

The point is that well-intentioned, ostensibly neutral public policies can have unequal effects in higher education, as in the case of Georgia's HOPE and Zell Miller scholarship programs. We do not argue that merit-based scholarships have no place in higher education, nor are we opposed to the notion that it is in the best interests of a state to convince its best and brightest to go to one of its colleges. Rather, what concerns us is the opportunity cost of the amount of money involved (now approaching $900 million annually in Georgia) and the method by which the money is generated.

The bottom line is that policies such as just described place HBCUs and Black students at a relative disadvantage . The University of Georgia (with 7 percent Black students in fall 2020)[41] alone captured more than 28 percent of all the HOPE scholarship dollars, and no HBCU finished in the top ten institutions with HOPE scholarship recipients.[42]

The HOPE and Zell Miller scholarship programs provide another example of a policy that appears to be neutral but has a disparate impact on HBCUs and Black students.[43] There is a better way to spend almost $900 million on student financial aid, and it involves maximizing the proportion that addresses need.

NONGOVERNMENTAL ORGANIZATIONS

Gasman, in her 2007 history of the United Negro College Fund,[44] noted that the fund, founded in 1944, took off slowly and collected only about $14 million in its first decade. This performance reflected a variety of factors: HBCUs' underdeveloped institutional advancement operations, ignorance of the predominantly white holders of wealth about HBCUs, and simple racism. To some degree, each of these conditions remains relevant.

After *Brown v. the Board of Education* decision in 1954, some individuals, both Black and white, questioned the need for HBCUs. As Gasman put it, "If integration now was mandated by law, what was the purpose of a Black college?"[45] This question continues to be posed by some today (and may affect fundraising), but it substantially ignores the specific contributions of HBCUs and the superior performance of Black students who have attended HBCUs compared with what these students would have achieved at a PWI.

Whatever the state of knowledge of prospective donors about HBCUs, it is fair to say that only a few major foundations and private donors have made the support of HBCUs and Black college students a high priority. This must change, and our hope is that the empirical evidence supplied in this book will reorient thinking and hasten change. However, at this juncture, one can detect more evolution in thinking about HBCUs on the part of federal and state governments than appears to hold true for major foundations and donors.

It is not easy to render a precise judgment about the funding priorities of foundations and wealthy individuals, because the reporting requirements imposed on foundations are modest and often one must work diligently to ascertain what they have accomplished. The disposition of individuals' wealth can remain out of the public eye if they decide to spurn publicity. Nevertheless, we once again observe that the median endowment value of an HBCU was slightly less than $25 million in 2020. This number would not be so small if making gifts to HBCUs were a higher priority.

Nothing less than a reorientation of the thinking of donors about HBCUs and a reprioritization of their giving practices is required to change this funding situation. HBCUs need to be viewed as valuable national resources that accomplish certain higher education tasks better than PWIs. This is an important selling point. HBCUs represent a portion of a rational, intelligent solution to several important societal problems involving race and inequality rather than being the source of those problems.

We believe that the findings we report in this book can assist in this transformation—first by thought and discourse, then by deed. Attending an HBCU is not for everyone, and for a variety of reasons, they do not represent the optimal campus choice for a portion of Black students. Nevertheless, HBCUs provide Black students with a welcoming atmosphere, an increased probability of graduation, a demonstrated ability to generate upward economic mobility, and an invaluable choice that forces PWIs to up their games.

This is the paradigm that nongovernmental institutions must come to understand and ultimately honor in terms of how they allocate their resources. This transformation will require that non-Black America open its eyes and hearts, reexamine its history, and reorder its priorities. But in addition, HBCUs and Black citizens must recognize that in substantial segments of the United States, both their deeds and their needs are unknown or currently constitute very low priorities. There must be recognition that the vote of a U.S. senator from South Dakota (with zero HBCUs and a Black population of 2.3 percent) counts just as much in determining critical federal policies as the vote of a senator from Alabama (which hosts eight HBCUs and has a Black population of 26.8 percent).[46]

The activities of the business community are crucial for accomplishing the desired transformation. Firms need to increase their support of HBCUs by means of direct gifts but also internships, programs for executives in residence, summer jobs, and speakers. They must consult on issues about curriculum and be willing to recruit employees at HBCUs and hire HBCU graduates. Let the job performance of HBCU graduates be the judge of their value to the firm rather than preestablished attitudes that reflect centuries of tragic history.

We are not recommending that employers ignore institutional affiliations, grade point averages, Graduate Record Examination scores, grades, course selections, and the like. Rather, we believe it is in the best interests of employers to cast their nets more widely and heed the evidence we have presented in this book. If they do so, they will discover individuals who can be strong performers and make a positive difference in their organizations. Businesses must move out of their comfort zones and recognize that ultimately, our recommendations likely coincide with their long-term welfare in a rapidly evolving society. It is in the nation's best interest as well as that of individual businesses that they do so. Every investment in an HBCU or its students is not guaranteed to pay off, but society wide, the evidence that we have presented in earlier chapters suggests that investing in HBCUs and their students is likely to yield attractive returns for investors, recipients, and the nation.

SUMMING IT UP

DuBois put it succinctly: "The problem of the twentieth century is the problem of the color line."[47] Whether or not one agrees with his assessment, there can be little argument that issues of color and race have been at the center of attention in the United States for many centuries. Americans expended hundreds of billions of dollars to establish and maintain racially segregated institutions (such as HBCUs) and to enforce inequality. The nation slowly began to shift gears and expend similar amounts to extinguish the segregationist institutions that had been created and to fine-tune their subtle cultural and economic successors. This task is ongoing.

Historically Black Colleges and Universities were established either to maintain segregation (for example, the wave of 1890 Black land-grant institutions) or to do battle with its effects (for example, Cheyney University and Wilberforce University). Whatever their motivations and origins, however, HBCUs are still with us and occupy an important strategic role in American higher education. They educate approximately 300,000 students annually and do so with documented skill. Nineteen-year-old Black persons with a given SAT score (let's say 1,000) who come to an HBCU campus from a household with a given annual income (say, $35,000) are more likely to graduate than if they attended a PWI. Further, after they graduate, their mid-career income will be higher if they attended an HBCU rather than a PWI.

This is not to suggest that the average HBCU student graduates at the same rate as the average PWI student or that they earn the same income. Instead, the evidence we have presented in this book tells us that if we compare like to like and control for critical variables such as standardized test scores and family income, we will find that the typical HBCU is doing a sparkling job—one that is vital to future of our society. The alternative may be chaos, social disintegration, and widening of existing racial gaps.

An Asian Indian fable describes a group of six blind men and their reactions on confronting an elephant. One touches the elephant's trunk and concludes that the elephant is squirmy like a snake; another touches a leg and thinks the elephant is stout and like a wall; yet another touches a tusk and believes the elephant to be shaped like a spear. Together, they come up with six very different versions of what that elephant is.

The fable concludes,

> So, oft in theologic wars
> The disputants, I ween,
> Rail on in utter ignorance
> Of what each other mean;
> And prate about an Elephant
> No one of them has seen![48]

The fable has obvious relevance to the environment in which HBCUs live and operate today. Many individuals know little or nothing about HBCUs, and their only connection to an HBCU may be via an intercollegiate athletic team. Even in Black communities, however, some individuals are not well informed about the strengths and weaknesses of institutions that might be nearby and that they or their relatives might have attended had they been more aware.

A primary goal of this book has been to provide the HBCU equivalent of an accurate picture of the elephant—or at least to illuminate parts of the HBCU elephant that previously were obscured by racial mist and distance. We hope that we have succeeded in this task, but the most critical measure of our success will be what you, the reader, do with the information and understanding you have acquired. The jury is out.

APPENDIX A

HISTORICALLY BLACK COLLEGES AND UNIVERSITIES (HBCUs) IN THE SAMPLE

IPEDS ID*	Institution Name	City	State	ZIP Code
100654	Alabama A&M University	Normal	AL	35762
100724	Alabama State University	Montgomery	AL	36104–0271
138716	Albany State University	Albany	GA	31705
175342	Alcorn State University	Alcorn State	MS	39096–7500
132602	Bethune-Cookman University	Daytona Beach	FL	32114–3099
162007	Bowie State University	Bowie	MD	20715–9465
201690	Central State University	Wilberforce	OH	45384–1004
162283	Coppin State University	Baltimore	MD	21216–3698
130934	Delaware State University	Dover	DE	19901
158802	Dillard University	New Orleans	LA	70122
198507	Elizabeth City State University	Elizabeth City	NC	27909
198543	Fayetteville State University	Fayetteville	NC	28301–4298
220181	Fisk University	Nashville	TN	37208–4501
133650	Florida A&M University	Tallahassee	FL	32307
139719	Fort Valley State University	Fort Valley	GA	31030–4313
159009	Grambling State University	Grambling	LA	71245
232265	Hampton University	Newport News	VA	23668–0099
131520	Howard University	Washington	DC	20059
175856	Jackson State University	Jackson	MS	39217

(*continued*)

IPEDS ID*	Institution Name	City	State	ZIP Code
157058	Kentucky State University	Frankfort	KY	40601–2355
220598	Lane College	Jackson	TN	38301–4598
101675	Miles College	Fairfield	AL	35064–2621
176044	Mississippi Valley State University	Itta Bena	MS	38941–1400
140553	Morehouse College	Atlanta	GA	30314
163453	Morgan State University	Baltimore	MD	21251–0001
232937	Norfolk State University	Norfolk	VA	23504–8000
199102	North Carolina A&T State University	Greensboro	NC	27411
199157	North Carolina Central University	Durham	NC	27707
227429	Paul Quinn College	Dallas	TX	75241
227526	Prairie View A&M University	Prairie View	TX	77446
176318	Rust College	Holly Springs	MS	38635
199582	Saint Augustine's University	Raleigh	NC	27610–2298
140960	Savannah State University	Savannah	GA	31404–5310
199643	Shaw University	Raleigh	NC	27601
218733	South Carolina State University	Orangeburg	SC	29117–0001
160621	Southern University and A&M College	Baton Rouge	LA	70813
141060	Spelman College	Atlanta	GA	30314–4399
102270	Stillman College	Tuscaloosa	AL	35401
102298	Talladega College	Talladega	AL	35160
221838	Tennessee State University	Nashville	TN	37209–1561
229063	Texas Southern University	Houston	TX	77004
176406	Tougaloo College	Tougaloo	MS	39174
106412	University of Arkansas at Pine Bluff	Pine Bluff	AR	71601
163338	University of Maryland Eastern Shore	Princess Anne	MD	21853–1299
234155	Virginia State University	Petersburg	VA	23806
234164	Virginia Union University	Richmond	VA	23220
206491	Wilberforce University	Wilberforce	OH	45384–1001
229887	Wiley College	Marshall	TX	75670
199999	Winston-Salem State University	Winston-Salem	NC	27110–0001
160904	Xavier University of Louisiana	New Orleans	LA	70125–1098

*IPEDS = U.S. Department of Education, Integrated Postsecondary Data System, https://nces.ed.gov
/ipeds.

APPENDIX B

OBSERVATIONS ON PANEL LEAST SQUARES, RANDOM EFFECTS, AND FIXED EFFECTS

O ur data set consists of a panel of annual observations from FY 2004 through FY 2019 of a large number of variables describing 236 American colleges and universities, 50 of which are HBCUs.

With a data set such as ours, one can develop a plausible argument in favor of using ordinary least-squares, fixed-effects, or random-effects estimation to generate reliable statistical results. An immediate problem is that these terms do not have standard definitions; one observer has catalogued five different ways to define them.[1]

Determining which estimation technique is best suited to a situation depends primarily on the assumptions one makes about the nature of the estimation being undertaken. Assuming that one's estimating equation contains all the relevant influences on the dependent variable, omitting no variables, random-effects estimation likely is the best choice. But if there are omitted variables, or causal influences that cannot be known or measured, then fixed estimation is a superior choice.

We rely on seventeen years of annual panel data that describe 236 institutions. Some analysts might choose fixed-effects estimation models in situations such as this because they believe there may be unobserved factors influencing institutional behavior in a given year that are not included in our equations as independent variables. This is referred to as "unobserved heterogeneity," and if one believes it is problematically large, then one can use period fixed-effects estimation models to address it. We do so in several circumstances. However, period fixed-effects models preclude the use of the dummy variables that are central to our analysis. They would be considered an instance of unobserved heterogeneity if we did not take them into account. Ordinary least-squares and random-effects estimations do not have this limitation.

An econometric test, the Hausman test, often is utilized to determine if unobserved heterogeneity is problematic. We applied it repetitively, and the test never generated results that came close to causing us to reject its null hypothesis (that no unobserved heterogeneity was present).

In our situation, a key determination is how much variability there is in our major explanatory influences over time. To the extent that important explanatory variables exhibit major changes in value over time, random-effects estimation is superior to fixed-effects estimation. On the other hand, if there is substantial variation in key variables among institutions in a single year, fixed-effects estimating techniques would be preferable.

Both circumstances exist with our data set. For some variables (such as FTE student enrollment or state appropriations per FTE student), the variability among institutions in a single year is substantial, which militates in favor of fixed-effects estimation. For other variables (for example, whether or not an institution is a flagship or the percentage of women in the student body), within-year variations across institution are much smaller or zero, which favors use of variable-effects estimation.

Given the deficiency of fixed-effects estimation that time-invariant variables cannot be used, virtually all our dichotomous 0,1 dummy variables reflecting institution type (for example, is the institution an HBCU?) are prohibited. This is a serious limitation because many of the most important explanatory variables in our analysis do not vary over time. An example is HBCU status, which does not change. Because we know that is an important consideration, ignoring it would be a greater mistake than using ordinary least-squares and random-effects estimating techniques and encountering other, less obvious heterogeneity.

Ordinary least-squares estimation using panel data is a dependable workhorse, though it will fall short if important explanatory variables have been omitted from the estimating equation, if the variables have not been measured accurately, if simultaneity exists (for example, if there is feedback in both directions between the dependent variable and independent variables). It seems likely that all these conditions exist to some extent in our estimations, a sufficient reason to supply random-effects and fixed-effects estimations along with ordinary least squares where possible and appropriate.

APPENDIX C
DATA TABLES

TABLE C.1 DETERMINANTS OF HBCU INSTITUTIONAL ENROLLMENTS, FY 2005–FY 2018

Variable	(1) Football divisions (cross-section random effects)	(2) Athletic expenditures (cross-section random effects)	(3) Football divisions and distance learning (cross-section random effects)	(4) Football divisions and private dummy (cross-section random effects)	(5) Athletic expenditures (cross-section fixed effects)
CONSTANT	4.5472 (.3531)***	5.4701 (.3792)***	3.9797 (.3061)***	6.6110 (.1998)***	–.2531 (.2782)
NHSGRADS (000s)	.0010 (.0013)	.0013 (.0016)	.000001 (.0015)		
STATEBLACK (000,000s)	.0814 (.1047)	.0587 (.1344)	.1507 (.0821)*	.1095 (.0484)**	.0425 (.0593)
UNEMP	.0294 (.0064)***	.0286 (.0070)***	.0544 (.006i4)***	.0344 (.0029)**	.0223 (.0044)***
HOMEPOP (000,000s)	.0222 (.0434)	.0049 (.0497)	.0620 (.0437)	.0579 (.0247)**	–.0679 (.0424)
PCTHCWHITE	–.0054 (.0061)	–.0050 (.0055)	–.0037 (.0061)		
PCTHCWOMEN	.0089 (.0050)*	–.0027 (.0043)	.0186 (.0044)***	.0017 (.0036)	.0120 (.0030)***
PCTHC25+	.0074 (.0013)***	.0077 (.0016)***	.0046 (.0023)**	.0066 (.0018)***	.0032 (.0022)
SATMID	.000006 (.0002)	.000009 (.0002)	.0001 (.0002)	.000002 (.0001)***	
NETT&F (000s)	–.0286 (.0077)***	–.0323 (.0087)***	–.0134 (.0051)***	–.0278 (.0067)***	
HHINC	.0473 (.0053)***	.0441 (.0069)***	.0490 (.0048)***	.0219 (.0071)***	

TABLE C.1 (CONTINUED)

Variable	(1) Football divisions (cross-section random effects)	(2) Athletic expenditures (cross-section random effects)	(3) Football divisions and distance learning (cross-section random effects)	(4) Football divisions and private dummy (cross-section random effects)	(5) Athletic expenditures (cross-section fixed effects)
MOBILITY	−.0478 (.0854)	.0236 (.0798)	−.1003 (.0413)**		
INSTRUCTEXPEND	.0128 (.0026)***	.0127 (.0030)***	0083 (.0038)**	.0067 (.0037)*	.0077 (.0046)*
STUDSERVEXPEND					.0133 (.0055)**
GRADRATE	.0002 (.0015)	−.0002 (.0015)	.0003 (.0015)		
FCSFB	.6908 (.1423)***		.8534 (.1370)***	.2261 (.1036)**	
DIVII/III	−.1321 (.1086)		−.0604 (.1184)	−.2111 (.0474)***	
NODISTANCE			−.0026 (.0010)***		
PRIVATE				−.5442 (.1410)***	
ATHEXPEND (000s)		.0309 (.0050)***			
R^2 adj.	.482	.455	.544	.324	.950
F-statistic	21.0***	19.6	16.1	22.2	194.0
Observations	323	313	203	531	502

The dependent variable is the logarithm of institutions' calendar year FTE student enrollments. White adjusted standard errors are in parentheses.

***Statistically significant at the .01 level; **statistically significant at the .05 level; *statistically significant at the .10 level.

TABLE C.2 PUBLIC HBCU ENROLLMENTS IN CONTEXT, FY 2004–FY 2018

Variable	(1) Public HBCUs plus control group institutions (panel least squares)	(2) Public HBCUs plus control group institutions, distance learning (cross-section fixed effects)
CONSTANT	−.9293 (.2808)***	1.8439 (.2742)***
HSGRADS	.0000001 (.000000007)***	.0000005 (.0000001)***
STATEBLACK	.0320 (.0030)***	.6599 (.1492)***
UNEMP	.0055 (.0035)	.0045 (.0024)*
HOMEPOP	.0119 (.0010)***	.1059 (.0302)***
STATEAPPRFTE	−.000002 (.00000008)***	−.000003 (.0000002)***
PCTHCWOMEN	.00001 (.0006)	.0043 (.0019)**
PCTHC25+	.0079 (.0007)***	.0043 (.0015)***
SATMID	.0011 (.000008)***	.0000009 (.00001)
HHINC	1.7579 (.3226)***	.1536 (.0948)
KIDS/PAR	.4411 (.1591)***	.0891 (.0758)
INSTRUCTEXPEND	.0093 (.0010)***	.0013 (.0005)***
NETT&F	−.0056 (.0010)***	−.0058 (.0038)
FLAGSHIP	.5896 (.0157)***	
METROLEADER	.3041 (.0105)***	

TABLE C.2 (CONTINUED)

Variable	(1) Public HBCUs plus control group institutions (panel least squares)	(2) Public HBCUs plus control group institutions, distance learning (cross-section fixed effects)
HBCU	−.4511 (.0290)***	
FBS	.6393 (.0241)***	
FCS	.2938 (.0215)***	
NOFB	.2128 (.0330)***	
NODISTANCE	−.0016 (.0003)***	−.0003 (.0003)
R^2 adj.	.825	.992
F-statistic	310.6	845.8
Cross-sections	171	171
Observations	1,316	1,316

The dependent variable is the logarithm of institutions' calendar year FTE student enrollments.
White adjusted standard errors are in parentheses.
***Statistically significant at the .01 level; **statistically significant at the .05 level; *statistically significant at the .10 level.

TABLE C.3 DETERMINANTS OF GRADUATION RATES AT HBCUs AND CONTROL GROUP INSTITUTIONS

Variable	(1) Entire sample with HBCU dummy (panel cross-section)	(2) Entire sample (cross-section fixed effects)	(3) Entire sample with multiple institution dummies (panel cross-section)	(4) Entire sample with institution dummies and additional controls (cross-section random effects)
CONSTANT	2.3007 (.1687)***	3.0206 (.1108)***	2.3378 (.1641)***	2.3507 (.1848)***
ENR	.0051 (.0006)***	.0025 (.0015)*	.0053 (.0004)***	.0051 (.0005)***
STATEBLACK	.0038 (.0033)	.1656 (.0745)**	.0150 (.0018)***	.0147 (.0023)***
HHINC	.0000046 (.0000052)			.0022 (.0015)
SATMID	.0017 (.0002)***		.0016 (.0002)***	.0014 (.0001)***
PELLPCT	−.0055 (.0007)***	.0015 (.0016)	−.0051 (.0007)***	−.0028 (.0007)***
NETT&F	−.0086 (.0058)	−.0141 (.0049)***	−.0089 (.0059)	.0034 (.0010)***
FLAGSHIP			.0512 (.0148)***	.0765 (.0083)***
METRO LEADER			−.0353 (.0090)***	−.0007 (.0107)
HBCU	.1067 (.0230)***		.0748 (.0214)***	.0295 (.0264)
PCTWOMEN				.0005 (.0004)
PCTHC25+				−.0046 (.0017)***

TABLE C.3 (CONTINUED)

Variable	(1) Entire sample with HBCU dummy (panel cross-section)	(2) Entire sample (cross-section fixed effects)	(3) Entire sample with multiple institution dummies (panel cross-section)	(4) Entire sample with institution dummies and additional controls (cross-section random effects)
INSTRUCTEXPEND				.0032 (.0005)***
STUDSERV				-.0037 (.0011)***
FBS			.0090 (.0150)	-.039 (.0078)***
FCS			.0489 (.0155)***	.0099 (.0085)
NOFB			.0479 (.0169)***	.0158 (.0233)
R^2 adj.	.659	.889	.662	.726
F-statistic	682.3***	85.6	441.3	330.2
Cross-sections	229	230	230	187
Observations	2,467	2,478	2,478	1,987

The dependent variable is each institution's first-time full-time six-year graduation rate. White adjusted standard errors are in parentheses.

***Statistically significant at the .01 level; **statistically significant at the .05 level; *statistically significant at the .10 level.

TABLE C.4 DETERMINANTS OF FIRST-TIME FULL-TIME STUDENT RETENTION RATES, FRESHMAN TO SOPHOMORE YEARS, FY 2004–2019

Variables	Full sample: retention rate (panel least squares)	HBCUs: retention rate (panel least squares)	HBCUs: retention rate (cross-section fixed effects)
CONSTANT	3.7075	4.8604	3.4716
	(.0739)***	(.3119)***	(.2011)***
ENR(–1)	.0023	–.0070	.0145
	(.0002)***	(.0085)	(.0031)***
NBLACK(–1)	.0055	.0233	.0145
	(.0025)**	(.1370)	(.0056)**
UNEMPL(–1)	.0060	–.0052	.0041
	(.0026)**	(.0047)	(.0040)
HOMEPOP(–1)	.0063	–.0138	–.0061
	(.0005)***	(.0460)	(.0032)*
NETPRICE(–1)	–.0017	.0007	–.0017
	(.0006)***	(.0006)	(.0018)
SAT(–1)	.0005	–.0001	.0002
	(.000006)***	(.0002)	(.0001)
PELLPCT(–1)	–.0015	.0013	–.0015
	(.0004)***	(.0019)	(.0010)
INSTRUCTEXPEND (–1)	.0010	.0017	–.0002
	(.0003)***	(.0012)	(.0009)
STUDSERVEXPEND (–1)	–.0031	.0052	–.0038
	(.0004)***	(.0028)*	(.0013)***
PCTBLACK INDIVIDUALSTUD(–1)	–.0002	–.0014	.0015
	(.0001)**	(.0019)	(.0008)*
PCTBLACKFAC(–1)	–.0008	–.0019	–.0011
	(.0004)*	(.0013)	(.0006)*
PCTWOMENTUD(–1)	.0014	–.0079	.0101
	(.0002)***	(.0060)	(.0011)***

TABLE C.4 (CONTINUED)

Variables	Full sample: retention rate (panel least squares)	HBCUs: retention rate (panel least squares)	HBCUs: retention rate (cross-section fixed effects)
PCT25+STUD(-1)	-.0019 (.0002)***	-.0038 (.0018)**	-.0028 (.0006)***
HBCU	.0667 (.0261)**		
NOFB	-.0105 (.0043)**		
ATHEXPEND(-1)		-.0013 (.0032)	.0012 (.0012)
R^2 adj.	.700	.621	.379
F-statistic	230.2***	9.6***	14.3***
Panels	227	45	45
Observations	1,478	306	306

The dependent variable is the logarithm of full-time student retention rate. White adjusted standard errors are in parentheses.

***Statistically significant at the .01 level; **statistically significant at the .05 level; *statistically significant at the .10 level.

TABLE C.5 STUDENT-FACULTY RATIO REGRESSIONS, ALL INSTITUTIONS AND HBCUs, FY 2012–FY 2019

Variable	(1) Entire sample (panel cross-section)	(2) HBCUs (panel cross-section)
CONSTANT	36.0498 (.6943)***	29.3764 (3.9152)***
ENR (000s)	.1602 (.0046)***	.3454 (.0819)***
ENDOW (000)	−.00000003 (.000000003)***	−.000001 (.0000002)***
INSTRUCT	−.0595 (.0048)***	−.0766 (.0213)***
PCTUGWOMEN	−.0223 (.0072)***	−.0917 (.0410)**
PCTUG25+	−.0571 (.0054)***	.0154 (.0182)
NODISTANCE	−.0245 (.0073)***	−.0141 (.0126)
NOFB	−.4712 (.0966)***	
ATHEXPEND		−.0190 (.0507)
FLAGSHIP	−.9755 (.1712)***	
METROLEADER	1.3958 (.1129)***	
HBCU	−3.3211 (.3713)***	
NETTFFTE (000s)	−.1693 (.0213)***	.0136 (.0897)
SAT	−.0101 (.0008)***	−.0009 (.0031)
HHINC	−.0312 (.0087)***	−8.7422 (2.8538)***
R^2 adj.	.459	.746
F-statistic	71.6***	29.4***
Cross-sections	180	8
Observations	1,163	98

The dependent variable is institutional student-faculty ratios. White adjusted standard errors are in parentheses.

***Statistically significant at the .01 level; **statistically significant at the .05 level; *statistically significant at the .10 level.

TABLE C.6 ADMISSIONS YIELDS

Variables	(1) % Admissions enrolled, expanded sample (cross-section random effects)	(2) % Admissions enrolled, HBCUs (cross-section, random effects)	(3) % Admissions enrolled, expanded sample (cross-section fixed effects)	(4) % Admissions enrolled, HBCUs only (cross-section fixed effects)
CONSTANT	5.1119 (.3194)***	3.2128 (.4856)***	3.7458 (.2126)***	3.1713 (1.6578)*
ENR	.0000004 (.0000004)	.0000008 (.000001)	.0056 (.0006)***	−.0181 (.0265)
NBLACK	−.0332 (.0261_	.2245 (.0582)***	.0525 (.0088)***	.2760 (.4548)
UNEMPLOY	.0058 (.0059)	.0884 (.0172	−.0306 (.0044)***	.0924 (.0185)***
HOMEPOP	.0042 (.0064)	−.0380 (.0163)**	−.0111 (.0015)***	−.0692 (.1493)
NETPRICE	−.000002 (.0000003)***	−.000005 (.0000007)***	−.000001 (.000002)***	−.000003 (.0000008)***
FLAGSHIP	−.0546 (.0709)			
METROLEADER	−.0627 (.0423)			
REGIONAL	−.1436 (.0423)**			
FCSFB		.4846 (.0808)***		
NOFB	−.0342 (.0343)_	.1354 (.3365)		
SAT	−.0013 (.0002)***	−.0002 (.0004)	.000007 (.0002)	2.3005 (.4356)***
HHINC	−.0050 (.0008)***	1.1309 (.7456)	−.6894 (.1795)***	−.0010 (.0004)**
PELLPCT				−.0099 (.0103)

(*continued*)

TABLE C.6 (CONTINUED)

Variables	(1) % Admissions enrolled, expanded sample (cross-section random effects)	(2) % Admissions enrolled, HBCUs (cross-section, random effects)	(3) % Admissions enrolled, expanded sample (cross-section fixed effects)	(4) % Admissions enrolled, HBCUs only (cross-section fixed effects)
INSTRUCTEXPEND	.0004 (.0017)	−.0049 (.0024)**	.0002 (.0006)	−.0004 (.0041)
STUDSERVEXPEND	−.0115 (.0027)***	−.0044 (.0065)	−.0085 (.0009)***	.0060 (.0130)
PCTWHITE	.0082 (.009)***		.0051 (.0003)***	
PCTBLACK INDIVIDUALSTUD		−.0072 (.0061)		
PCTBLACKFAC		−.0021 (.0020)		−.0009 (.0030)
PCTTWOMEN	−.0059 (.0022)***	−.0044 (.0020)**	.0014 (.0013)	
PCT25+	−.000004 (.000002**)	.0015 (.0033)	.000002 (.000004)	
ATHLEXPEND				.0127 (.0139)
R^2 adj.	.246	.345	.240	.731
F-statistic	52.6***	9.9***	17.7***	16.9***
Cross-sections	187	38	155	35
Observations	2,692	256	1,062	270

The dependent variable is the logarithm of the percentage yield. White adjusted standard errors are in parentheses.

***Statistically significant at the .01 level; **statistically significant at the .05 level; *statistically significant at the .10 level.

TABLE C.7 REGRESSIONS FOCUSING ON GENDER DIFFERENCES IN GRADUATION RATES, ENTIRE SAMPLE, FY 2004–FY 2019

Variable	(1) Entire sample: men and women (panel cross-section)	(2) Entire sample: men only (panel cross-section)	(3) Entire sample: women only (panel cross-section)
CONSTANT	1.6911 (.1237)***	1.3504 (.1235)***	2.1552 (.1138)***
ENR	.0039 (.0004)***	.0041 (.0003)***	.0039 (.0003)***
SAT	.0020 (.0001)***	.0022 (.0001***	.0019 (.000004)***
HHINC	.0057 (.0042)	.0059 (.0049)	.0039 (.0033)
HBCU	.0673 (.0324)	–.0671 (.0317)**	.0791 (.0340)**
R^2 adj.	.669	.572	.530
F-statistic	1479.2	976.4***	822.8***
Cross-sections	190	189	189
Observations	2,933	2,921	2,921

The dependent variable is the logarithm of first-time full-time six-year graduation rates. White adjusted standard errors are in parentheses.

***Statistically significant at the .01 level; **statistically significant at the .05 level; *statistically significant at the .10 level.

TABLE C.8 DETERMINANTS OF JUNE 30, 2018, ENDOWMENT VALUES BY INSTITUTION TYPE

Variable	Entire sample: June 30, 2018, endowment value (period fixed effects)
CONSTANT	3.4218
	(2.1995)
ENR	.000003
	(.000002)**
INCGRADS	.0340
	(.0181)*
KIDS/PAR	−.5283
	(.9130)
PELL	−.0146
	(.0101)
INSTRUCT	−.0162
	(.0075**
STUDSERV	−.0223
	(.01197)*
PCTWOMEN	.0131
	(.0125)
PCT25+	.0018
	(.0073)
PCTSTEM	.0062
	(.0046)
UNEMPLOY	−.0884
	(.1076)
FBSFB	.4932
	(.1793)***
FLAGSHIP	.4948
	(.2748)*
METROLEADER	.0123
	(.1871)
REGIONAL	−.6453
	(.1839)***
R^2 adj.	.807
F-statistic	36.5***
Cross-sections	128
Observations	128

The dependent variable is the logarithm of institutional endowment values on June 30, 2018. White adjusted standard errors are in parentheses.

***Statistically significant at the .01 level; **statistically significant at the .05 level; *statistically significant at the .10 level.

TABLE C.9 IMPACT OF HBCUs AND OTHER INSTITUTION TYPES ON STUDENTS' UPWARD INCOME MOBILITY

Variable	Entire sample: 2018–19 (panel least squares)
CONSTANT	36.8505
	(14.6297)
ENR	.0252
	(.0266)
HOMEPOP	.2067
	(.1320)
MEDHHINC	.000007
	(.000003)*
PELL	−.2979
	(.1206)**
SAT	.0004
	(.0030)
PCTWOMEN	.1135
	(.0643)*
PCT25+	−.0899
	(.0460)*
PARENTINC	−.5089
	(.1970)**
HBCU	−2.4227
	(1.66365)
ATHEXPEND	.0017
	(.0069)
INSTRUCTEXPEND	−.0449
	(.0292)
STUDSERVEXPEND	−.0271
	(.0474)
R^2 adj.	.609
F-statistic	16.82***
Cross-sections	123
Observations	123

The dependent variable is the ratio of the kids' income percentile to the parents' income percentile (KIDS/PAR). White adjusted standard errors are in parentheses.

***Statistically significant at the .01 level; **statistically significant at the .05 level; *statistically significant at the .10 level.

NOTES

1. REMOVING THE VEIL

1. U.S. Department of Education, Integrated Postsecondary Data System (hereafter cited as IPEDS), https://nces.ed.gov/ipeds.
2. This number represents an update of the United Negro College Fund's 2020 report, *HBCUs Make America Strong: The Positive Economic Impact of Historically Black Colleges and Universities*, https://cdn.uncf.org/wp-content/uploads/HBCU_Consumer_Brochure_FINAL_APPROVED.pdf.
3. Opportunity Insights, Data Library, mrc_table 2, , https://opportunity insights.org/data/.
4. This point was made by an HBCU student in the excellent Stanley Nelson/Marco Williams 2017 documentary featured on PBS, "Tell Them We Are Rising: The Story of Historically Black Colleges and Universities," https://www.pbs.org/independentlens/documentaries/tell-them-we-are -rising.
5. U.S. Department of Education, College Scorecard, https://collegescorecard .ed.gov/data.
6. Adam Harris, *The State Must Provide: Why America's Colleges Have Always Been Unequal—and How to Set Them Right* (New York: HarperCollins, 2021).
7. *Berea College v. Kentucky*, 211 U.S. 45 (1908).
8. *Plessy v. Ferguson*, 163 U.S. 537 (1896). *Plessy* dealt with railroad accommodations and had nothing to do per se with higher education.
9. *Brown v. Board of Education of Topeka*, 347 U.S. 483 (1954).

10. These data come from the U.S. Department of Education, National Center for Education Statistics, College Navigator, https://nces.ed.gov/collegenavigator.

11. Professor William A. Darity Jr., of Duke University pointed out the especially significant role played by Shaw University in the civil rights struggle.

12. Benedict College has gained notice for an additional reason. Beginning in 2004, it began to base a portion of a student's grade in each course on that student's effort. The complicated interactions between effort and knowledge have been examined by Omari H. Swinton, "The Effect of Effort Grading on Learning," *Economics of Education Review* 29, no. 6 (December 2010): 1176–82.

13. *Edwards v. South Carolina*, 372 U.S. 299 (1963).

14. Jelani M. Favors, *Shelter in a Time of Storm: How Black Colleges Fostered Generations of Leadership and Activism* (Chapel Hill: University of North Carolina Press, 2019).

15. Favors, *Shelter in a Time of Storm*, 251.

16. Martin Luther King, quoted in Brian McClure, "Heart and Soul of the Movement: Influence of Historically Black Colleges and Universities on the Civil Rights Movement," State of HBCUs: Past, Present and Future, August 26, 2013, https://stateofhbcus.wordpress.com/2013/08/26/heart-and-soul-of-the-movement-influence-of-historically-black-colleges-and-universities-on-the-civil-rights-movement.

17. "Tell Them We Are Rising."

18. Eric Hoover, "The Demographic Cliff: 5 Findings from New Demographic Projections of High-School Graduates," *Chronicle of Higher Education*, December 15, 2020, https://www.chronicle.com/article/the-demographic-cliff-5-findings-from-new-projections-of-high-school-graduates.

19. Hoover, "The Demographic Cliff."

20. Western Interstate Commission for Higher Education, "Projections Data from the 10th Edition of *Knocking at the College Door*, https://knocking.wiche.edu/data/knocking-10th-data.

21. Ted Sedmak, "Undergraduate Enrollment Declines Show No Signs of Recovery from 2020" (press release), National Student Clearinghouse, October 26, 2021, https://www.studentclearinghouse.org/blog/undergraduate-enrollment-declines-show-no-signs-of-recovery-from-2020.

22. This observation was made by an HBCU admissions director who prefers not to be identified.

23. The number of students enrolled at HBCUs increased by 47 percent to 327,000 between 1976 and 2010 but then receded by 11 percent between 2010 and 2018. National Center for Education Statistics, Fast Facts, "Historically Black Colleges and Universities," https://nces.ed.gov/fastfacts /display.asp?id=667#:~:text=The%20number%20of%20HBCU%20 students,2010%20and%202018%20.

24. Talia Richman, "A Historically Black College in Maryland Is Growing— by Enrolling Hispanic, White and International Students," *Washington Post*, October 9, 2019, https://www.washingtonpost.com/local/education /a-historically-black-college-in-maryland-is-growing--by-enrolling -hispanic-white-and-international-students/2019/10/09/64185318-def3 -11e9-be96-6adb81821e90_story.html.

25. Chris Burt, "What One HBCU Credits for Record Surge in Applications," University Business, May 3, 2021, https://universitybusiness.com /what-one-hbcu-credits-for-record-surge-in-applications.

26. IPEDS.

27. Joelle Davis Carter and Tiffany Patrice Fountaine, "An Analysis of White Student Engagement at Public HBCUs," *Educational Foundations* (Summer–Fall 2012): 49–66, https://files.eric.ed.gov/fulltext /EJ1000230.pdf.

28. Deja Dennis, "What Does Diversity Look Like at HBCUs?" *Nation*, June 7, 2018, https://www.thenation.com/article/archive/diversity-look -like-hbcus.

29. David J. Dent, "Inside the Lives of White Students at Historically Black Colleges," *Vice*, June 27, 2018, https://www.vice.com/en/article /a3ampj/inside-the-lives-of-white-students-at-historically-black -colleges.

30. Monica Anderson, "A Look at Historically Black Colleges and Universities as Howard Turns 150," February 28, 2017, Pew Research Center, https:// www.pewresearch.org/fact-tank/2017/02/28/a-look-at-historically-black -colleges-and-universities-as-howard-turns-150.

31. Data from IPEDS.

32. IPEDS. For a success story, see Richman, "A Historically Black College in Maryland Is Growing."

33. U.S. Department of Education, College Scorecard.

34. Expressed mathematically, the coefficient of variation of enrollments in our sample of 50 HBCUs is .697, whereas it is .536 for the 186 PWIs in our sample. Hence, HBCU enrollments are relatively more variable than PWI enrollments.

35. For example, the average fiscal year full-time equivalent student body of the 50 HBCUs that make up our primary sample was 3,713 in 2019–20. Meanwhile, the comparable average for the 186 non-HBCUs in our sample was 23,112 (IPEDS).

2. A PRÉCIS OF THE CASE FOR HBCUs

1. *Brown v. Board of Education of Topeka*, 347 U.S. 483 (1954).

2. U.S. Department of Education, White House Initiative on Advancing Educational Equity, Excellence, and Economic Opportunity through Historically Black Colleges and Universities, "What is an HBCU?," accessed June 8, 2022, https://sites.ed.gov/whhbcu/one-hundred-and -five-historically-black-colleges-and-universities.

3. James T. Minor, "Contemporary HBCUs: Considering Institutional Capacity and State Priorities" (research report, Michigan State University, College of Education, Department of Educational Administration, 2008), https://research.steinhardt.nyu.edu/scmsAdmin/uploads /002/151/MINOR_Contemporary_HBCU_Report_2008.pdf. Also see Marybeth Gasman, "Comprehensive Funding Approaches for Historically Black Colleges and Universities" (Graduate School of Education, University of Pennsylvania, 2010), https://repository.upenn.edu /gse_pubs/331/; Donald Mitchell, Jr., "Funding U.S. Historically Black Colleges and Universities: A Policy Recommendation," *EJournal of Education Policy* (Fall 2013), https://files.eric.ed.gov/fulltext/EJ1158554 .pdf.

4. All data are expressed in July 2018 prices.

5. Danielle Douglas-Gabriel and Ovetta Wiggins, "Hogan Signs Off on $577 Million for Maryland's Historically Black Colleges and Universities," *Washington Post*, March 24, 2021, https://www.washingtonpost .com/education/2021/03/24/maryland-hbcus-lawsuit-settlement. The settlement was interesting for two reasons. First, Maryland already provided its institutions of higher education with funding per FTE student support well above the national average. Comparatively speaking, HBCUs in other states occupied funding positions substantially

inferior to those of Maryland's. Second, prior to the agreement, all of Maryland's HBCUs were receiving more funding per FTE student than nearby PWI institutions such as Towson State University.

6. U.S. Department of Education, Integrated Postsecondary Data System (hereafter cited as IPEDS), https://nces.ed.gov/ipeds.

7. IPEDS.

8. Mary Alice McCarthy, "Who Owns the Bachelor's Degree?" *Inside Higher Education*, April 12, 2019, https://www.insidehighered.com/views /2019/04/12/community-college-four-year-degrees-are-smart-policy -not-mission-creep-opinion.

9. C. J. Libassi, "The Neglected College Race Gap: Racial Disparities Among College Completers" (report, Center for American Progress, Washington, DC, May 23, 2018), https://www.americanprogress.org /issues/education-postsecondary/reports/2018/05/23/451186/neglected -college-race-gap-racial-disparities-among-college-completers.

10. U.S. Department of Education, National Center for Education Statistics, College Navigator, https://nces.ed.gov/collegenavigator.

11. Richard Fry and Anthony Cilluffo, "A Rising Share of Undergraduates Are from Poor Families, Especially at Less Selective Colleges," Pew Research Center, May 22, 2019, https://www.pewresearch.org/social -trends/2019/05/22/a-rising-share-of-undergraduates-are-from-poor -families-especially-at-less-selective-colleges.

12. College Navigator.

13. College Navigator.

14. Libassi, "The Neglected College Race Gap."

15. College Navigator.

16. *Fisher v. University of Texas at Austin*, 579 U.S __ (2016).

17. IPEDS.

18. IPEDS.

19. Richard V. Reeves and Sarah Nzau, "Poverty Hurts the Boys the Most: Inequality at the Intersection of Class and Gender" (report, Brookings, Washington, DC, June 14, 2021), https://www.brookings.edu/research /poverty-hurts-the-boys-the-most-inequality-at-the-intersection-of -class-and-gender.

20. Thurgood Marshall College Fund, "Most Expensive HBCUs Keep Tuition Costs Lower Than National Average," https://www.tmcf.org /events-media/tmcf-in-the-media/most-expensive-hbcus-keep -tuition-costs-lower-than-national-average.

21. Opportunity Insights, Data Library, "Income Segregation and Inter-generational Mobility Across Colleges in the United States," https://opportunityinsights.org/data. See especially MRC tables 2, 3, and 4.

22. James V. Koch, *The Impoverishment of the American College Student* (Washington, DC: Brookings Institution, 2019), provides details on this practice in American higher education.

23. College Navigator.

24. That is, ($16,904 − $7,968) × 2,760 = $24,663,360.

25. That is, ($33,150 − $13,160) × 12,000 = $239,880,000.

26. College Navigator. Note that this exercise assumes all students attend full-time and that no scholarship or grant aid is given to nonresident students. Even if we were to deduct one-quarter of the University of Delaware's revenue premium to recognize this, almost $180 million in semi-discretionary revenue would remain available for whatever purposes the university deemed appropriate, including grants and scholarships to lower-income students.

27. W. E. B. DuBois, *The Souls of Black Folks,* 2nd ed. (Chicago: A. G. McClurg, 1908).

28. Marissa Stubbs, "My HBCU Experience Has Been Life-Changing," Andscape, February 13, 2021, https://andscape.com/features/my-hbcu-experience-has-been-life-changing.

29. Jayla Jones, "The Difference Between and HBCU and a PWI: I see myself," Andscape, February 10, 2021, https://theundefeated.com/features/the-difference-between-an-hbuc-and-a-pwi-i-see-myself.

30. Nick Chiles, "HBCUs Graduate More Poor Black Students Than White Colleges," NPR Code Switch, March 1, 2017, www.npr.org/sections/codeswitch/2017/03/01/517770255/hbcus-graduate-more-poor-black-students-than-white-colleges.

31. Gallup began college satisfaction polling early in the past decade and sometimes conducts polls in cooperation with Purdue University. Gallup Alumni Survey, "Measuring College and University Outcomes," accessed April 14, 2022, https://www.gallup.com/education/194264/gallup-alumni-survey.aspx.

32. Walter M. Kimbrough, "Why Historically Black Colleges Should Be a Choice," *Education Week*, April 18, 2017, https://www.edweek.org/teaching-learning/opinion-why-historically-black-colleges-should-be-a-choice/2017/04.

33. Precious M. Hardy, Elizabeth J. Kaganda, and Mara S. Aruguete, "Below the Surface: HBCU Performance, Social Mobility, and College Ranking," *Journal of Black Studies*, 50, no. 5 (2019): 468–93.

34. Mels de Zeeuw, Samera Fazili, and Julie L. Hotchkiss, "Decomposing Outcome Differences Between HBCU and Non-HBCU Institutions" (Working Paper Series No. 2020–10, Federal Reserve Bank of Atlanta, July 2020), https://www.frbatlanta.org/-/media/documents/research/publications/wp/2020/07/16/10-decomposing-outcome-differences-between-hbcu-non-hbcu-institutions.pdf.

35. Ronald G. Ehrenberg and Donna S. Rothstein, "Do Historically Black Institutions of Higher Education Confer Unique Advantages on Black Students? An Initial Analysis," in *Choices and Consequences: Contemporary Policy Issues in Education*, ed. Ronald G. Ehrenberg (Ithaca, NY: IRL Press, 1994), 89–137.

36. Andrew H. Nichols and Denzel Evans-Bell, "A Look at Black Student Success: Identifying Top- and Bottom-Performing Institutions" (report, Education Trust, 2017), https://vtechworks.lib.vt.edu/handle/10919/83663.

37. David A. R. Richards and Janet T. Awokoya, "Understanding HBCU Retention and Completion" (Patterson Research Institute, UNCF, 2014), https://eric.ed.gov/?id=ED562057.

38. Ray Franke and Linda DeAngelo, "Degree Attainment for Black Students at Historically Black Colleges and Universities and Predominantly White Institutions: A Propensity Score Matching Approach" (paper presented at American Educational Research Association Meeting, New York City, April 13–17, 2018), https://www.aera.net/Publications/Online-Paper-Repository/AERA-Online-Paper-Repository.

39. This model is $G_{ij} = a + b_{ijk}X_{ijk}$, where G_{ij} is the six-year graduation rate of first-time full-time freshmen at institution i in year j, and X_{ijk} is a vector of n variables for institution i in year j as $n = 1 \ldots k$.

40. This sample was used in James V. Koch and Richard J., *Runaway College Costs: How College Governing Boards Fail to Protect Their Students* (Baltimore: Johns Hopkins University Press, 2020) and contains 186 PWIs, 76 of which are flagship state universities.

41. PayScale's estimates are imperfect but respected and based on very large samples. See PayScale, "College Salary Report, 2021–22," https://www.payscale.com/college-salary-report.

42. This point was made with emphasis in the documentary by Stanley Nelson and Marco Williams featured on PBS, "Tell Them We Are Rising: The Story of Historically Black Colleges and Universities," https://www. pbs.org/independentlens/documentaries/tell-them-we-are-rising.

43. In this case, Opportunity Insights (table 1) measures household income over the five years when a student was age fifteen to nineteen.

44. Opportunity Insights adopted admissions selectivity categories. Complete data were available for 192 institutions in its top two selectivity categories for private nonprofit institutions (from of a total of 792 institutions). See table mrc_2.

45. Opportunity Insights.

46. Opportunity Insights.

47. Opportunity Insights.

48. Opportunity Insights.

49. Opportunity Insights.

50. Thomas Mortenson, as quoted in Karin Fischer, "Engine of Inequality," *Chronicle of Higher Education*, January 17, 2016, https://www.chronicle.com/article/engine-of-inequality.

51. Andrea Widener, "Who Has the Most Success Preparing Black Students for Careers in Science? Historically Black Colleges and Universities," *Chemical and Engineering News*, September 4, 2020, https://cen.acs.org/education/success-preparing-Black-students-careers/98/i34.

52. Widener, "Who Has the Most Success Preparing Black Students."

53. IPEDS.

54. The population data are derived from Data USA, Itta Bena, MS, https://datausa.io/profile/geo/itta-bena-ms, and the enrollment data come from IPEDS.

55. U.S. Census Quick Facts, LeFlore County, MS, www.census.gov/quickfacts/fact/table/leflorecountymississippi,US/PST045221.

56. IPEDS.

57. Among many sources, see Marianne Bertrand and Sendil Mullainathan, "Are Emily and Greg More Employable Than Lakisha and Jamal? A Field Experiment on Labor Market Discrimination," *American Economic Review* 94 (September 2004): 991–2013; and Sonia K. Kang, Katherine A. DeCelles, András DeCelles, and Sora Jun, "Whitened Resumes: Race and Self-Presentation in the Labor Market," *Administrative Science Quarterly* 61, no. 3 (2016): 469–502.

58. One of the very few instances is the 2015–16 merger of Georgia HBCU Albany State University with two-year PWI Darton State College. Both are located in Albany. Darton became Albany State's College of Health Professions. This is the most important reason that Albany State's headcount enrollment surged from 3,041 in 2017 to 6,615 in 2018. See IPEDS.
59. Mississippi Governor Haley Barbour once proposed merging Mississippi Valley State University and Alcorn State University, the state's two smallest HBCUs, into much the much larger HBCU, Jackson State University. As the respected website Governing wryly commented, Barbour's proposal was "unlikely to gain traction in the Legislature." See Josh Goodman, "Merging Historically Black Universities," Governing, March 24, 2010, https://www.governing.com/archive/Merging-Historically-Black-Universities.html.
60. Grambling State University's head football coach, Broderick Fobbs, hired his father as an assistant coach. M. Shuler, "GSU Football Coach, Father Facing Ethics Charges," Advocate, October 30, 2015, https://www.theadvocate.com/baton_rouge/news/politics/article_c02c71ea-7b62-57a5-bf07-4a9a12630e1d.html. Fobbs survived this situation and went on to win 22 games over the next two seasons and had a 51–21 record as head coach at Grambling as of spring 2021. Whether at an HBCU or PWI, winning coaches have a way of avoiding major grief. Andrea Lewis Miller's contract as president of LeMoyne-Owen College in Memphis, Tennessee, was not renewed after her board alleged a variety of offenses, including nepotism. "HBUC President Ousted After Accusations of Plagiarism, Nepotism," Richmond Free Press, August 23, 2019, http://richmondfreepress.com/news/2019/aug/23/hbcu-president-ousted-after-accusations-plagiarism.
61. Bill Maxwell, "FAMU Should Look Outside for Leadership, " Tampa Bay Times, July 14, 2012, https://www.tampabay.com/opinion/columns/famu-should-look-outside-for-leadership/1240193.
62. Susan Svrluga, "How to Make Top-Heavy Historically Black Colleges Better, More Nimble," Washington Post, September 11, 2015, https://www.washingtonpost.com/news/grade-point/wp/2015/09/11/how-to-make-top-heavy-historically-black-colleges-better-more-nimble/.
63. U.S. Department of Education, Integrated Postsecondary Data System, "IPEDS Survey Components," https://nces.ed.gov/ipeds/use-the-data/survey-components-glossary/2.

64. Jason Coupet, "Historically Black Colleges and Universities and Resource Dependence: A Chow Test of Production Functions," *Journal of Higher Education Policy and Management* 35, no. 4 (2013): 355–69.

3. DECLINING HBCU ENROLLMENTS—A MYSTERY OR NOT?

1. Among many others, see Peter Jacobs, "There's an Unprecedented Crisis Facing America's Historically Black Colleges," *Insider*, March 30, 2015, https://www.businessinsider.com/hbcus-may-be-more-in-danger-of -closing-than-other-schools-2015-3; Delece Smith-Barrow, "Many HBCUs Are Teetering Between surviving and Thriving," *Hechinger Report*, October 23, 2019, https://hechingerreport.org/many-hbcus-are-teetering -between-surviving-and-thriving; and Gregory N. Price, "1 in 10 HBCUs Were Financially Fragile Before COVID-19 Endangered All Colleges and Universities," *The Conversation*, June 24, 2020, https://theconversation .com/1-in-10-hbcus-were-financially-fragile-before-covid-19-endangered -all-colleges-and-universities-140528.

2. Leaders who are effective seldom please everyone. President Hawkins's decision to have the Talladega College marching band perform in the festivities attached to Donald Trump's inauguration provoked some critics to insist that he resign. He did not.

3. However, IPEDS data reveal that the newly merged institution's head-count enrollment declined more than 25 percent below the sum of the two institutions' premerger enrollments. Not all students regarded the merger as an improvement.

4. U.S. Department of Education, Integrated Postsecondary Data System (hereafter cited as IPEDS), https://nces.ed.gov/ipeds.

5. Arkansas's 800-student Philander Smith College, facing a $3.5 million budget deficit, laid off 22 of its 185 employees, including 15 faculty members. Neale Earley, "Philander Smith College Sees Enrollment Fall, Lays Off 22 Employees," *Arkansas Democrat Gazette*, January 7, 2021, https://www.arkansas online.com/news/2021/jan/07/lr-college-sees-enrollment-fall-lays-off-22.

6. See Don Calloway, "Opinion: Don't Let the Less Famous HBCUs Get Left Behind," *Washington Post*, July 12, 2021, https://www.washington post.com/opinions/2021/07/12/its-great-time-be-howard-what-about -struggling-hbcus/.

7. National Association of College and University Business Officers (NACUBO).

8. National Student Clearinghouse Research Center, "Current Term Enrollment Estimates," https://nscresearchcenter.org/current-term-enrollment -estimates, for various years.

9. Not the Department of Education, which misread economic fundamentals and continued to pump out projections of enrollment growth even in the face of almost a decade of consecutive annual declines.

10. IPEDS.

11. Susan Adams and Hank Tucker, "For HBCUs Cheated Out of Billions, Bomb Threats Are the Latest Indignity," *Forbes*, February 1, 2022, https:// www.forbes.com/sites/susanadams/2022/02/01/for-hbcus-cheated-out -of-billions-bomb-threats-are-latest-indignity/?sh=2aca2889640c.

12. Kentucky Council on Postsecondary Education, "Current Financial Status of Kentucky State University," November 2021, https://governor .ky.gov/attachments/Nov2021_CPE-Assessment-of-KSU-Finances .pdf.

13. One should not attribute all of the increased enrollment at PWIs to their greater interest in enrolling Black students. Enrollment is a two-way street, and Black students had to show an interest in the PWIs to enroll. It appears that many have become more willing to do so.

14. Census Reporter, Virginia Beach-Norfolk-Newport News-VA-NC Metro Area, https://censusreporter.org/profiles/31000US47260-virginia-beach -norfolk-newport-news-va-nc-metro-area.

15. IPEDS.

16. NACUBO, "Historic Endowment Study Data, 2019," https://www .nacubo.org/Research/2021/Historic-Endowment-Study-Data.

17. U.S. Department of Education, National Center for Education Statistics, College Navigator, https://nces.ed.gov/collegenavigator.

18. National Center for Education Statistics, "Fast Facts: Distance Learning," https://nces.ed.gov/fastfacts/display.asp?id=80.

19. College Navigator.

20. IPEDS.

21. National Center for Education Statistics, U.S. Department of Education, "Transferability of Postsecondary Credit Following Student Transfer or Co-enrollment: Statistical Analysis Report," August 2014, https://nces.ed.gov/pubs2014/2014163.pdf, table 4.

22. National Center for Education Statistics, "Transferability of Postsecondary Credit," table 6.
23. College Navigator.
24. Federal Reserve Bank of St. Louis Economic Data (FRED), "Crude Birth Rate for the United States," 2019, updated April 27, 2021, https://fred.stlouisfed.org/series/SPDYNCBRTINUSA.
25. FRED, "Crude Birth Rate for the United States."
26. Peace Bransberger, Colleen Falkenstern, and Patrick Lane, Western Interstate Commission for Higher Education, *Knocking at the College Door, 10th Edition*, https://knocking.wiche.edu/wp-content/uploads/sites/10/2020/12/Knocking-pdf-for-website.pdf.
27. Bransberger et al., *Knocking at the College* Door, figure 4b, at 9.
28. William Roberts and Marissa Parker-Bair, "Predatory For-Profit Colleges Benefit from Washington's Culture of Corruption," Center for American Progress, July 29, 2019, https://www.americanprogress.org/article/predatory-profit-colleges-benefit-washingtons-culture-corruption/.
29. Paul Fain, "The Long View," *Inside Higher Education*, October 31, 2014, https://www.insidehighered.com/news/2014/10/31/obama-administration-has-helped-weaken-and-change-profit-industry.
30. Mitchell A. Fletcher, "Obama's Roller-Coaster Relationship with HBCUs," *Andscape*, October 10, 2016, https://theundefeated.com/features/obamas-roller-coaster-relationship-with-hbcus/.

4. THE SAMPLE AND THE DATA

1. James V. Koch and Richard J. Cebula, *Runaway College Costs: How College Governing Boards Fail to Protect Their Students* (Baltimore: Johns Hopkins University Press, 2020).
2. National Association of College and University Business Officers (NACUBO), "2020 NACUBO-TIAA Study of Endowments," February 23, 2021, http://www.nacubo.org/Research/2021/Historic-Endowment-Study-Data.
3. Federal Reserve Bank of St. Louis Economic Data (FRED), https://fred.stlouisfed.org.
4. U.S. Department of Education, National Center for Education Statistics, *Digest of Education Statistics*, "Public High School Graduates," various years, https://nces.ed.gov.

5. NACUBO, "2020 NACUBO-TIAA Study of Endowments."
6. U.S, Department of Education, College Scorecard, https://college scorecard.ed.gov.
7. U.S. Department od Education, Equity in Athletics, accessed May 19, 2022, https://ope.ed.gov/athletics/#/.
8. More than 1,200 institutions are members of the NCAA. The membership in each NCAA division is provided at https://web3.ncaa.org /directory. The nature of the divisions is explained in Justin Berkman, "What Are NCAA Divisions? Division 1 vs. 2 vs. 3," Prep Scholar, January 20, 2020, https://blog.prepscholar.com/what-are-ncaa-divisions -1-vs-2-vs-3.
9. National Center for Education Statistics, "College Enrollment Rates," May 2020, https://nces.ed.gov/programs/coe/indicator_cpb.asp.
10. Although the experiential level of HBCU private sector presidents is higher, their number is smaller ($N = 20$), and the standard deviation of their estimate is larger than the experience estimate itself.
11. Benjamin E. Mays, "The Role of the Negro Liberal Arts College in Post-War Reconstruction," *Journal of Negro Education* 11 (July 1942): 400–11.
12. Walter M. Kimbrough, "A Warning to Anyone Thinking About Being the Next TSU President," *Diverse Issues in Education*, March 2, 2020, https://diverseeducation.com/article/168520.
13. A well-publicized example is Kentucky State University's hiring of Christopher Brown II as its president in 2017 despite his having resigned "under pressure" from the presidency of Alcorn State University. Brown subsequently resigned from Kentucky State, again apparently for matters relating to his financial management, in July 2021. Sylvia Goodman, "Gov. Beshear Calls for Review of Kentucky State Finances After President Abruptly Resigns," *Louisville Courier Journal*, July 20, 2021, https:// www.courier-journal.com/story/news/local/2021/07/20/kentucky-state -university-president-m-christopher-brown-ii-resigns/8025138002.
14. "The Tradition of White Presidents at Black Colleges," *Journal of Black Individuals in Higher Education* 16 (Summer 1997): 93–99.
15. Pete Adrian, a white man, was head football coach at Norfolk State University between 2005 and 2014 after serving as head coach at Pennsylvania's Bloomsburg University. He won two Coach of the Year Awards in the FCS-level Mid-Eastern Athletic Conference and garnered a 54–60 won-loss record during his time at Norfolk State.

16. Shorter presidential tenures at HBCUs would not be a new circumstance. See James L. Fisher and James V. Koch, *Presidential Leadership: Making a Difference* (Phoenix, AZ: American Council on Education and Oryx Press, 1996); and Fisher and Koch, *The Entrepreneurial College President* (Westport, CT: American Council on Education and Praeger, 2004).

5. ENROLLMENT, RETENTION, AND GRADUATION

1. Curtis Bunn, "Enrollment Declines Threaten Future of HBCUs, Disheartening Alumni," *NBC News*, March 23, 2020, https://www.nbcnews.com /news/nbcblk/enrollment-declines-threaten-future-hbcus-disheartening -alumni-n1158191.

2. Jeffrey M. Wooldridge, *Introductory Econometrics: A Modern Approach*, 7th ed. (Boston: Cengage, 2021).

3. Our typical regression estimating equation will be of the form

$$\log \text{FTE}_{ijk} = a + \sum_{i}^{n} \sum_{j}^{m} \sum_{k}^{p} bijk X_{ijk} + e,$$ where $\log Y_{ijk}$ = logarithm

of dependent variable k in year i for institution j, a = constant term, b_{ijk} = estimated regression coefficient for independent variable k in year i for institution j, X_{ijk} = value of independent variable k in year i for institution j, and e = a random error term. There are two reasons we express our dependent variables in logarithms. First, doing so will make it much easier to translate our estimated regression coefficients (the b_{ijk} terms) into understandable estimates that show how much (or little) one variable affects another. The second reason is econometric and technical in nature. Expressing the variables in logarithms increases the confidence we may have in the statistical quality of our regression estimates. In addition, doing so frequently reduces heteroskedasticity, which occurs when there is a systematic change in the spread of the regression residuals over the range of measured values. The conventional regression model assumes that the residuals are drawn from a population that has constant variance. When this is not so (and extreme values in variables can be a cause), the regression results are less precise, and the usual statistical tests may overestimate the quality of the estimates. Expressing the dependent variable in logarithms frequently (though not always) brings one closer to the constant variance assumption. So does expressing variable values in per capita terms, which we frequently do. Appendix B speaks to our choices of estimating techniques and models.

4. Appendix C table C.1 presents five regression estimates that seek to explain HBCU annual enrollments between FY 2005 and FY 2018. Regressions 1 and 2 rely on cross-section fixed effects estimations, regression 4 presents a cross-section random effects estimate, and regressions 3 and 5 are ordinary least-squares estimates. We acknowledge that one can mount an argument in favor of each and present results that rely on all three approaches.
5. Michael Martin, "Veblen Saw It Coming," *Inside Higher Education*, July 3, 2019, https://www.insidehighered.com/views/2019/07/03/thorstein-veblens-writings-about-rich-are-relevant-ongoing-admission-scandal.
6. Harvey Leibenstein, "Bandwagon, Snob and Veblen Effects in the Theory of Consumers' Demand," *Quarterly Journal of Economics* 64 (May 1950): 183–207.
7. In one of our regressions, we used as an explanatory variable the percentage of undergraduate students who received a Pell Grant—an inverse measure of household incomes. The estimated coefficient on this argument assumed the expected negative sign and was statistically significant at the 0.01 level.
8. This is total expenditure on instruction per FTE divided by the sum of total expenditures on instruction + total expenditures on student services + total expenditures on academic support + total expenditures on research + total expenditures on institutional support.
9. Shortly, we also will provide evidence that the proportion of Black students on an HBCU campus seems unrelated to HBCU enrollments.
10. U.S. Department of Education, National Center for Education Statistics, College Navigator, "Southern New Hampshire University," https://nces.ed.gov/collegenavigator/?q=southern+new+hampshire&s=all&id=183026.
11. U.S. Department of Education, Integrated Postsecondary Data System (hereafter cited as IPEDS), https://nces.ed.gov/ipeds.
12. IPEDS.
13. Manna Zelealem, "Why Choosing Not to Attend an HBCU Doesn't Define Your Blackness," *TeenVogue*, June 28, 2016, https://www.teenvogue.com/story/hbcus-and-pwis-does-not-define-blackness.

14. Robert Zemsky, Susan Shaman, and Susan Campbell Baldridge, *The College Stress Test* (Baltimore: Johns Hopkins University Press, 2020).

15. U.S. Department of Education, "Heightened Cash Monitoring," March 1, 2021, https://studentaid.gov/data-center/school/hcm.

16. Delice Smith-Barrow, "Many HBCUs Are Teetering Between Surviving and Thriving," Hechinger Report, October 23, 2019, https://hechinger report.org/many-hbcus-are-teetering-between-surviving-and -thriving.

17. U.S. Department of Education, National Center for Education Statistics, Digest of Education Statistics, table 303.40: Total Fall Enrollment in Degree-Granting Postsecondary Institutions, by Attendance Status, Sex, and Age of Student: Selected Years, 1970 Through 2029, https:// nces.ed.gov/programs/digest/d19/tables/dt19_303.40.asp.

18. National Center for Education Statistics, Digest of Education Statistics, table 303.40.

19. American Association of Colleges & Universities, "Transfer and Mobility: A National View of Student Movements," *AAC&U News*, August 2015, https://www.aacu.org/aacu-news/newsletter/transfer-and -mobility-national-view-student-movements.

20. See in particular Ethan K. Gordon, Zackary B. Hawley, Ryan Carrasco Kobler, and Jonathan C. Rork, "The Paradox of HBCU Graduation Rates," *Research in Higher Education* 62 (2021): 332–58.

21. Roland G. Fryer Jr. and Michael Greenstone, "The Changing Consequences of Attending Historically Black Colleges and Universities," *American Economic Journal: Applied Economics* 2, no. 1 (2010): 116–48; Gregory N. Price, William Spriggs, and Omari H. Swinton, "The Relative Returns to Graduating from a Historically Black College/University: Propensity Score Matching Estimates from the National Survey of Black Americans," *Review of Black Political Economy* 38 (2011): 103–30.

22. Gordon et al., "The Paradox of HBCU Graduation Rates."

23. All appropriate variables were lagged two periods (years) on the assumption that this year's graduation rate reflects past years' activities.

24. Alexander Astin, *What Matters in College: Four Critical Years Revisited* (San Francisco: Jossey-Bass, 1993).

25. Vincent Tinto, "Dropout in Higher Education: A Review of Recent Research" (report prepared for the Office of Planning, Budgeting and Evaluation, U.S. Office of Education, Washington, DC, 1973); and

Tinto, *Leaving College: Rethinking the Causes and Cures of Student Attrition* (Chicago: University of Chicago, 1993).

26. The most sophisticated assessment of this issue was supplied by Ann M. Gansemer-Topf and John M. Schuh, "Institutional Grants: Investing in Student Retention and Graduation," *Journal of Student Financial Aid* 35, no. 3 (2005): 5–20; and Gansemer-Topf and Schuh, "Institutional Selectivity and Institutional Expenditures: Examining Organizational Factors that Contribute to Retention and Graduation," *Research in Higher Education* 47, no. 6 (2006): 613–42.

27. Among the hypotheses offered by C. J. Libassi concerning differences in institutional graduation rates is "The Neglected College Race Gap: Racial Disparities Among College Completers" (report, Center for American Progress, Washington, DC, May 23, 2018), https://www.americanprogress.org/issues/education-postsecondary/reports/2018/05/23/451186/neglected-college-race-gap-racial-disparities-among-college-completers.

28. National Association of College and University Business Officers, "2020 NACUBO-TIAA Study of Endowments," www.nacubo.org/Research/2021/Historic-Endowment-Study-Data.

29. Philip Oreopoulos and Uros Petronijevic, "Making College Worth It: A Review of Research on the Returns to Higher Education," *Future of Children* 23, no. 1 (2013): 41–65.

30. See Sara Weissman, "Can Coaching Bring Students Back to HBCUs?" *Inside Higher Education*, May 25, 2021, https://www.insidehighered.com/news/2021/05/25/new-initiative-re-enroll-thousands-hbcu-students.

31. Specifically, our estimates are about 10 percent higher than those found in IPEDS.

32. "Tobler's First Law of Geography," *GISGeography* (January 2, 2021), . For many years, Tobler, now deceased, held a geography and statistics professorship at the University of California, Santa Barbara.

33. Specifically, the percentage of major expenditures devoted to institutional support is institutional support expenditures per FTE student divided by the sum of institutional support expenditures per student FTE + instruction expenditures per FTE student + academic support expenditures per FTE student + student services expenditures per FTE student + research expenditures per FTE student. These are the IPEDS definitions.

34. About half of all federal student debt is owed by graduate students. Anthony P. Carnevale and Emma Wenzinger, "The Student Debt Dilemma," May 24, 2021, Georgetown University Center on Education and the Workforce, https://medium.com/georgetown-cew/the-student -debt-dilemma-6db2f56039eb.

35. Weissman, "Can Coaching Bring Students Back to HBCUs?"

36. See James V. Koch, *The Impoverishment of the American College Student* (Washington DC: Brookings, 2019), 51–68 for a summary of the evidence.

37. Mike Brown, "Student Loan Default Rates by School & State," *Lend-EDU*, November 22, 2019 .

38. Koch, *The Impoverishment of the American College Student*, chapter 3, which includes a review of the evidence.

39. For example, Andre M. Perry, Marshall Steinbaum, and Carl Romer, "Student Loans, the Racial Wealth Divide, and Why We Need Full Student Debt Cancellation" (report, Brookings, Washington, DC, June 23, 2021, https://www.brookings.edu/research/student-loans-the-racial -wealth-divide-and-why-we-need-full-student-debt-cancellation.

40. Adam Looney, "Putting Student Loan Forgiveness in Perspective: How Costly Is It and Who Benefits?" (Up Front, Brookings, Washington, DC, February 12, 2021), https://www.brookings.edu/blog/up-front/2021 /02/12/putting-student-loan-forgiveness-in-perspective-how-costly-is -it-and-who-benefits.

41. Looney, "Putting Student Loan Forgiveness in Perspective."

42. This point is disputed by Perry et al., "Student Loans, the Racial Wealth Divide, and Why We Need Full Student Debt Cancellation."

43. College Board, *Trends in College Pricing*, tables CP-9 and CP-10, accessed April 23, 2022, https://research.collegeboard.org/trends/college -pricing.

44. For a complete discussion of the issues, see James V. Koch and Richard J. Cebula, *Runaway College Costs: How College Governing Boards Fail to Protect Their Students* (Baltimore: Johns Hopkins University Press, 2020).

45. According to IPEDS, in FY 2018, the median calendar year FTE student enrollments were 3,254 for HBCUs and 21,329 for PWIs.

46. IPEDS shows that Ohio State's institutional cost per calendar year FTE student was $4,667 in FY 2019.

47. IPEDS.

6. A DEEPER DIVE INTO HBCU DYNAMICS

1. Some HBCUs, however, have open admissions and therefore admit almost every student applicant with a high school diploma.
2. U.S. Department of Education, Integrated Postsecondary Data System (hereafter cited as IPEDS), https://nces.ed.gov/ipeds.
3. Dominique Johnson of Old Dominion University suggested to the authors that if the median percentage of Black students on an HBCU campus is 86.0, it may not make much difference if that percentage declines to 76.0 percent or rises to 96.0 percent. The dominant campus culture will not change.
4. Robert Morse and Eric Brooks, "A More Detailed Look at the Ranking Factors," *U.S. News and World Report*, September 13, 2020, https:// www.usnews.com/education/best-colleges/articles/ranking-criteria -and-weights.
5. National Association of College and University Business Officers (NACUBO), "2020 NACUBO-TIAA Study of Endowments," April 22, 2021, www.nacubo.org/Research/2021/Historic-Endowment -Study-Data.
6. Lorelle L. Espinosa, Robert Kelchen, and Morgan Taylor, "Minority Serving Institutions as Engines of Upward Mobility" (American Council on Education, Washington, DC, 2018), https://vtechworks.lib .vt.edu/bitstream/handle/10919/86902/MSIEnginesUpwardMobility .pdf?sequence=1&isAllowed=y.
7. Robert A. Nathanson, Andrés Castro Samayoa, and Marybeth Gasman, "Moving Upward and Onward: Income Mobility at Historically Black Colleges and Universities" (Rutgers Graduate School of Education, Center for Minority Serving Institutions, New Brunswick, NJ, 2019), https://cmsi.gse.rutgers.edu/sites/default/files/EMreport_R4_0 .pdf.
8. Roland Fryer and Michael Greenstone, "The Causes and Consequences of Attending Historically Black Colleges and Universities," *American Economic Journal: Applied Economics* 2, no. 1 (2010): 116–48.
9. Gregory N. Price, William Spriggs, and Omari H. Swinton, "The Relative Returns to Graduating from a Historically Black College/University: Propensity Score Matching Estimates from the National Survey of Black Americans," *Review of Black Political Economy* 38 (2011): 103–30.

10. Once one controls for the parental incomes of students, however, HBCU's KID/PAR advantage declines. Starting-point incomes make a difference.

7. A ROADMAP FOR THE FUTURE

1. Maya Rhodan, "The Secretary of Education Equated Historically Black Colleges to 'School Choice,'" *Time*, February 17, 2017, https://time .com/4685456/betsy-devos-black-colleges-school-choice/.
2. Analogously, and thinking historically, many Americans have been ignorant of the history, culture, and economics of the continent of Africa. The academic study of Africa was underdeveloped. Created in 1948, the African Studies program at Northwestern University was the only such academic program or center in the United States for several decades (though some work in this area was being done at Howard University). This circumstance speaks to what must be labeled a general lack of interest among the white establishment (and higher education) in things Black.
3. U.S. Census Bureau, Income and Poverty in the United States: 2000, Figure 1, Median Household Income and Percent Change by Selected Characteristics, www.census.gov/content/dam/Census/library /publications/2021/demo/p60-273.pdf.
4. For a rendition of some of these discrepancies see Adam Harris, *The State Must Provide: Why America's Colleges Have Always Been Unequal—and How to Set Them Right* (New York: HarperCollins, 2021). .
5. In our sample, the 21 HBCUs that sponsor NCAA FCS football programs spent $3,042 per FTE student on intercollegiate athletics in FY 2019, while the 44 PWIs that fielded similar programs spent only $1,600 per FTE student, and the 99 PWIs that offered NCAA FBS football spent $2,264. Data on expenditures are from U.S. Department of Education, Equity in Athletics Data Analysis, https://ope.ed.gov /athletics/#/; for FTE students, Integrated Postsecondary Data System (hereafter cited as IPEDS), https://nces.ed.gov/ipeds.
6. These endowment data come from U.S. Department of Education, College Scorecard, https://collegescorecard.ed.gov/data.
7. Emily A. Shrider, Melissa Kollar, Frances Chen, and Jessica Semega, "Income and Poverty in the United States: 2020" (report no. P60-273, September 14, 2021, U.S. Census Bureau), https://www.census.gov

/library/publications/2021/demo/p60-273.html, table A-2, "Households by Total Money Income, Race, and Hispanic Origin of Householder: 1967 to 2020."

8. Shrider et al., , "Income and Poverty in the United States: 2020," table B-5, "Poverty Status of People by Age, Race, and Hispanic Origin: 1959 to 2020."

9. See, for example, Jeffrey T. Denning, Benjamin M. Marx, and Lesley J. Turner, "ProPelled: The Effects of Grants on Graduation, Earnings, and Welfare," *American Economic Journal: Applied Economics* 11, no. 3 (July 2019): 199–224.

10. U.S. Department of Education, National Center for Education Statistics, College Navigator, https://nces.ed.gov/collegenavigator.

11. College Navigator.

12. U.S. Department of Education, Federal Student Aid, "Apply for Financial Aid," https://studentaid.gov/h/apply-for-aid.

13. Student Loan Hero, "A Look at the Shocking Student Loan Debt Statistics for 2021," *Lending Tree*, January 27, 2021, Student Loan Hero, January 27, 2021, https://studentloanhero.com/student-loan-debt-statistics/.

14. U.S. Department of Education, Federal Student Aid.

15. Kim Cook, Kristin Hultquist, Bridget Terry Long, and Judith Scott-Clayton, "FAFSA: Ask Any College Student. The Federal Student Aid Application Is Needlessly Complex," *USA Today*, December 5, 2019, https://www.usatoday.com/story/opinion/2019/12/05/fafsa-ask-any-college-student-federal-student-aid-application-column/2598151001.

16. Andy Johnston, "One Surprising Barrier to College Success: Dense Higher Education Lingo," *Hechinger Report*, June 2019, https://hechinger report.org/one-surprising-barrier-to-success-in-college-understanding-higher-education-lingo.

17. Michael T. Nietzel, "HBCUs Team Up With Wells Fargo to Improve Financial Wellness for College Students of Color," *Forbes*, June 9, 2021, https://www.forbes.com/sites/michaeltnietzel/2021/06/09/hbcus-team-up-with-wells-fargo-to-improve-financial-wellness-for-college-students-of-color/?sh=3b926f3d3507.

18. Susan Dynarski and Judith Scott-Clayton, "There Is a Simpler way for Students to Apply for Financial Aid," *New York Times*, June 20, 2014, https://www.nytimes.com/2014/06/21/upshot/a-simple-way-to-help-financial-aid-do-its-job.html.

19. Mathew Chingos and Susan Dynarski, "An International Final Four: Which Country Handles Student Debt Better?" *New York Times*, April 2, 2018, https://www.nytimes.com/2018/04/02/upshot/an-international -final-four-which-country-handles-student-debt-best.html.

20. Susan Dynarski, "$20 Billion in Tax Credits Fails to Increase College Attendance," *New York Times*, April 19, 2016, https://www.nytimes.com /2016/04/20/upshot/how-to-use-tax-credits-to-increase-college-attendance .html.

21. Federal Reserve Bank of St. Louis Economic Data (FRED), "Real Median Household Income in the United States," https://fred.stlouisfed .org/series/MEHOINUSA672N.

22. There are, of course, other reasons that college costs have increased so dramatically. For a lengthy discussion of the hypotheses and evidence in this area, see James V. Koch and Richard J. Cebula, *Runaway College Costs: How College Governing Boards Fail to Protect Their Students* (Baltimore: Johns Hopkins University Press, 2020).

23. All data in this paragraph came from IPEDS.

24. Melanie Hanson, "Student Loan Debt by Race," *Education Data Initiative*, December 12, 2021, updated March 10, 2022, https://educationdata .org/student-loan-debt-by-race.

25. Judith Scott-Clayton and Jing Li, "Black-White Disparity in Student Loan Debt More Than Triples After Graduation" (report, Brookings, Washington, DC, October 20, 2016), https://www.brookings.edu/research /black-white-disparity-in-student-loan-debt-more-than-triples-after -graduation.

26. The deterioration reflects a variety of factors including Black graduates have lower employment rates and occupying lower paying jobs than white graduates. Scott-Clayton and Li, "Black-White Disparity in Student Loan Debt More Than Triples After Graduation."

27. Robert Kelchen, "Examining Long-Term Student Loan Default Rates by Race and Ethnicity" (blog), February 13, 2018, https://robertkelchen .com/2018/02/13/examining-long-term-student-loan-default-rates-by -race-and-ethnicity/.

28. For a concise recitation of this evidence, most of which has been generated by research units of the Federal Reserve System, see James V. Koch, *The Impoverishment of the American College Student* (Washington, DC: Brookings, 2019), chap. 5.

29. Terrance M. McAdoo, "The Leadership Behind the Leader: Examining Boards of HBCUs and the Potential Effect That These Members Are Having on HBCUs' Success and/or Failure," in *Improving the Viability and Perception of HBCUs*, ed. Comfort O. Okpala and Kimberly Young Walker (Lanham, MD: Lexington, 2018), 11.

30. *Code of Virginia*, §23.1-2700, https://law.lis.virginia.gov/vacode/title23.1/.

31. One of the authors has been involved in more than fifty evaluations of governing boards and presidents. He has observed board meetings in many governance situations and locations. This statement is based on that experience.

32. Marybeth Gasman, "At Morehouse: When College Boards of Trustees Won't Let Presidents Do Their Jobs," *Washington Post*, March 28, 2017, https://www.washingtonpost.com/news/grade-point/wp/2017/03/28 /at-morehouse-when-college-boards-of-trustees-wont-let-presidents -do-their-jobs.

33. Lindsay Ellis, "This University's Board Now Has the Power to Fire Anyone—'Even Down to the Janitor,'" *Chronicle of Higher Education*, February 3, 2020, https://www.chronicle.com/article/this-universitys -board-now-has-the-power-to-fire-anyone-even-down-to-the-janitor.

34. College Board, *Trends in College Pricing and Student Aid 2021*, https:// research.collegeboard.org/media/pdf/trends-college-pricing-student -aid-2021.pdf, figure SA-17A.

35. College Board, *Trends in College Pricing and Student Aid 2021*, figure CP-9.

36. College Board, *Trends in College Pricing and Student Aid 2021*, figure SA-17B.

37. Jennifer Lee, "Moving HOPE Forward Into the 21st Century," Georgia Budget & Policy Institute, September 14, 2020, https://gbpi.org/moving -hope-forward-into-the-21st-century/.

38. Ross Rubenstein and Benjamin Scafidi, "Who Pays and Who Benefits? Examining the Distributional Consequences of the Georgia Lottery for Education," *National Tax Journal* 55, no. 2 (2002), 223–38.

39. Lee, "Moving HOPE Forward Into the 21st Century."

40. Emma Whitford, "The Dark Side of Lottery-Funded Scholarships," *Inside Higher Education*, November 30, 2021, https://www.insidehighered .com/news/2021/11/30/low-income-people-pay-more-lottery-funded -scholarships.

41. College Navigator, University of Georgia.

42. Lee, "Moving HOPE Forward Into the 21st Century."
43. The existence of disparate circumstances in a situation does not constitute evidence of discriminatory intent or actions. Thus, the absence of 5'6" players in the National Basketball Association is a disparate impact that has arisen because of the roster choices made by NBA team managers. Those roster choices appear to have nothing to do with any protected class and have legitimate statistical grounding.
44. Marybeth Gasman, *Envisioning Black Colleges: A History of the United Negro College Fund* (Baltimore: Johns Hopkins University Press, 2007).
45. Gasman, *Envisioning Black* Colleges, 86.
46. The Black population estimates come from U.S. Census, "Quick Facts."
47. W. E. B. DuBois, *The Souls of Black Folk* (New York: Penguin, 1903), 13.
48. All About Philosophy, "Blind Men and the Elephant," https://www.allaboutphilosophy.org/blind-men-and-the-elephant.htm.

APPENDIX B. OBSERVATIONS ON PANEL LEAST SQUARES, RANDOM EFFECTS, AND FIXED EFFECTS

1. Stack Exchange, Cross Validated, "What Is the Difference Between Fixed Effect, Random Effect and Mixed Effect Models?," https://stats.stackexchange.com/questions/4700/what-is-the-difference-between-fixed-effect-random-effect-and-mixed-effect-mode.

INDEX

labor force, 65, 89–90, 92
labor force participation rates
  (LFPRs), *89*, 92
land-grant institution, Black, 73–74,
  176
Langston University, 192
layoffs, 67
leadership, 62, 111–14, 242n2
least-squares estimation, 213, 215
Lee, Kurtis, 159
LeFlore County, Mississippi, 52
legislatures, state, 195
Lehman College, 168
Leibenstein, Harvey, 124
LFPRs. *See* labor force participation
  rates
Lifetime Learning Credit, 187–88
limits, for federal loans, 184–85
linear regression analysis, 120,
  134–35, 246n3
list, at-risk, 132
literacy, financial, 186, 187
loans. *See* federal loans
location, HBCU sample data, *99*
Los Angeles, California, 172
Los Angeles Times, 159
loss, financial, 115
lottery, 204, 205
Louisiana Tech University, 35
low-cost medical education, 80
lower income, 33, 34–35, 171,
  175, 180

Making College Work (Holzer and
  Baum), 152
Malveaux, Julianne, 155
management, principles of, 117–18

market share, HBCUs, 68–74, 177–78
Marshall, Thurgood, 19
mathematics, 119, 239n39, 246n3
matriculation, 133
Maxwell, Bill, 53–54
Mays, Benjamin, 111
McAdoo, Terrance M., 194–95
McCaskill, Claire, 172–73
medical education, low-cost, 80
merger, 62–63, 241n58, 242n3
metro leader institutions, 29, 105;
  Black populations and Black
  student percentages at, *30*;
  flagship institutions *versus*, 31
micromanagement, 112, 199, 200
Microsoft, 115
midcareer income, HBCU
  graduates, 42–43, *43*
missions, HBCUs, 64
Mississippi, 26, 52
Mississippi Valley State University
  (MVSU), 22, 52
mobility: coefficient, 101, 103, 109;
  income, *45*, 45–47, *47–48*, 167–68,
  170. *See also* economic mobility
morals, debt forgiveness, 151
Morehouse College, 9, 63, 148, 154,
  163, 199
Morgan State University, 6, 11, 63,
  154, 194
Morrill Act, U.S., 19
Mortensen, Thomas, 50
motivation, for governing boards,
  201
MVSU. *See* Mississippi Valley State
  University
mystery, of HBCUs, 4–5

rates and, 136, 137, 182–83; representation minima for, 183; student debt and, *148*
Petronijevic, Uros, 140
Pew Research Center, 26
Pew Trust, 12
philanthropy, 180
pipeline, Black talent, 50–51
Plessy v. Ferguson, 6, 233n8
policy recommendations, 96
politics, governing boards and, 200–201
polls, Gallup, 39, 238n31
populations, 102
post-racial society, 58
power: diffused, 117; governing boards, 196; of institutional presidents, 199
Prairie View A&M University, 119, 194
predominantly white institutions (PWIs), 2, 13, 14, 20, 130–31; Black male student enrollment at, 90–91, *91*; Black student enrollment at, 77–81, *79*, 243n13; Black students underperforming at, 37–44; enrollment, 70; graduation rates by gender, 161–62; HBCUs affordability *versus*, 33–37; HBCUs competing with, 77–81; HBCUs located near, 44; Jones on, 38; open admission, 26; price discrimination at, 35, 108–9; retention rates, 174; revenue, 191–92

presidents, institutional, 61–62, 104, 110, 111, 112, 245n10; governing boards and, 197–98; median tenure, *114*; power of, 199; recycling of, 113; white, 113
price discrimination, 116; at HBCUs, 108; at PWIs, 35, 108–9
priorities, 173, 206, 207
private HBCUs, 23, 24, 70, 131–32, 177
private loans, 185
public awareness, of HBCUs, 2, 3–5
public-sector HBCUs, 23, 128–31
PWIs. *See* predominantly white institutions

race: admissions yield and, 158; HBCUs and, 172–73
racial differences: college-bound high school graduates, *32*, 32–33; for scholarship programs, 203–4, *204*, 205; for tax credits, 188
racism, 4, 174
random-effects estimation, 213, 215
ratios: income, *47–48*, 169, *170*, 171; student-faculty, *143*, 143–44, *226*
recognition, name, 173
recruitment, 11–12; flagship institutions, 163; strategies, 92, 128
recycling, of presidents, 113
redemption, 9
regional institutions, 105, 136
religion, 18
repayment plans, loan, 186, 187
reputations, 125

Printed and bound by CPI Group (UK) Ltd, Croydon, CR0 4YY

22/04/2024

14487065-0001